Truly Yours

Oliver Wolcott

Andrews Pr.

EXTRACTS

FROM THE

DIARY AND CORRESPONDENCE

OF THE LATE

AMOS LAWRENCE;

WITH A

Brief Account of Some Incidents in his Life.

EDITED BY HIS SON,

WILLIAM R. LAWRENCE, M. D.

BOSTON:
GOULD AND LINCOLN,
59 WASHINGTON STREET.
NEW YORK: SHELDON AND COMPANY.
CINCINNATI: GEO. S. BLANCHARD
1860.

Entered according to Act of Congress, in the year 1855, by
WILLIAM R. LAWRENCE,
In the Clerk's Office of the District Court of the District of Massachusetts

BOSTON:
Stereotyped by
HOBART & ROBBINS,
New England Type and Stereotype Foundery.

Press of George C. Rand & Avery.

To his

ONLY SURVIVING BROTHER,

AMOS A. LAWRENCE,

OF BOSTON,

This Volume is Affectionately Inscribed,

BY

THE EDITOR.

LETTERS,

REQUESTING PUBLICATION.

Rooms of the Boston Young Men's Christian Union,
6 Bedford-street, Boston, June 22, 1855

WILLIAM R. LAWRENCE, ESQ.

DEAR SIR: The undersigned, members of the Government of the Boston Young Men's Christian Union, some of whom have perused the excellent memoir of your honored father, feel deeply impressed with the desire that it should be published and circulated, knowing that its publication and perusal would greatly benefit the young, the old, and all classes of our busy mercantile community.

Remembering with pleasure the friendship which your father expressed, not only in kind words, but in substantial offerings to the treasury and library of our Society, the Union would be most happy, should it comport with your feelings, to be made the medium of the publication and circulation of the memoir, which you have compiled with so much ability and faithfulness.

Hoping to receive a favorable response to our desire,

We are most truly yours,

THOMAS GAFFIELD,	H. K. WHITE,
JOHN SWEETSER,	J. F. AINSWORTH,
JOSEPH H. ALLEN,	W. H. RICHARDSON,
CHAS. C. SMITH,	FRANCIS S. RUSSELL,
C. J. BISHOP,	FREDERIC H. HENSHAW,
F. H. PEABODY,	CHARLES F. POTTER,
W. IRVING SMITH,	THORNTON K. LOTHROP,
ARTHUR W. HOBART.	GEO. S. HALE.

Rooms of the Boston Young Men's Christian Association,
Tremont Temple, Boston, July 10, 1855.

DEAR SIR:

The Committee on the Library of the Boston Young Men's Christian Association beg leave, in its behalf, to tender you sincere thanks for your donation of a copy of the "Diary and Correspondence of Amos Lawrence." It will remain to the members of the Association a valued memorial of one of its earliest benefactors. It will be yet more prized for its record of his invaluable legacy, — the history of a long life — a bright example.

The Committee, uniting with the subscribers, managers of the Association, are happy to improve this opportunity to express the hope that you may be induced to give the book a more general circulation. The kindly charities of your late lamented parent are still fresh in impressions of gratitude upon their recipients. They require no herald to give them publicity. The voice of fame would do violence to their spirit.

Yet, now that "the good man" can no more utter his words of sympathy and counsel, — that his pen can no more subscribe its noble benefactions, or indite its lessons of wisdom and experience, — the press may silently perpetuate those which survive him.

We must assure you of our pleasure in the knowledge that the liberal interest in the Association, so constantly manifested by your revered father, is actively maintained by yourself.

We remain, in the fraternal bonds of Christian regard,

Yours, truly,

JACOB SLEEPER,	FRANCIS D. STEDMAN,
J. S. WARREN,	ELIJAH SWIFT,
SAMUEL GREGORY,	B. C. CLARK, JR.,
LUTHER L. TARBELL,	JOSEPH P. ELLICOTT,
ALONZO C. TENNEY,	GEO. N. NOYES,
MOSES W. POND,	PEARL MARTIN,
STEPHEN G. DEBLOIS,	W. H. JAMESON,
HENRY FURNAS,	W. F. STORY.

FRANKLIN W. SMITH,
E. M. PUTNAM,
CHAS. L. ANDREWS,
GEO. C. RAND,
H. C. GILBERT,
} *Committee on Library and Rooms*

To

WILLIAM R. LAWRENCE, M.D.

Williams College, June 30, 1855.

DEAR SIR:

The students of Williams College having learned that you have prepared, for private distribution, a volume illustrating the character of the late Amos Lawrence, whose munificence to this Institution they appreciate, and whose memory they honor; the undersigned, a Committee appointed for the purpose, express to you their earnest desire that you would allow it to be published.

Very truly yours,

SAMUEL B. FORBES,
E. C. SMITH,
FRED. W. BEECHER,
HENRY HOPKINS.

To
W. R. LAWRENCE, M.D., *Boston*

PREFACE.

AMONG the papers of the late Amos Lawrence were found copies of a large number of letters addressed to his children.

With the hope that the good counsels there given, during a succession of years, extending from their childhood to adult age, might still be made profitable to their descendants, he had caused them to be carefully preserved.

These letters, as well as an irregular record of his daily experience, were scattered through many volumes, and required arrangement before they could be of use to those for whom they were intended.

As no one else of the immediate family could conveniently undertake the task, the editor considered it his duty to do that which could not properly be committed to one less nearly connected with the deceased.

The present volume, containing what was thought most interesting among those letters and extracts, was accordingly prepared for private circulation; and an edition of one hundred copies was printed and distributed among the nearest relatives and friends.

It has been thought by many that the record of such a life as is here portrayed would be useful to other readers, and especially to young men, — a class in whom Mr. Lawrence was deeply interested, and with whom circumstances in his own life had given him a peculiar bond of sympathy.

Although many, among both friends and strangers, have urged the publication of the present memorial, and some have even questioned the moral right of withholding from the view of others the light of an example so worthy of imitation, much hesitation has been felt in submitting to the public the recital of such domestic incidents as are treasured in the memory of every family; those incidents which cast a sunbeam or a shadow across every fireside, and yet possess little or no interest for the busy world without.

At the solicitation of the "Boston Young Men's Christian Union," the "Boston Young Men's Christian Association," and the students of Williams College, through their respective committees, and at the request of many esteemed citizens, the pages which were prepared for the eye of kindred and friends alone are now submitted to the public. Personal feeling is forgotten in the hope that the principles here inculcated may tend to promote the ends for which the subject of this memorial lived and labored.

The interest manifested in his life, and the tributes rendered to his memory, have been a source of sincere gratification to his family; and they would here tender their acknowledgments to all those who have expressed their interest and their wishes in regard to this publication.

The present volume is submitted with a few unimportant omissions, and with the addition of some materials, received after the issue of the first edition, which will throw light upon the character and principles of Mr. Lawrence during his early business career.

His course was that of a private citizen, who took but little part in public measures or in public life.

To the general reader, therefore, there may be but little to amuse in a career so devoid of incident, and so little connected with the stirring events of his times; but there cannot fail to be something to interest those who can appreciate the spirit which, in this instance, led to a rare fidelity in the fulfilment of important trusts, and the consecration of a life to the highest duties.

Mr. Lawrence was eminently a religious man, and a deep sense of accountability may be discovered at the foundation of those acts of beneficence, which, during his lifetime, might have been attributed to a less worthy motive.

It has been the object of the editor to allow the subject of this memorial to tell his own story, and to add merely what is necessary to preserve the thread of the narrative, or to throw light upon the various matters touched upon in the correspondence.

It is designed to furnish such materials as will afford a history of Mr. Lawrence's charitable efforts, rather than give a detailed account of what was otherwise an uneventful career.

Such selections from his correspondence are made as seemed best adapted to illustrate the character of the man; such as exhibit his good and valuable traits, without attempting to conceal those imperfections, an exemption from which would elevate him above the common sphere of mortals.

Most of his letters are of a strictly private nature, and involve the record of many private details. His domestic tastes, and his affection for his family, often led him to make mention of persons and events in such a way that few letters could be wholly given without invading the precincts of the family circle.

The engraving at the commencement of the volume is from an original portrait, by Harding, in the possession of the editor, a copy of which hangs in the library of Williams College.

It seems also fitting to include a portrait of the Hon. Abbott Lawrence, who, for forty-three years, was so intimately associated with the subject of this memorial in all the trials, as well as in the triumphs, of business life, and who was still more closely connected by the bonds of fraternal affection and sympathy. A few days only have elapsed since he was removed from the scene of his earthly labors.

The grave has rarely closed over one who to such energy of character and strength of purpose united a disposition so gentle and forbearing. Amidst the perplexities attending his extended business relations, and in the excitement of the political struggles in which he was called to take part, he was never tempted to overstep the bounds of courtesy, or to regard his opponents otherwise than with feelings of kindness.

His wealth was used freely for the benefit of others, and for the advancement of all those good objects which tended to promote the welfare of his fellow-men.

That divine spark of charity, which burned with such ceaseless energy in the bosom of his elder brother, was caught up by him, and exhibited its fruits in those acts of munificence which will make him long remembered as a benefactor of his race.

BOSTON, *September* 1st, 1855.

CONTENTS.

CHAPTER I.
                                                          PAGE
BIRTH. — ANCESTRY. — PARENTS, ... 15

CHAPTER II.
EARLY YEARS. — SCHOOL DAYS. — APPRENTICESHIP, ... 20

CHAPTER III.
ARRIVAL IN BOSTON. — CLERKSHIP. — COMMENCES BUSINESS. — HABITS, ... 28

CHAPTER IV.
BUSINESS HABITS. — HIS FATHER'S MORTGAGE. — RESOLUTIONS. — ARRIVAL OF BROTHERS IN BOSTON, ... 35

CHAPTER V.
VISITS AT GROTON. — SICKNESS. — LETTER FROM DR. SHATTUCK. — ENGAGEMENT. — LETTER TO REV. DR. GANNETT. — MARRIAGE, ... 40

CONTENTS

CHAPTER VI.

BRAMBLE NEWS. — JUNIOR PARTNER GOES TO ENGLAND. — LETTERS TO BROTHER, ... 47

CHAPTER VII.

DEATH OF SISTER. — LETTERS, ... 54

CHAPTER VIII.

DOMESTIC HABITS. — ILLNESS AND DEATH OF WIFE, ... 59

CHAPTER IX.

JOURNEYS. — LETTERS. — JOURNEY TO NEW YORK, ... 68

CHAPTER X.

MARRIAGE. — ELECTED TO LEGISLATURE. — ENGAGES IN MANUFACTURES. — REFLECTIONS, ... 77

CHAPTER XI.

REFLECTIONS. — BUNKER HILL MONUMENT. — LETTERS, ... 82

CHAPTER XII.

JOURNEY TO CANADA. — LETTERS. — DIARY. — CHARITIES, ... 89

CHAPTER XIII.

CORRESPONDENCE WITH MR. WEBSTER. — LETTERS, ... 96

CHAPTER XIV.

TESTIMONIAL TO MR. WEBSTER. — DANGEROUS ILLNESS. — LETTERS, ... 102

CHAPTER XV.

OURNEY TO NEW HAMPSHIRE. — LETTERS. — RESIGNS OFFICE OF TRUSTEE AT HOSPITAL. — LETTERS, ... 109

CHAPTER XVI.

DAILY EXERCISE. — REGIMEN. — IMPROVING HEALTH. — LETTERS, ... 122

CHAPTER XVII.

REFLECTIONS. — VISIT TO WASHINGTON. — VISIT TO RAINSFORD ISLAND. REFLECTIONS. — VIEW OF DEATH. — REFLECTIONS, ... 137

CHAPTER XVIII.

BROTHER'S DEATH. — LETTERS. — GIFTS. — LETTERS. — BIRTH-PLACE. - DIARY. — APPLICATIONS FOR AID. — REFLECTIONS. — LETTER FROM REV. DR. STONE. — DIARY, ... 147

CHAPTER XIX.

REFLECTIONS. — LETTERS. — ACCOUNT OF EFFORTS TO COMPLETE BUNKER HILL MONUMENT, ... 165

CHAPTER XX.

INTEREST IN MOUNT AUBURN. — REV. DR. SHARP. — LETTER FROM BISHOP McILVAINE. — LETTER FROM JUDGE STORY, ... 175

CHAPTER XXI.

ACQUAINTANCE WITH PRESIDENT HOPKINS.—LETTERS.—AFFECTION FOR BRATTLE-STREET CHURCH.—DEATH OF MRS. APPLETON.—LETTERS.—AMESBURY CO., ... 182

CHAPTER XXII.

DEATH OF HIS DAUGHTER.—LETTERS.—DONATION TO WILLIAMS COLLEGE.—BENEFICENCE.—LETTERS, ... 193

CHAPTER XXIII.

LETTER FROM DR. SHARP.—ILLNESS AND DEATH OF HIS SON.—LETTERS.—AFFLICTIONS, ... 203

CHAPTER XXIV.

REFLECTIONS.—EXPENDITURES.—LETTERS.—DONATION FOR LIBRARY AT WILLIAMS COLLEGE.—VIEWS ON STUDY OF ANATOMY, ... 212

CHAPTER XXV.

DONATION TO LAWRENCE ACADEMY.—CORRESPONDENCE WITH R. G. PARKER.—SLEIGH-RIDES.—AVERSION TO NOTORIETY.—CHILDREN'S HOSPITAL, 221

CHAPTER XXVI.

CAPTAIN A. S. McKENZIE.—DIARY.—AID TO IRELAND.—MADAM PRESCOTT.—SIR WILLIAM COLEBROOKE. 234

CHAPTER XXVII.

MR. LAWRENCE AS AN APPLICANT. — LETTERS. — DIARY. — PRAYER AND MEDITATIONS. — FAC-SIMILE OF HAND-WRITING. — LIBERALITY TO A CREDITOR. — LETTERS, ... 242

CHAPTER XXVIII.

REFLECTIONS. — VIEWS ON HOLDING OFFICE. — LETTERS. — CAPT. A. SLIDELL McKENZIE. — DEATH OF BROTHER AND OF HON. J. MASON, ... 255

CHAPTER XXIX.

SYSTEM IN ACCOUNTS. — LETTER FROM PROF. STUART. — LETTERS. — DIARY. — DR. HAMILTON. — FATHER MATHEW, ... 262

CHAPTER XXX.

CODICIL TO WILL. — ILLNESS. — GEN. WHITING. — LETTERS. — DIARY, ... 271

CHAPTER XXXI.

DIARY. — REFLECTIONS. — SICKNESS. — LETTER FROM DR. SHARP. — CORRESPONDENCE, ... 278

CHAPTER XXXII.

AMIN BEY. — AMOUNT OF DONATIONS TO WILLIAMS COLLEGE, ... 285

CHAPTER XXXIII.

LETTERS — LIKENESS OF ABBOTT LAWRENCE. — DIARY, ... 292

CHAPTER XXXIV.

SIR T. F. BUXTON. — LETTER FROM LADY BUXTON. — ELLIOTT CRESSON. — LETTERS, ... 298

CHAPTER XXXV.

LETTERS. — REV. DR. SCORESBY. — WABASH COLLEGE, ... 304

CHAPTER XXXVI.

DIARY. — AMOUNT OF CHARITIES. — LETTERS. — THOMAS TARBELL. — UNCLE TOBY. — REV. DR. LOWELL, ... 311

CHAPTER XXXVII.

CORRESPONDENCE. — DIARY, ... 324

CHAPTER XXXVIII.

MR. LAWRENCE SERVES AS PRESIDENTIAL ELECTOR. — GEN. FRANKLIN PIERCE. — SUDDEN DEATH. — FUNERAL, ... 334

CHAPTER XXXIX.

SKETCH OF CHARACTER BY REV. DRS. LOTHROP AND HOPKINS, ... 343

CHAPTER XL.

CONCLUSION, ... 352

INDEX, ... 361

DIARY AND CORRESPONDENCE.

CHAPTER I.

BIRTH. — ANCESTRY. — PARENTS

AMOS LAWRENCE was born in Groton, Mass., on the 22d of April, 1786. His ancestor, John Lawrence, was baptized, according to the records, on the 8th of October, 1609, at Wisset, County of Suffolk, England, where the family had resided for a long period, though originally from the County of Lancaster.

Butler, in his "History of Groton," has, among other details, the following:

"The first account of the ancestor of the numerous families of this name in Groton and Pepperell, which can be relied upon as certain, is, that he was an inhabitant of Watertown as early as 1635. He probably came in the company which came with Governor Winthrop, in 1630. His given name was John, and that of his wife was Elizabeth. Whether they were married in England or not, has not been ascertained. Their eldest child was born in Watertown, January 14, 1635. He removed to Groton, with probably all his family, at an early period of its settlement, as his name is found in the records there in 1663. He was an original proprietor, having a twenty-acre right."

Of the parents of the subject of this memoir, the same author writes:

"Samuel Lawrence, the son of Captain Amos Lawrence, sen., was an officer in the continental army, in the former part of the Revolutionary War. He was in the battle of Bunker Hill, where a musket-ball passed through his beaver hat. He was also in the battle in Rhode Island, where he served as adjutant under General Sullivan. On the 22d day of July, 1777, being at home, on a furlough, for the express purpose, he was married to Susanna Parker. * * * *

"Having faithfully served in the cause of his country during the term of his engagement, he returned to his native town, to enjoy the peace and quiet of domestic life on his farm. He was elected by his townsmen to some of the highest offices in their gift; he was a deacon of the church, and a justice of the peace *quorum unus*. He took a deep interest in providing means for the education of youth, particularly in establishing and supporting the seminary in Groton, which now, in gratitude to him and his sons, bears the family name. Of this institution he was a trustee thirty-three years, and in its benefits and advantages he gave ample opportunities for all his children to participate. Here their minds undoubtedly received some of those early impressions, the developments and consequences of which it will be the work of their biographers hereafter to portray. No deduction, however, should here be made from the importance of parental instruction, to add to the merit of academical education. The correct lessons given by the mother in the nursery are as necessary to give the right inclination to the tender mind as are those of the tutor in the highest seminary to prepare it for the business of life and intellectual greatness. In the present case, all the duties incumbent on a mother to teach her offspring to be good, and consequently great, were discharged with fidelity and success. Both parents lived to see, in the subject of their care, all that they could reasonably hope or desire. He died November 8, 1827, æt. seventy-three; and his venerable widow, May 2, 1845, æt. eighty-nine."

Mr. Lawrence writes, in 1849, to a friend:

"My father belonged to a company of *minute-men* in Groton, at the commencement of the Revolution. On the morning of the 19th of April, 1775, when the news reached town that the British troops were on the road from Boston, General Prescott, who was a neighbor, came towards the house on horseback, at rapid speed, and cried out, 'Samuel, notify your men: *the British are coming.*' My father mounted the general's horse, rode a distance of seven miles, notified the men of his circuit, and was back again at his father's house in forty minutes. In three hours the company was ready to march, and on the next day (the 20th) reached Cambridge. My father was in the battle of Bunker Hill; received a bullet through his cap, which cut his hair from front to rear; received a spent grape-shot upon his arm, without breaking the bone; and lost a large number of men. His veteran Captain Farwell was shot through the body, was taken up for dead, and was so reported by the man who was directed to carry him off. This report brought back the captain's voice, and he exclaimed, with his utmost power, 'It *an't true; don't let my poor wife hear of this; I shall live to see my country free.*' And so it turned out. This good man, who had served at the capture of Cape Breton in 1745, again in 1755, and now on Bunker Hill in 1775, is connected with everything interesting in my early days. The bullet was extracted, and remains, as a memento, with his descendants. My father and mother were acquainted from their childhood, and engaged to be married some time in 1775. They kept up a correspondence through 1776, when he was at New York; but, on a visit to her, in 1777 (his mother having advised them to be married, as Susan had better be Sam's widow than his forlorn damsel), they were married; but, while the ceremony was going forward, the signal was given to call all soldiers to their posts; and, within the hour, he left his wife, father, mother, and friends, to join his regiment, then at Cambridge. This was on the 22d day of July, 1777. In consideration of the circumstances, his colonel allowed him to return to his wife, and to join the army at Rhode Island in a brief time (two or three days). He did so, and saw nothing more of home until the last day of that year. The army being in winter quarters, he got a furlough for a short period, and reached home in time to assist at the ordination of the Rev. Daniel Chaplin, of whose church both my parents were then members. His return was a season of great joy to all his family. His stay was brief, and nothing more was seen of him until the autumn of 1778, when he retired from the army, in time to be with his wife at the birth of their first child. From that time he was identified with everything connected with the good of the town. As we children came forward, we were carefully looked after, but were taught to use the talents intrusted to us; and every nerve was strained to provide for us the academy which is now doing so much there. We *sons* are doing less for education *for our means* than our father for his means."

Of his mother Mr. Lawrence always spoke in the

strongest terms of veneration and love, and in many of his letters are found messages of affection, such as could have emanated only from a heart overflowing with filial gratitude. Her form bending over their bed in silent prayer, at the hour of twilight, when she was about leaving them for the night, is still among the earliest recollections of her children.

She was a woman well fitted to train a family for the troubled times in which she lived. To the kindest affections and sympathies she united energy and decision, and in her household enforced that strict and unhesitating obedience, which she considered as the foundation of all success in the education of children. Her hands were never idle, as may be supposed, when it is remembered that in those days, throughout New England, in addition to the cares of a farming establishment, much of the material for clothing was manufactured by the inmates of the family. Many hours each day she passed at the hand-loom, and the hum of the almost obsolete spinning-wheel even now comes across the memory like the remembrance of a pleasant but half-forgotten melody.

CHAPTER II.

EARLY YEARS. — SCHOOL DAYS. — APPRENTICESHIP.

THE first public instruction received by Mr. Lawrence was at the district school kept at a short distance from his father's house. Possessing a feeble constitution, he was often detained at home by sickness, where he employed himself industriously with his books and tools, in the use of which he acquired a good degree of skill, as may be seen from a letter to his son, at Groton, in 1839 :

" Near the barn used to be an old fort, where the people went to protect themselves from the Indians; and, long since my remembrance, the old cellar was there, surrounded by elder-bushes and the like. I made use of many a piece of the elder for pop-guns and squirts, in the preparation of which I acquired a strong taste for the use of the pen-knife and jack-knife. I like the plan of boys acquiring the taste for tools, and of their taking pains to learn their use; for they may be so situated as to make a very slight acquaintance very valuable to them. And, then, another advantage is that they may have exercise of body and mind in some situations where they would suffer without. How do you employ yourself? Learn as much as you can of farming; for the work of your hands in this way may prove the best resource in securing comfort to you. The beautiful images of early life come up in these bright moonlight nights, the like of which I used to enjoy in the fields below our old mansion, where I was sent to watch the cattle. There I studied astronomy to more account than ever afterwards; for the heavens were impressive teachers of the goodness of that Father who is ever near to each one of his children. May you never lose sight of this truth, and so conduct yourself that at any moment you may be ready to answer when He calls!"

He did not allow himself to be idle, but, from his earliest years, exhibited the same spirit of industry which led to success in after life. With a natural quickness of apprehension, and a fondness for books, he made commendable progress, in spite of his disadvantages. His father's social disposition and hospitable feelings made the house a favorite resort for both friends and strangers; and among the most welcome were old messmates and fellow-soldiers, to whose marvellous adventures and escapes the youthful listener lent a most attentive ear. In after life he often alluded to the intense interest with which he hung upon these accounts of revolutionary scenes, and times which "tried men's souls." The schoolmaster was usually billeted upon the family; and there are now living individuals high in political and social life who served in that capacity, and who look back with pleasure to the days passed under that hospitable roof.

At a later period, he seems to have been transferred

to another school, in the adjoining district, as will be seen by the following extract of a letter, written in 1844, to a youth at the Groton Academy:

"More than fifty years ago, your father and I were school children together. I attended then at the old meeting-house, or North Barn, as it was called, by way of derision, where I once remember being in great tribulation at having lost my spelling-book on the way. It was afterwards restored to me by Captain Richardson, who found it under his pear-tree, where I had been, without leave, on my way to school, and with the other children helped myself to his fruit."

From the district school, Mr. Lawrence entered the Groton Academy, of which all his brothers and sisters were members at various times. As his strength was not sufficient to make him useful upon the farm, in the autumn of 1799 he was placed in a small store, in the neighboring town of Dunstable. There he passed but a few months; and, on account, perhaps, of greater facilities for acquiring a knowledge of business, he was transferred to the establishment of James Brazer, Esq., of Groton, an enterprising and thrifty country merchant, who transacted a large business, for those times, with his own and surrounding towns. The store was situated on the high road leading from Boston to New Hampshire and Canada, and was, consequently, a place of much resort, both for travellers and neighbors who took an interest in passing events. Several clerks were employed; and, as Mr. Brazer did not take a very active part in the management of the business, after a year or two nearly the whole responsibility of the establishment rested upon young Lawrence. The stock consisted of the usual variety kept in the country stores of those days, when neighbors could not, as now, run down to the city, thirty or forty miles distant, for any little matter of fancy, and return before dinner-time. Puncheons of rum and brandy, bales of cloth, kegs of tobacco, with hardware and hosiery, shared attention in common with silks and thread, and all other articles for female use. Among other duties, the young clerk was obliged to dispense medicines, not only to customers, but to all the physicians within twenty miles around, who depended on this establishment for their supply.

The confidence in his good judgment was such that he was often consulted, in preference to the physician, by those who were suffering from minor ails; and many were the extemporaneous doses which he administered for the weal or woe of the patient. The same confidence was extended to him in all other matters, no one doubted his assertion; and the character for probity and fairness which accompanied him through life was here established.

The quantity of rum and brandy sold would surprise the temperance men of modern days. At eleven o'clock, each forenoon, some stimulating beverage, according to the taste of the clerk who compounded it, was served out for the benefit of clerks and customers. Mr. Lawrence partook with the others; but, soon finding that the desire became more pressing at the approach of the hour for indulgence, he resolved to discontinue the habit altogether:

"His mind was soon made up. Understanding perfectly the ridicule he should meet with, and which for a time he did meet with in its fullest measure, he yet took at once the ground of *total abstinence*. Such a stand, taken at such an age, in such circumstances of temptation, before temperance societies had been heard of, or the investigations had been commenced on which they are based, was a practical instance of that judgment and decision which characterized him through life." *

In regard to this resolution, he writes, many years afterward, to a young student in college:

"In the first place, take this for your motto at the commencement of your journey, that the difference of going *just right*, or a *little wrong*, will be the difference of finding yourself in good quarters, or in a miserable bog or slough, at the end of it. Of the whole number educated in the Groton stores for some years before and after myself, no one else, to my knowledge, escaped the bog or slough; and my escape I trace to the simple fact of my having put a restraint upon my appetite. We five boys were in the habit, every forenoon, of making a drink compounded of

---

* President Hopkins's Sermon in commemoration of Amos Lawrence

rum, raisins, sugar, nutmeg, &c., with biscuit, — all palatable to eat and drink. After being in the store four weeks, I found myself admonished by my appetite of the approach of the hour for indulgence. Thinking the habit might make trouble if allowed to grow stronger, without further apology to my seniors I declined partaking with them. My first resolution was to abstain for a week, and, when the week was out, for a month, and then for a year. Finally, I resolved to abstain for the rest of my apprenticeship, which was for five years longer. During that whole period, I never drank a spoonful, though I mixed gallons daily for my old master and his customers. I decided not to be a slave to tobacco in any form, though I loved the odor of it then, and even now have in my drawer a superior Havana cigar, given me, not long since, by a friend, but only to smell of. I have never in my life smoked a cigar; never chewed but one quid, and that was before I was fifteen; and never took an ounce of snuff, though the scented rappee of forty years ago had great charms for me. Now, I say, to this simple fact of starting *just right* am I indebted, with God's blessing on my labors, for my present position, as well as that of the numerous connections sprung up around me. I have many details that now appear as plain to me as the sun at noonday, by which events are connected together, and which have led to results that call on me to bless the Lord for all his benefits, and to use the opportunities thus permitted to me in cheering on the generation of young men who have claims upon my sympathies as relations, fellow-townsmen, or brethren on a more enlarged scale."

Of this period he writes elsewhere, as follows:

"When I look back, I can trace the small events which happened at your age as having an influence upon all the after things. My academy lessons, little academy balls, and eight-cent expenses for music and gingerbread, the agreeable partners in the hall, and pleasant companions in the stroll, all helped to make me feel that I had a character even then; and, after leaving school and going into the store, there was not a month passed before I became impressed with the opinion that restraint upon appetite was necessary to prevent the slavery I saw destroying numbers around me. Many and many of the farmers, mechanics, and apprentices, of that day, have filled drunkards' graves, and have left destitute families and friends.

"The knowledge of every-day affairs which I acquired in my business apprenticeship in Groton has been a source of pleasure and profit even in my last ten years' discipline."

The responsibility thrown upon the young clerk was very great; and he seems cheerfully to have accepted it, and to have given himself up entirely to the performance of his business duties. His time, from early dawn till evening, was fully taken up; and, although living in the family of his employer, and within a mile of his father's house, a whole week would sometimes pass without his having leisure to pay even a flying visit.

But few details of his apprenticeship can now be gathered either from his contemporaries or from any allusions in his own writings. He was disabled for a time by an accident which came near being fatal. In assisting an acquaintance to unload a gun, by some means the charge exploded, and passed directly through the middle of his hand, making a round hole like that of a bullet. Sixty-three shot were picked out of the floor after the accident, and it seemed almost a miracle that he ever again had the use of his hand.

CHAPTER III.

ARRIVAL IN BOSTON. — CLERKSHIP. — COMMENCES BUSINESS. — HABITS. — LETTERS.

On the 22d of April, 1807, Mr. Lawrence became of age; and his apprenticeship, which had lasted seven years, was terminated.

On the 29th of the same month, he took his father's horse and chaise, and engaged a neighbor to drive him to Boston, with, as he says, many years afterwards,—

"Twenty dollars in my pocket, but feeling richer than I had ever felt before, or have felt since; so rich that I gave the man who came with me two dollars to save him from any expense, and insure him against loss by his spending two days on the journey here and back (for which he was glad of an excuse)."

His object was to make acquaintances, and to establish a credit which would enable him to commence business in Groton on his own account, in company with a fellow-apprentice.

A few days after his arrival in Boston, he received the offer of a clerkship from a respectable house; and, wishing to familiarize himself with the modes of conducting mercantile affairs in the metropolis, and with the desire of extending his acquaintance with business men, he accepted the offer. His employers were so well satisfied with the capacity of their new clerk, that, in the course of a few months, they made a proposition to admit him into partnership. Without any very definite knowledge of their affairs, he, much to their surprise, declined the offer. He did not consider the principles on which the business was conducted as the true ones. The result showed his sagacity; for, in the course of a few months, the firm became insolvent, and he was appointed by the creditors to settle their affairs. This he did to their satisfaction; and, having no further occupation, decided upon commencing business on his own account. He accordingly hired a small store in what was then called Cornhill, and furnished it by means of the credit which he had been able to obtain through the confidence with which he had inspired those whose acquaintance he had made during his brief sojourn in Boston.

On the 17th of December, 1807, he commenced business, after having engaged as his clerk Henry Whiting, in after years well and honorably known as Brigadier-General Whiting, of the United States Army.

Mr. Lawrence writes to General Whiting, in 1849, as follows:

"I have just looked into my first sales-book, and there see the entries made by you more than forty-one years ago. Ever since, you have been going up from the cornet of dragoons to the present station. Abbott, who took your place, is now the representative of his country at the Court of St. James."

In a memorandum in one of his account-books, he thus alludes to his condition at that time:

"I was then, in the matter of property, not worth a dollar. My father was comfortably off as a farmer, somewhat in debt; with perhaps four thousand dollars. My brother Luther was in the practice of law, getting forward, but not worth two thousand dollars; William had nothing; Abbott, a lad just fifteen years old, at school; and Samuel, a child seven years old."

Of the manner in which he occupied himself when not engaged about his business, he writes to his son in 1832:

"When I first came to this city, I took lodgings in the family of a widow who had commenced keeping boarders for a living. I was one of her first, and perhaps had been in the city two months when I went to this place; and she, of course, while I remained, was inclined to adopt any rules for the boarders that I prescribed. The only one I ever made was, that, after supper, all the boarders who remained in the public room should remain quiet at least for one hour, to give those who chose to study or read an opportunity of doing so without disturbance. The consequence was, that we had the most quiet and improving set of young men in the town. The few who did not wish to comply with the regulation went abroad after tea, sometimes to the theatre, sometimes to other places, but, to a man, became bankrupt in after life, not only in fortune, but in reputation; while a majority of the other class sustained good characters, and some are now living who are ornaments to society, and fill important stations. The influence of this small measure will perhaps be felt throughout generations. It was not less favorable on myself than on others."

Mr. Lawrence was remarkable through life for the most punctilious exactness in all matters relating to business. Ever prompt himself in all that he undertook, he submitted with little grace to the want of the same good trait in others. He writes to a friend:

"And now having delivered the message, having the power at the present moment, and not having the assurance that I shall be able to do it the next hour, I will state that I practised upon the maxim, '*Business before friends*,' from the commencement of my course. During the first seven years of my business in this city, I never allowed a bill against me to stand unsettled over the Sabbath. If the purchase of goods was made at auction on Saturday, and delivered to me, I always examined and settled the bill by note or by crediting it, and having it clear, so that, in case I was not on duty on Monday, there would be no trouble for my boys; thus keeping the business *before* me, instead of allowing it to *drive* me."

Absence from his home seemed only to strengthen the feelings of attachment with which he regarded its inmates

"My interest in home, and my desire to have something to tell my sisters to instruct and improve them, as well as to hear their comments upon whatever I communicated, was a powerful motive for me to spend a portion of each evening in my boarding-house, the first year I came to Boston, in reading and study."

During the same month in which he commenced his business, he opened a correspondence with one of his sisters by the following letter:

"BOSTON, December, 1807.

"DEAR E.: Although the youngest, you are no less dear to me than the other sisters. To you, therefore, I ought to be as liberal in affording pleasure (if you can find any in reading my letters) as to S. and M.; and, if there is any benefit resulting from them, you have a claim to it as well as they. From these considerations, and with the hope that you will write to me whenever you can do so with convenience, I have begun a correspondence which I hope will end only with life. To be able to write a handsome letter is certainly a very great accomplishment, and can best be attained by practice; and, if you now begin, I have no hesitation in saying, that, by the time you are sixteen, you will be mistress of a handsome style, and thrice the quantity of ideas you would otherwise possess, by omitting this part of education. At present, you can write about any subject that will afford you an opportunity of putting together a sentence, and I shall read it with pleasure. I mention this, that you need not fear writing on subjects not particularly interesting to me; the manner at present being of as much consequence as the matter.

"For our mutual pleasure and benefit, dear E., I hope you will not fail to gratify your affectionate brother AMOS."

To show the nature of the correspondence between the parties, extracts are given below from a letter dated within a few days of the preceding, and addressed to another sister ·

"From you, my dear sister, the injunction not to forget the duties of religion comes with peculiar grace. You beg I will pardon you for presuming to offer good advice. Does a good act require pardon? Not having committed an offence, I can grant you no pardon; but my thanks I can give, which you will accept, with an injunction never to withhold any caution or advice which you may think necessary or beneficial on account of fewer years having passed over your head.   *   *   *   *

"Many, when speaking of perfection, say it is not attainable, or hitherto unattainable, and it is therefore vain to try or hope for it. To such I would observe, that, from motives of duty to our Creator, and ambition in ourselves, we ought to strive for it, at least so far as not to be distanced by those who have preceded us. Morality is strict justice between man and man; therefore, a man being moral does not imply he is a Christian, but being a Christian implies he is a moral man.   *   *   *   *

"We ought to use our utmost endeavors to conquer our passions and evil propensities, to conform our lives to the strict rules of morality and the best practice of Christianity. I cannot go further, without introducing the subject of evil speaking, which you will perhaps think I have exhausted.   *   *   *

"I do not, my dear M., set myself up as a reformer of human nature, or to find fault with it; but these observations (which have occurred to me as I am writing) may serve to show how apt we are to do things which afford us no pleasure, and which oftentimes are attended with the most disagreeable consequences. If you receive any improvement from the sentiments, or pleasure from the perusal, of this letter, the time in writing will be considered as well spent by your affectionate brother

AMOS."

CHAPTER IV.

BUSINESS HABITS. — HIS FATHER'S MORTGAGE. — RESOLUTIONS. — ARRIVAL OF BROTHERS IN BOSTON.

MR. LAWRENCE had early formed, in the management of his affairs, certain principles, to which he rigidly adhered till the close of life. He writes:

"I adopted the plan of keeping an accurate account of merchandise bought and sold each day, with the profit as far as practicable. This plan was pursued for a number of years; and I never found my merchandise fall short in taking an account of stock, which I did as often at least as once in each year. I was thus enabled to form an opinion of my actual state as a business man. I adopted also the rule always to have property, after my second year's business, to represent forty per cent. at least more than I owed; that is, never to be in debt more than two and a half times my capital. This caution saved me from ever getting embarrassed. If it were more generally adopted, we should see fewer failures in business. Excessive credit is the rock on which so many business men are broken.

"When I commenced, the embargo had just been laid, and with such restrictions on trade that many were induced to leave it. But I felt great confidence, that, by industry, economy, and integrity, I could get a living; and the experiment showed that I was right. Most of the young men who commenced at that period failed by spending too much money, and using credit too freely.

"I made about fifteen hundred dollars the first year, and more than four thousand the second. Probably, had I made four thousand the first year, I should have failed the second or third year. I practised a system of rigid economy, and never allowed myself to spend a fourpence for unnecessary objects until I had acquired it."

It is known to many of Mr. Lawrence's friends that his father mortgaged his farm, and loaned the proceeds to his son; thereby enabling him, as some suppose, to do what he could not have done by his own unaided efforts. To show how far this supposition is correct, the following extract is given. It is copied from the back of the original mortgage deed, now lying before the writer, and bearing date of September 1, 1807. The extract is dated March, 1847:

"The review of this transaction always calls up the deep feelings of my heart. My honored father brought to me the one thousand dollars, and asked me to give him my note for it. I told him he did wrong to place himself in a situation to be made unhappy, if I lost the money. He told me he *guessed I would n't lose it*, and I gave him my note. The first thing I did was to take four per cent. premium on my Boston bills (the difference then between passable and Boston money), and send a thousand dollars in bills of the Hillsborough Bank to Amherst, New Hampshire, by my father, to my brother L. to carry to the bank and get specie, as he was going there to attend court that week. My brother succeeded in getting specie, principally in silver change, for the bills, and returned it to me in a few days. In the mean time, or shortly after, the bank had been sued, the bills discredited, and, in the end, proved nearly worthless. I determined not to use the money, except in the safest way; and therefore loaned it to Messrs. Parkman, in whom I had entire confidence. After I had been in business, and had made more than a thousand dollars, I felt that I could repay the money, come what would of it; being insured against fire, and trusting nobody for goods. I used it in my business, but took care to pay off the mortgage as soon as it would be received. The whole transaction is deeply interesting, and calls forth humble and devout thanksgiving to that merciful Father who has been to us better than our most sanguine hopes."

In alluding to this transaction in another place, he says:

"This incident shows how dangerous it is to the independence and comfort of families, for parents to take pecuniary responsibilities for their sons in trade, beyond their power of meeting them without embarrassment. Had my Hillsborough Bank notes not been paid as they were, nearly the whole amount would have been lost, and myself and family might probably have been ruined. The incident was so striking, that I have uniformly discouraged young men who have applied to me for credit, offering their fathers as bondsmen; and, by doing so, I have, I believe, saved some respectable families from ruin. My advice, however, has been sometimes rejected with anger. A young man who cannot get along without such aid will not be likely to get along with it. On the first day of January, 1808, I had been but a few days in business; and the profits on all my sales to that day were one hundred and seventy-five dollars and eighteen cents. The expenses were to come out, and the balance was my capital. In 1842, the sum had increased to such an amount as I thought would be good for my descendants; and, from that time, I have been my own executor. How shall I show my sense of responsibility? Surely by active deeds more than by unmeaning words. God grant me to be true and faithful in his work!"

Having become fairly established in Boston, Mr. Lawrence concluded to take his brother Abbott, then fifteen years of age, as an apprentice. On the 8th of October, 1808, Abbott accordingly joined his brother, who says of him:

"In 1808, he came to me as my apprentice, bringing his bundle under his arm, with less than three dollars in his pocket (and this was his fortune); a first-rate business lad he was, but, like other bright lads, needed the careful eye of a senior to guard him from the pitfalls that he was exposed to."

In his diary of February 10, 1847, he writes:

"In the autumn of 1809, I boarded at Granger's Coffee House, opposite Brattle-street Church; and, in the same house, Mr. Charles White took up his quarters, to prepare his then new play, called the 'Clergyman's Daughter.' He spent some months in preparing it to secure a *run* for the winter; and used to have Tennett, Canfield, Robert Treat Paine, and a host of others, to dine with him very often. I not unfrequently left the party at the dinner-table, and found them there when I returned to tea. Among the boarders was a fair proportion of respectable young men, of different pursuits; and, having got somewhat interested for White, we all agreed to go, and help bring out his Clergyman's Daughter.' Mrs. Darley was the lady to personate her, and a more beautiful creature could not be found. She and her husband (who sung his songs better than any man I had ever heard then) had all the spirit of parties in interest. We filled the boxes, and encored, and all promised a great run. After three nights, we found few beside the friends, and it was laid aside a failure. In looking back, the picture comes fresh before me; and, among all, I do not recollect one who was the better, and most were ruined. The theatre is no better now."

In 1849, he resumes:

"About this time, my brother William made me a little visit to recruit his health, which he had impaired by hard work on the farm, and by a generous attention to the joyous meetings of the young folks of both sexes, from six miles around, which meetings he never allowed to break in upon his work. He continued his visit through the winter, and became so much interested in my business that I agreed to furnish the store next my own for his benefit. Soon after that, I was taken sick; and he bought goods for himself to start with, and pushed on without fear. From that time, he was successful as a business man. He used his property faithfully, and I trust acceptably to the Master, who has called him to account for his talents. Our father's advice to us was,

"'Do not fall out by the way, for a three-fold cord is not quickly broken.'"

CHAPTER V.

VISITS AT GROTON. — SICKNESS. — LETTER FROM DR. SHATTUCK. — ENGAGEMENT. — LETTER TO REV. DR. GANNETT. — MARRIAGE.

DURING these years, Mr. Lawrence was in the habit of making occasional visits to his parents in Groton, thirty-five miles distant. His custom was to drive himself, leaving Boston at a late hour on Saturday afternoon, and often, as he says, encroaching upon the Sabbath before reaching home. After midnight, on Sunday, he would leave on his return; and thus was enabled to reach Boston about daybreak on Monday morning, without losing a moment's time in his business.

In 1810, Mr. Lawrence was seized with an alarming illness, through which he enjoyed the care and skill of his friend and physician, the late Dr. G. C. Shattuck, who, shortly before his own death, transmitted the following account of this illness to the editor of these pages, who also had the privilege of enjoying a friendship so much prized by his father:

"Feb. 28, 1853.

"More than forty years ago, New England was visited with a pestilence. The people were stricken with panic. The first victims were taken off unawares. In many towns in the interior of the commonwealth, the people assembled in town meeting, and voted to pay, from the town treasury, physicians to be in readiness to attend on any one assailed with the premonitory symptoms of disease. The distemper was variously named, cold plague, spotted fever, and malignant remittent fever. After a day of unusual exercise, your father was suddenly taken ill. The worthy family in which he boarded were prompt in their sympathy. A physician was called: neighbors and friends volunteered their aid. Remedies were diligently employed. Prayers in the church were offered up for the sick one. A pious father left his home, on the banks of the Nashua, to be with his son. To the physician in attendance he gave a convulsive grasp of the hand, and, with eyes brimful of tears, and choked utterance, articulated, 'Doctor, if Amos has not money enough, I have!' To the anxious father his acres seemed like dust in the balance contrasted with the life of his son. He was a sensible man, acting on the principle that the stimulus of reward is a salutary adjunct to the promptings of humanity. God rebuked the disorder, though the convalescence was slow. A constitution with an originally susceptible nervous temperament had received a shock which rendered him a long time feeble. An apprentice, with a discretion beyond his years, maintained a healthy activity in his mercantile operations, to the quiet of his mind. He did not need great strength; for sagacity and decision supplied every other lack. Supply and demand were as familiar to him as the alphabet. He knew the wants of the country, and sources of supply. Accumulation followed his operations, and religious principle regulated the distribution of the cumbrous surplus. A sensible and pious father, aided by a prudent mother, had trained the child to become the future man. You will excuse my now addressing you, when you recur to the tradition that I had participated in the joy of the house when you first opened your eyes to the light. That God's promises to the seed of the righteous may extend to you and yours, is the prayer of your *early* acquaintance,

"GEORGE C. SHATTUCK."

But few details of Mr. Lawrence's business from this date until 1815 are now found. Suffice it to say, that, through the difficult and troubled times in which the United States were engaged in the war with England, his efforts were crowned with success. Dark clouds sometimes arose in the horizon, and various causes of discouragement from time to time cast a gloom over the mercantile world; but despondency formed no part of his character, while cool sagacity and unceasing watchfulness and perseverance enabled him to weather many a storm which made shipwreck of others around him.

Amidst the engrossing cares of business, however, Mr. Lawrence found time to indulge in more genial pursuits, as will be seen from the following lines, addressed to his sister:

"BOSTON, March 17, 1811.

"My not having written to you since your return, my dear M., has proceeded from my having other numerous avocations, and partly from a carelessness in such affairs reprehensible in me. You will, perhaps, be surprised to learn the extent and importance of my avocations; for, in addition to my usual routine of mercantile affairs, I have lately been engaged in a negotiation of the first importance, and which I have accomplished very much to my own satisfaction. It is no other than having offered myself as a husband to your very good friend Sarah Richards, which offer she has agreed to accept. So, next fall, you must set your mind on a wedding. Sarah I have long known and esteemed: there is such a reciprocity of feelings, sentiments, and principles, that I have long thought her the most suitable person I have seen for me to be united with. Much of my time, as you may well suppose, is spent in her society; and here I cannot but observe the infinite advantage of good sense and good principles over the merely elegant accomplishments of fashionable education. By the latter we may be fascinated for a time; but they will afford no satisfaction on retrospection. The former you are compelled to respect and to love. Such qualities are possessed by Sarah; and, were I to say anything further in her favor, it would be that she is beloved by you. Adieu, my dear sister, A. L."

As this volume is intended only for the perusal of the family and friends of the late Amos Lawrence, no apology need be made for introducing such incidents of his life, of a domestic nature, as may be thought interesting, and which it might not seem advisable to introduce under other circumstances. Of this nature are some details connected with this engagement. The young lady here alluded to, whose solid qualities he thus, at the age of twenty-five and in the first flush of a successful courtship, so calmly discusses, in addition to these, possessed personal charms sufficient to captivate the fancy of even a more philosophical admirer than himself. Her father, Giles Richards, was a man of great ingenuity, who resided in Boston at the close of the Revolutionary War. He owned an establishment for the manufactory of cards for preparing wool. A large number of men were employed; and, at that time, it was considered one of the objects worthy of notice by strangers. As such, it was visited by General Washington on his northern tour; and may be found described, in the early editions of Morse's Geography, among the industrial establishments of Boston. As in the case of many more noted men of inventive genius, his plans were more vast than the means of accomplishment; and the result was, loss of a handsome competency, and embarrassment in business, from which he retired with unsullied reputation, and passed his latter years in the vicinity of Boston. Here the evening of his life was cheered by the constant and watchful care of his wife, whose cheerful and happy temperament shed a radiance around his path, which, from a naturally desponding character, might otherwise have terminated in gloom. She had been the constant companion of her husband in all his journeyings and residences in nearly every State in the Union, where his business had called him; and, after forty years, returned to die in the house where she was born, — the parsonage once occupied by her father, the Rev. Amos Adams, of Roxbury, who, at the time of the Revolution, was minister of the church now under the pastoral care of the Rev. Dr. Putnam.

Sarah had been placed in the family of the Rev. Dr. Chaplin, minister of the church at Groton, and was a member of the academy when Mr. Lawrence first made her acquaintance. "The academy balls, the agreeable partners in the hall, the pleasant companions in the stroll," remembered with so much pleasure in after life, were not improbably associated with this acquaintance, who had become a visitor and friend to his own sisters. After a separation of four years, the acquaintance was accidentally renewed in the year 1807. Sarah was on a visit at Cambridge to the family of Caleb Gannett, Esq., then and for many years afterwards Steward of Harvard University. In a letter to Rev. Dr. Gannett, dated February 15, 1845, Mr. Lawrence thus alludes to this interview:

"My first interview with you, thirty-eight years ago, when you were led by the hand into the store where I then was, in Cornhill, by that friend (who was afterwards my wife), unconscious of my being within thirty miles, after a four years' separation, connects you in my thoughts with her, her children and grandchildren, in a way that no one can appreciate who has not had the experience."

Enclosed in this letter was a faded paper, on which were written several verses of poetry, with the following explanation:

"Only think of your sainted mother writing this little scrap thirty-eight years ago, when on her death-bed, for her young friend, then on a visit to her, to teach to you, who could not read; and this scrap, written upon a blank term-bill without premeditation, being preserved by that friend while she lived, and, after her death, by her daughter while she lived, and, after her death, being restored to me as the rightful disposer of it; and my happening, within four days after, to meet you under such circumstances as made it proper to show it to you."

MRS. GANNETT'S HYMN FOR HER LITTLE BOY IN 1807.

How can a child forgetful prove
Of all that wakes the heart to love,
And from the path of duty stray,
To spend his time in sport and play;
Neglectful of the blessing given,
Which marks the path to peace and heaven?

O! how can I, who daily share
A mother's kind, assiduous care,
Be idle, and ungrateful too;
Forsake the good, the bad pursue;
Neglectful of the blessings given,
Which mark the path to peace and heaven?

O! how can I such folly show,
When faults indulged to vices grow, —
Who know that idle days ne'er make
Men that are useful, good, or great?
Dear mother, still be thou my guide,
Nor suffer me my faults to hide;
And O may God his grace impart
To fix my feeble, foolish heart,
That I may wait the blessing given,
Which marks the path to peace and heaven!

MEM. — Mrs. Gannett died soon after writing this on a blank term-bill of Harvard College, in 1807. — A. L., 1847.

The marriage of Mr. Lawrence took place in Boston, on the 6th of June, 1811, three months after announcing his engagement to his sister.

CHAPTER VI.

BRAMBLE NEWS. — JUNIOR PARTNER GOES TO ENGLAND. — LETTERS TO BROTHER.

IN 1849, Mr. Lawrence writes as follows.

"On the 1st of January, 1814, I took my brother Abbott into partnership on equal shares, putting fifty thousand dollars, that I had then earned, into the concern. Three days afterwards, the 'Bramble News' came, by which the excessive high price of goods was knocked down. Our stock was then large, and had cost a high price. He was in great anguish, considering himself a bankrupt for at least five thousand dollars. I cheered him by offering to cancel our copartnership indentures, give him up his note, and, at the end of the year, pay him five thousand dollars. He declined the offer, saying I should lose that, and more beside, and, as he had enlisted, would do the best he could. This was in character, and it was well for us both. He was called off to do duty as a soldier, through most of the year. I took care of the business, and prepared to retreat with my family into the country whenever the town seemed liable to fall into the hands of the British, who were very threatening in their demonstrations. We still continue mercantile business under the first set of indentures, and under the same firm, merely adding '& Co.,' as new partners have been admitted."

In March, 1815, the junior partner embarked on

board the ship Milo, the first vessel which sailed from Boston for England after the proclamation of peace On the eve of his departure, he received from his brother and senior partner a letter containing many good counsels for his future moral guidance, as well as instructions in relation to the course of business to be pursued. From that letter, dated March 11th, the following extracts are taken:

"MY DEAR BROTHER: I have thought best, before you go abroad, to suggest a few hints for your benefit in your intercourse with the people among whom you are going. As a first and leading principle, let every transaction be of that pure and honest character that you would not be ashamed to have appear before the whole world as clearly as to yourself. In addition to the advantages arising from an honest course of conduct with your fellow-men, there is the satisfaction of reflecting within yourself that you have endeavored to do your duty; and, however greatly the best may fall short of doing all they ought, they will be sure not to do more than their principles enjoin.

"It is, therefore, of the highest consequence that you should not only cultivate correct principles, but that you should place your standard of action so high as to require great vigilance in living up to it.

"In regard to your business transactions, let everything be so registered in your books, that any person, without difficulty, can understand the whole of your concerns. You may be cut off in the midst of your pursuits, and it is of no small consequence that your temporal affairs should always be so arranged that you may be in readiness.

"If it is important that you should be well prepared in this point of view, how much more important is it that you should be prepared in that which relates to eternity!

"You are young, and the course of life seems open, and pleasant prospects greet your ardent hopes; but you must remember that the race is not always to the swift, and that however flattering may be your prospects, and however zealously you may seek pleasure, you can never find it except by cherishing pure principles, and practising right conduct. My heart is full on this subject, my dear brother, and it is the only one on which I feel the least anxiety.

"While here, your conduct has been such as to meet my entire approbation; but the scenes of another land may be more than your principles will stand against. I say, *may be*, because young men, of as fair promise as yourself, have been lost by giving a small latitude (innocent in the first instance) to their propensities. But I pray the Father of all mercies to have you in his keeping, and preserve you amid temptations.

* * * * * *

"I can only add my wish to have you write me frequently and particularly, and that you will embrace every opportunity of gaining information. Your affectionate brother,

"AMOS LAWRENCE.
"To ABBOTT LAWRENCE."

Again, on the 28th of the month, he writes to the same, after his departure:

"I hope you will have arrived in England early in April; and if so, you will be awaiting with anxious solicitude the arrival of the 'Galen,' by which vessel you will receive letters from *home*, a word which brings more agreeable associations to the mind and feelings of a young stranger in a foreign land than any other in our language. I have had many fears that you have had a rough passage, as the weather on the Friday following your departure was very boisterous, and continued so for a number of days, and much of the time since has been uncomfortable. I trust, however, that the same good Hand which supplies our daily wants has directed your course to the desired port.

"With a just reliance on that Power, we need have no fear, though winds and waves should threaten our destruction. The interval between the time of bidding adieu and of actual departure called into exercise those fine feelings which those only have who can prize friends, and on that account I was happy to see so much feeling in yourself.

"Since your departure nothing of a public nature has transpired of particular interest. All that there is of news or interest among us you will gather from the papers forwarded.

"Those affairs which relate particularly to ourselves will be of as much interest as any; I shall therefore detail our business operations.

*　　*　　*　　*　　*　　*

"My next and constant direction will be to keep a particular watch over yourself, that you do not fall into any habits of vice; and, as a means of preserving yourself, I would most strictly enjoin that your Sabbaths be not spent in noise and riot, but that you attend the public worship of God. This you may think an unnecessary direction to you, who have always been in the habit of doing so. I hope it may be; at any rate, it will do no harm.

"That you may be blessed with health, and enjoy properly the blessings of life, is the wish of your ever affectionate brother,

"A. L

"To Abbott Lawrence"

(TO ABBOTT LAWRENCE.)

"Boston, April 15th, 1815.

"MY DEAR BROTHER: By the favor of Heaven I trust ere this you have landed upon the soil from which sprang our forefathers. In the contemplation of that wonderful 'Isle' on your first arrival, there must be a feeling bordering on devotion. The thousand new objects, which make such constant demand on your attention, will not, I hope, displace the transatlantic friends from the place they should occupy in your remembrance. Already do I begin to count the days when I may reasonably hear from you.

"I pray you to let no opportunity pass without writing, as you will be enabled to appreciate the pleasure your letters will give by those which you receive from home. Since your departure, our father has been dangerously ill; he seems fast recovering, but we much fear a relapse, when he would, in all probability, be immediately deprived of life, or his disease would so far weaken him as to terminate his usefulness. Our mother continues as comfortable as when you left us. Should you live to return, probably one or both our parents may not be here to welcome you; we have particular reason for thankfulness that they have both been spared to us so long, and have been so useful in the education of their children.

"All others of our connection have been in health since your departure, and a comfortable share of happiness seems to have been enjoyed by all.

*   *   *   *   *   *

"Now for advice: you are placed in a particularly favorable situation, my dear brother, for improving yourself in the knowledge of such things as will hereafter be useful to you. Let no opportunity pass without making the most of it. There are necessarily many vacant hours in your business, which ought not to pass unemployed. I pretend not to suggest particular objects for your attention, but only the habit generally of active employment, which, while making your time useful and agreeable to yourself, will be the best safeguard to your virtue. The American character, I trust, is somewhat respected in England at this time, notwithstanding it was lately at so low an ebb; and I would wish every American to endeavor to do something to improve it. Especially do I wish you, my dear A., who visit that country under circumstances so favorable, to do your part in establishing a character for your country as well as for yourself. Thus prays your affectionate brother, A. L."

To his wife, at Groton, Mr. Lawrence writes, under date of June 4, 1815:

"The Milo got in yesterday, and brought letters from Abbott, dated 4th April. He was then in Manchester, and enjoyed the best health. He wrote to our father, which letter, I hope, will arrive at Groton by to-morrow's mail. I received from him merchandise, which I hope to get out of the ship and sell this week. I suspect there are few instances of a young man leaving this town, sending out goods, and having them sold within ninety days from the time of his departure. It is eighty-four days this morning since he left home."

(TO ABBOTT LAWRENCE.)

"BOSTON, June 7, 1815.

"DEAR BROTHER: By the arrival of the Milo last Saturday, and packet on Monday, I received your several letters, giving an account of your proceedings. You are as famous among your acquaintances here for the rapidity of your movements as Bonaparte. Mr. —— thinks that you leave Bonaparte entirely in the background. I really feel a little proud, my dear brother, of your conduct. Few instances of like despatch are known.

"The sensations you experienced in being greeted so heartily by the citizens of Liverpool, were not unlike those you felt on hearing the news of peace. I am happy to state to you that our father has so far recovered from his illness as to be able to attend to his farm. Our mother's health is much as when you left.

"Your friends here feel a good deal of interest in your welfare, and read with deep interest your letters to them. The opportunity is peculiarly favorable for establishing a reputation as a close observer of men and manners, and for those improvements which travelling is reputed to give.

"When writing to you sentences of advice, my heart feels all the tender sympathies and affections which bind me to my own children. This is my apology, if any be necessary, for so frequently touching on subjects for your moral improvement.

"In any condition I can subscribe myself no other than your ever affectionate brother, A. L."

CHAPTER VII.

DEATH OF SISTER. — LETTERS

On the 19th of August, 1815, Mr. Lawrence, in the following letter to his brother, announced the sudden death of a sister, who to youth and beauty united many valuable qualities of mind and character:

"To you, who are at such a distance from home, and employed in the busy pursuits of life, the description of domestic woe will not come with such force as on us who were eye-witnesses to an event which we and all our friends shall not cease to deplore. We have attended this morning to the last sad office of affection to our loved sister S. Although for ourselves we mourn the loss of so much excellence, yet for her we rejoice that her race is so soon run. We are permitted to hope that she is now a saint in heaven, celebrating before the throne of her Father the praises of the redeemed. She met death in the enjoyment of that hope which is the peculiar consolation of the believer. This event, I know, my dear brother, is calculated to awaken all the tender recollections of home, and to call forth all your sympathy for the anguish of friends; but it is also calculated to soften the heart, and to guide you in your own preparation for that great day of account. The admonition, I hope, may not be lost on any of us, and happy will it be for us if we use it aright."

(TO THE SAME.)

"Boston, October 19, 1815.

"Dear Abbott: By this vessel I have written to you, but am always desirous of communicating the last intelligence from home, therefore I write again. The situation of our town, our country, our friends, and all the objects of endearment, continues the same as heretofore. We are, to be sure, getting into a religious controversy which does not promise to increase the stock of charity among us, but good will undoubtedly arise from it. The passions of some of our brethren are too much engaged, and it would seem from present appearances that consequences unfavorable to the cause of our Master may ensue; but the wrath of man is frequently made subservient to the best purposes, and the good of mankind may in this case be greatly promoted by what at present seems a great evil. Men's passions are but poor guides to the discovery of truth, but they may sometimes elicit light by which others may get at the truth.

"It does seem to me that a man need only use his common sense, and feel a willingness to be instructed in the reading of the Scriptures, and there is enough made plain to his understanding to direct him in the way he should go.

"Others, however, think differently; but that should not be a reason with me for calling them hard names, especially if by their lives they show that they are followers of the same Master."

On December 2d, he writes again:

"I heard from you verbally on the 1st of October, in company with a platoon of New England Guards; and hope the head of the corps allowed Lord Wellington the honor of an introduction, and of inspecting this choice corps, which once had the honor of protecting the constitution and independence of the United States, when menaced by the 'proud sons of Britain.' This is a theme on which *you* may be allowed to dwell with some delight, although there are no recitals of hair-breadth escapes and hard-fought actions, when numbers bit the dust. Yet to you, who were active in performing duty, this should be a source of comfortable feeling, as the amount of human misery has not been increased by your means. Shakspeare's knight of sack thought 'the better part of valor was discretion,' but I do not believe the Guards would have confirmed this sentiment, had the opportunity offered for a trial. I am really glad to hear of you in Paris, and hope you will improve every moment of your time in acquiring information that will be agreeable and interesting; and, more particularly, I hope you will have gone over the ground where the great events have happened that now allow Europe to repose in peace. How much should I delight in a few hours' intercourse with you; but that must be deferred to another period, perhaps to a very distant period.

"I feel very healthy and very happy; my wife and children all enjoying health, and a good share of the bounties of Providence in various ways. Well you may be contented, you will say. What more is wanting? Such is not always the lot of man possessing those blessings. There is often a voracious appetite for other and greater blessings. The desire for more splendor, the possession of more wealth, is coveted, without the disposition to use it as an accountable creature; and too late the poor man finds that all his toil for these earthly objects of his worship fails in satisfying or giving a good degree of content. I, therefore, have reason for thankfulness that I am blessed with a disposition to appreciate tolerably the temporal blessings I enjoy. To the Father of all mercies I am indebted for this and every other good thing; even for the increased affection with which I think of you. That he may bless and keep you, dear Abbott, is the prayer of your brother, A. L."

On June 6th, 1817, a few days after the birth of a daughter, he writes to a friend:

"I am the richest man, I suppose, that there is on this side of the water, and the richest because I am the happiest. On the 23d ult. I was blessed by the birth of a fine little daughter; this, as you may well suppose, has filled our hearts with joy. S. is very comfortable, and is not less gratified than I am. I wish you were a married man, and then (if you had a good wife) you would know how to appreciate the pleasures of a parent. I have lately thought more than ever of the propriety of your settling soon. It is extremely dangerous to defer making a connection until a late period; for a man is in more and more danger of not forming one the longer he puts it off; and any man who does not form this connection grossly miscalculates in the use of the means which God has given him to supply himself with pleasures in the downhill journey of life.

"He is also foolish to allow himself to be cheated in this connection by the prospect of a few present advantages, to the exclusion of the more permanent ones. Every man's best pleasures should be at home; for there is the sphere for the exercise of his best virtues; and he should be particularly careful, in the selection of a partner, to get one who will jeopardize neither. On this subject, you know, I am always eloquent. But, at this time, there is reason for my being so, as it is the anniversary of my wedding day.

"S. has put her eye on a *rib* for you. The said person, you must know, is of a comely appearance (not beautiful), is rather taller than ——, has a good constitution, is perfectly acquainted with domestic economy, and has all the most desirable of the fashionable accomplishments, such as music, painting &c.; and my only objection to her is, as far as I have observed her, that she has a few thousand dollars in cash. This, however, might be remedied; for, after furnishing a house, the balance might be given to her near connections, or to some public institution. I will give no further description, but will only say that her connections are such as you would find pleasure in. No more on this subject. The subject of principal interest among us now is the new tariff of duties." * * * *

CHAPTER VIII.

DOMESTIC HABITS. — ILLNESS AND DEATH OF WIFE.

In searching for records of the business at this period, the first copied letters are found in a volume commencing with the date of March 10, 1815; since which period the correspondence, contained in many volumes, is complete. On the first page of this volume is a letter from the senior partner somewhat characteristic. It relates to a bill of exchange for two thousand rupees, which he knew was a doubtful one, but which he had taken to relieve the pressing necessities of a young Englishwoman from Calcutta, with a worthless husband. He writes to his friends in that city:

"We have been so particular as to send a clerk to her with the money, that we might be sure of her receiving it. Previous to her receiving the money from us, we were told her children were ragged, barefooted, and hungry; afterwards we knew they were kept comfortably clad."

In tracing the course of business as revealed by the perusal of the correspondence, it is evident that Mr. Lawrence's time and attention must have been engrossed by the increasing importance and magnitude of the mercantile operations of his firm. The cares and perplexities of the day did not, however, unfit him for the quiet enjoyments of domestic life ; and, however great and urgent were the calls upon his time and his thoughts from abroad, home, with its endearments, occupied the first place in his affections. So much did its interests transcend all others in his feelings, that he speaks in after life of having "watched night and day without leaving, for a fortnight," a sick child ; and then being rewarded for his care by having it restored to him after the diligent application of remedies, when the physician and friends had given up all hope of recovery.

With such affections and sources of happiness, connected with prosperity in his affairs, it may well be supposed that the current of life flowed smoothly on. His evenings were passed at home ; and urgent must have been the call which could draw him from his fireside, where the social chat or friendly book banished the cares of the day.

A gentleman, now a prominent merchant in New York, who was a clerk with Mr. Lawrence at this time, says of him :

"When the business season was over, he would sit down with me, and converse freely and familiarly, and would have something interesting and useful to say. I used to enjoy these sittings;

and, while I always feared to do anything, or leave anything undone, which would displease him, I at the same time had a very high regard, and I may say love, for him, such as I never felt for any other man beside my own father. He had a remarkable faculty of bringing the sterling money into our currency, with any advance, by a calculation in his mind, and would give the result with great accuracy in one quarter of the time which it took me to do it by figures. I used to try hard to acquire this faculty, but could not, and never saw any other person who possessed it to the degree he did. His mind was remarkably vigorous and accurate; and consequently his business was transacted in a prompt and correct manner. Nothing was left undone until to-morrow which could be done to-day. He was master of and controlled his business, instead of allowing his business to master and control him. When I took charge of the books, they were kept by single entry; and Mr. Lawrence daily examined every entry to detect errors. He was dissatisfied with this loose way of keeping the books; and, at his request, I studied book-keeping by double entry with Mr. Gershom Cobb, who had just introduced the new and shorter method of double entry. I then transferred the accounts into a new set of books on this plan, and well remember his anxiety during the process, and his expression of delight when the work was completed, and I had succeeded in making the first trial-balance come out right. This was the first set of books opened in Boston on the new system. While Mr. Lawrence required all to fulfil their engagements fully and promptly, so long as they were able to do so, he was lenient to those who were unfortunate, and always ready to compromise demands against such. No case occurred, while I was with him, in which I thought he dealt harshly with a debtor who had failed in business."

The year 1818 opened with cheering prospects; but a cloud was gathering which was destined to cast a shadow over all these pleasant hopes. During the spring, Mrs. Lawrence was troubled with a cough, which became so obstinate at the beginning of the summer, that she was persuaded to remain at Groton for a short period, in order to try the benefit of country air. Mr. Lawrence writes to her, July 16:

"I am forcibly reminded of the blessings of wife, children, and friends, by the privation of wife and children; and, when at home, I really feel homesick and lonesome. Here I am, in two great rooms, almost alone; so you must prepare at a minute's notice to follow your husband."

She remained in the country for several weeks, and was summoned suddenly home by the alarming illness of her husband; the result of which, for a time, seemed very doubtful. After a season of intense anxiety and unremitted watchings at his bedside, Mrs. Lawrence was seized during the night with a hemorrhage from the lungs. This symptom, which so much alarmed her friends, was hailed by herself with joy, as she now had no wish to outlive her husband, whose life she had despaired of. Mr. Lawrence's recovery was slow; and, as soon as it was deemed prudent, he was sent to Groton to recruit his strength. He writes, under date of November 5, 1818:

"DEAREST SARAH: We have heard of the fire on Tuesday evening, and hope the alarm has not impaired your health. I enjoy myself here as much as it is possible for any one to do under like circumstances. The idea of leaving the objects most dear to me, a wife and child sick, is too great a drawback upon my happiness to allow me as much quiet as is desirable. Yet I have great reason for thankfulness that I am at this time able to enjoy the society of friends, and that you are so comfortable as to give good reason to hope that the next season will restore to you a tolerable share of health."

Mrs. Lawrence writes, in reply to his letter:

"I have just received yours, and feel better to hear that you are so well. I hope that you will leave no means unimproved to regain health. Do not allow unreasonable fears on my account. I am as well as I was the week past; but we are uneasy mortals, and I do not improve as I could wish. You know me: therefore make all allowances. It is a cloudy day."

It soon became evident to all that the disease under which Mrs. Lawrence labored was a settled consumption, and that there could be little hope of recovery. To her mother Mr. Lawrence writes, Dec. 7:

"Since I last wrote to you, there has been no material change in Sarah's situation. She suffers less pain, and has more cheerful spirits than when you were here. She is very well apprised of her situation, and complains that those who are admitted to see her look so sorrowful, that it has a painful effect upon her feelings. She is desirous of being kept cheerful and happy; and, as far as I am capable of making her so, I do it. Yet I am a poor hand to attempt doing, with my feeble health, what is so foreign to my feelings. Although she is much more comfortable than she was, I cannot flatter myself that she is any better. She still retains a faint hope that she may be so; yet it is but a faint one. It takes much from my distress to see her so calm, and so resigned to the will of the Almighty. Although her attachments to life are as strong and as numerous as are the attachments of most, I believe the principle of resignation is stronger. She is a genuine disciple of Christ; and, if my children walk in her steps, they will all be gathered among the blest, and sing the song of the redeemed. Should it be the will of God that we be separated for a season, there is an animation in the hope that we shall meet again, purified from the grossness of the flesh, and never to be parted. 'God tempers the wind to the shorn lamb.' I shall have, therefore, no more put upon me than I am able to bear; yet I know not how to bring my mind to part with so excellent a friend, and so good a counsellor."

On Jan. 13, 1819, he writes:

"Sarah has continued to sink since you left, and is now apparently very easy, and very near the termination of her earthly career. She may continue two or three days; but the prospect is, that she will not open her eyes upon another morning. She suffers nothing, and it is, therefore, no trial to our feelings, compared with what it would be did she suffer. Her mind is a little clouded at times, but, in the main, quite clear. We shall give you early information of the event which blasts our dearest earthly hopes. *But God reigns: let us rejoice.*"

A few hours before her death, she called for a paper (now in possession of the writer), and, with a pencil, traced, in a trembling hand, some directions respecting small memorials to friends, and then added:

"Feeling that I must soon depart from this, I trust, to a better world, I resign very dear friends to God, who has done so much for me. I am in ecstacies of love. How can I praise him enough! To my friends I give these tokens of remembrance."

On the 14th of January, 1819, Mr. Lawrence closed the eyes of this most beloved of all his earthly objects, and immediately relapsed into a state of melancholy and gloom, which was, no doubt, greatly promoted by the peculiar state of health and physical debility under which he had labored since his last illness.

A valued friend writes, a few days after the death of Mrs. L.:

"It was my privilege to witness the closing scene; to behold faith triumphing over sense, and raising the soul above this world of shadows. It was a spectacle to convince the sceptic, and to animate and confirm the Christian. About a week before her death, her increasing weakness taught her the fallacy of all hope of recovery. From this time, it was the business of every moment to prepare herself and her friends for the change which awaited her. Serene, and even cheerful, she could look forward without apprehension into the dark valley, and beyond it she beheld those bright regions where she should meet her Saviour, through whose mediation she had the blessed assurance that her sins were pardoned, and her inheritance secure. God permitted a cloud to obscure the bright prospect; it was but for a moment, and the sun broke forth with redoubled splendor. On the last night of her life, she appeared to suffer extremely, though, when asked, she constantly replied in the negative. She repeated, in a feeble voice, detached portions of hymns of which she had been fond. Towards morning, as she appeared nearly insensible, Mrs. R. was persuaded to lie down and rest. Shortly after, Sarah roused herself, and said to L., 'I am going; call my mother.' Mrs. R. was at her bedside immediately, and asked her if she was sensible that she was leaving the world. She answered 'Yes,' and expressed her resignation.

"Mrs. R. then repeated a few lines of Pope's Dying Christian, and the expiring saint, in broken accents, followed her. On her mother's saying 'the world recedes,' she added, 'It disappears, — heaven opens.' These were the last words I heard her utter. She then became insensible, and in about ten minutes expired. Not a sound interrupted the sacred silence; the tear of affection was shed, but no lamentation was heard. The eye of affection dwelt on the faded form, but faith pointed to those regions where the blessed spirit was admitted to those joys which eye has not seen, nor ear heard, neither hath it entered into the heart of man to conceive. Mr. L. is wonderfully supported. He feels as a man and a Christian."

Upon this letter Mr. Lawrence has endorsed the following memorandum :

"I saw this letter to-day for the first time. My son-in-law handed to me yesterday a number of memorials of my beloved daughter, who was called home on the second day of December last, when only a few months younger than her mother, whose death is so beautifully described within. The description brought the scene back to my mind with a force that unmanned me for a time, and leads me to pray most earnestly and humbly that I may be found worthy to join them through the beloved, when my summons comes. A. L.

"February 5th, 1845."

CHAPTER IX.

JOURNEYS. — LETTERS. — JOURNEY TO NEW YORK.

THE sense of loss and the state of depression under which Mr. Lawrence labored were so great, that he was advised to try a change of scene; and accordingly, after having placed his three children with kind relatives in the country, he left Boston, on a tour, which lasted some weeks, through the Middle States and Virginia. He wrote many letters during this time, describing the scenes which he daily witnessed, and particularly the pleasure which he experienced in Virginia from the unbounded hospitality with which he was welcomed by those with whom he had become acquainted. He also visited Washington, and listened to some important debates on the admission of Missouri into the Union, which produced a strong and lasting influence upon his mind respecting the great questions then discussed.

In a letter to his brother from the latter city, dated Feb. 25th, after describing a visit to the tomb of Washington at Mount Vernon, he writes:

" Friend Webster has taken a stand here which no man can

surpass; very few are able to keep even with him. He has made a wonderful argument for the United States Bank. If he does not stand confessedly first among the advocates here, he does not stand second. Tell brother L. of this; it will do him good."

On March 30, he writes to his sister, after his return to Boston:

"I am once more near the remains of her who was lately more dear to me than any other earthly object, after an absence of two months; my health much improved,—I may say restored; my heart filled with gratitude to the Author of all good for so many and rich blessings, so rapidly succeeding such severe privations and trials."

A few days later, he writes to his sister-in-law:

"Sunday evening, April 4, 1819.

"DEAR S.: It is proper that I should explain to you why my feelings got so much the better of my reason at the celebration of the sacrament this morning. The last time I attended that service was with my beloved S., after an absence on her part of fifteen months, during which period you well know what passed in both our minds. On this occasion our minds and feelings were elevated with devotion, and (as I trust) suitably affected with gratitude to the Father of mercies for once more permitting her to celebrate with her husband this memorial of our Saviour. Then, indeed, were our hearts gladdened by the cheering prospect of her returning health and continued life. The consideration that I had since this period been almost within the purlieu of the grave, that my beloved Sarah had fallen a sacrifice to her care and anxiety for me, and that I was for the first time at the table of the Lord without her, with a view to celebrate the most solemn service of our religion, overwhelmed me as a torrent, and my feelings were too powerful to be restrained; I was almost suffocated in the attempt.

"Comment is unnecessary. God grant us a suitable improvement of the scene!

"Your affectionate brother,   A. L."

On April 6, he writes to a friend in England:

"Since I last wrote, family misfortunes, of which you have from time to time been apprised, have pressed heavily upon me. I am now in tolerable health, and hope soon to see it entirely confirmed."

After a visit to his parents, at Groton, he says, on April 9:

"I arrived at home last Saturday night, at eleven o'clock, after rather an uncomfortable ride. However, I had the satisfaction on Monday of exercising my right of suffrage, which, had I not done, I should have felt unpleasantly. I wrote to M., on Tuesday, under a depression of spirits altogether greater than I have before felt. The effect of hope upon my feelings, before I saw the little ones, was very animating; since that time (although I found them all I could desire), the stimulus is gone, and I have been very wretched. The principles I cherish will now have their proper effect, although nature must first find its level. Do not imagine I feel severely depressed all the time; although I certainly have much less of animal spirits than I had before my return, I do not feel positively unhappy. Under all the circumstances it is thought best for me to journey. Hitherto, I have experienced the kind protection of an almighty Friend; it will not hereafter be withheld. Commending all dear friends and myself to Him, I remain your truly affectionate brother,

"A. L."

To another sister he writes five days afterwards, before commencing a second journey:

"In a few moments I am off. I gladly seize the leisure they furnish me, to tell you I feel well, and have no doubt of having such a flow of spirits as will make my journey pleasant. At any rate, I start with this determination. You know not, dear E., the delight I feel in contemplating the situation of my little ones; this (if no higher principle) should be sufficient to do away all repining and vain regrets for the loss of an object so dear as was their mother. In short, her own wishes should operate very strongly against these regrets. I hope to be forgiven the offence, if such it be; and to make such improvement of it as will subserve the purposes of my heavenly Father, who doth not willingly afflict the children of men, but for their improvement. My prayer to God is, that the affliction may not be lost upon me; but that it may have the effect of making me estimate more justly the value of all temporal objects, and, by thus softening the heart, open it to the kind influences of our holy religion, and produce that love and charity well pleasing to our Father. I have no object in view further south than Baltimore; from thence I shall go across the Alleghanies, or journey through the interior to the northern border of this country. At Baltimore I remain a few days; my business there is as delegate from Brattle-street Church, in the settlement of a minister, a young gentleman named Sparks, from Connecticut."

(TO ABBOTT LAWRENCE.)

"PHILADELPHIA, April 26, 1819.

"DEAR BROTHER: When I see how people in other places are doing business, I feel that we have reason to thank God that we are not obliged to do as they do, but are following that regular and profitably safe business that allows us to sleep well o' nights, and eat the bread of industry and quietness. The more I see of the changes produced by violent speculation, the more satisfied I am that our maxims are the only true ones for a life together. Different maxims may prove successful for a part of life, but will frequently produce disastrous results just at the time we stand most in need; that is, when life is on the wane, and a family is growing around us.

"Two young brokers in —— have played a dashing game. They have taken nearly one hundred thousand dollars from the bank, without the consent of the directors. A clerk discounted for them. They have lost it by United States Bank speculations.

"Look after clerks well, if you wish to keep them honest. Too good a reputation sometimes tempts men to sin, upon the strength of their reputation.

"As to business, it must be bad enough; that is nothing new; but patience and perseverance will overcome all obstacles, and, notwithstanding all things look so dark, I look for a good year's work.

"You must remember that I have done nothing yet, and I have never failed of accomplishing more than my expectations; so I say again, we will make a good year's work of it yet, by the blessing of Heaven."

From Lancaster, Penn., April 29, he writes to his sister:

"My feelings are usually buoyant, except occasionally when imagination wanders back to departed days; then comes over me a shadow, which, by its frequency, I am now enabled to dispel without violence, and even to dwell upon without injury."

(TO ABBOTT LAWRENCE.)

"BALTIMORE, May 25, 1819.

"DEAR BROTHER: I arrived in this city this morning, in the steamboat, from Norfolk, and have found a number of letters from you and brother W. From the present aspect of affairs in this city, I fear that I shall make but a short stay. At no period has the face of affairs been more trying to the feelings of the citizens. Baltimore has never seen but two days which will compare with last Friday: one of those was the mob day, the other was the day of the attack by the British.

"Nearly one half the city, embracing its most active and hitherto wealthiest citizens, have stopped or must stop payment. Confidence is prostrated, capital vanished.

"I am rejoiced to hear of your easy situation, and hope it may continue. Avoid responsibilities, and all is well with us. I am in no wise avaricious, and of course care not whether we make five thousand dollars more or less, if we risk twenty thousand to do it.

"I have a high eulogium to pay the Virginians, which I must reserve for another letter; as also an account of my travels from Petersburg."

In a letter to a friend, dated at Baltimore, he says ·

"Since I have been here, I have been constantly occupied; and, although the heavy cloud which overhangs this city is discharging its contents upon their heads, they bear it well, resolving that, if they are poor, they will not be unsocial, nor uncivil, and on this principle they meet in little groups, without much style or ceremony, and pass sensible and sociable evenings together.

"I have really become very much interested in some of the people here.

"And now my advice to you is, get married, and have no fear about the expense being too great. If you have two children born unto you within a twelve-month, you will be the richer man for it. Nothing sharpens a man's wits, in earning property and using it, better than to see a little flock growing up around him. So I say again, man, fear not."

On his return, it seems to have been his object to interest himself as much as possible in business, and thus endeavor to divert his mind from those painful associations, which, in spite of all his efforts, would sometimes obtain the mastery. In the mean time, he had given up his house, and resided in the family of his brother Abbott; where he was welcomed as an inmate, and treated with so much sympathy and considerate kindness, that his mind, after a time, recovered its tone: his health was restored, and he was once more enabled to give his full powers to the growing interests of his firm. For the few succeeding years, he was engaged in the usual routine of mercantile affairs, and has left but few memorials or letters, except those relating to his business. In the winter of 1820, he made a visit to New York, which he describes in his diary under date of February 15, 1846:

"Yesterday was one of the most lovely winter days. To-day the snow drives into all the cracks and corners, it being a boisterous easterly snow-storm, which recalls to my mind a similar one, which I shall never forget, in February, 1820.

"I went to New York during that month, for the New England Bank, with about one hundred thousand dollars in foreign gold, the value of which by law at the mint was soon to be reduced from eighty-seven to eighty-five cents per pennyweight, or about that. I also had orders to buy bills with it, at the best rate I could. Accordingly I invested it, and had to analyze the standing of many who offered bills, as drawers or endorsers.

"Some of the bills were protested for non-acceptance, and were returned at once, and damages claimed. This was *new* law in New York, and resisted; but the merchants were convinced by suits, and paid the twenty per cent. damages. The law of damage was altered soon after.

"On my return, I took a packet for Providence, and came at the rate of ten knots an hour for the first seven hours of the night. I was alarmed by a crash, which seemed to me to be breaking in the side of the ship, within a few inches of my head. I ran upon deck, and it was a scene to be remembered. Beside the crew, on board were the officers of a wrecked vessel from Portsmouth, N. H., and some other old ship-masters, all at work, and giving directions to a coaster, which had run foul of us, and had lost its way. By favor and labor, we were saved from being wrecked; but were obliged to land at some fifteen miles from Providence, and get there as we could through the snow. I arrived there almost dead with headache and sickness. Madam

Dexter and her daughter left the day before, and reached home in perfect safety before the storm. Such are the scenes of human life! Here am I enjoying my own fireside, while all who were then active with me in the scenes thus recalled are called to their account, excepting Philip Hone, M. Van Schaick, N. Goddard, Chancellor Kent, and his son-in-law, Isaac Hone."

CHAPTER X.

MARRIAGE. — ELECTED TO LEGISLATURE. — ENGAGES IN MANUFACTURES. — REFLECTIONS.

IN April, 1821, Mr. Lawrence was married to Mrs. Nancy Ellis, widow of the late Judge Ellis, of Claremont, N. H., and daughter of Robert Means, Esq., of Amherst, in the same State. His children, who had been placed with his parents and sisters at Groton, were brought home; and he was now permitted again to unite his family under his own roof, and to enjoy once more those domestic comforts so congenial to his taste, and which each revolving year seemed to increase until the close of his life.

Mr. Lawrence was elected a representative from Boston to the Legislature for the session of 1821 and 22 ; and this was the only occasion on which he ever served in a public legislative body. Although deeply engaged in his own commercial pursuits, he was constantly at his post in the House of Representatives ; and attended faithfully to the duties of his office, although with much sacrifice to his own personal interests. Very little is found among his memoranda relating to this new experience. As a member of a committee of the Legislature having in charge the subject of the erection of wooden buildings in Boston, he seems to have had a correspondence with the late Hon. John Lowell, who took strong ground before the committee against the multiplication of buildings of this material, and backed his arguments with some very characteristic statements and observations. On one of these letters Mr. Lawrence made a memorandum, dated March, 1845, as follows:

"The *Boston Rebel* was a true man, such as we need more of in these latter days. The open-mouthed lovers of the *dear people* are self-seekers in most instances. Beware of such."

The following extract is taken from a letter, dated January 4th, 1822, addressed by Mr. Lawrence to Hon. Frederic Wolcott, of Connecticut, respecting a son who was about to be placed in his counting-room, and who, in after years, became his partner in business:

"H. will have much leisure in the evening, which, if he choose, may be profitably devoted to study; and we hope he will lay out such a course for himself, as to leave no portion of his time unappropriated. It is on account of so much leisure, that so many fine youths are ruined in this town. The habit of industry once well fixed, the danger is over.

"Will it not be well for him to furnish you, at stated periods, an exact account of his expenditures? The habit of keeping such an account will be serviceable, and, if he is prudent, the satisfaction will be great, ten years hence, in looking back and observing the process by which his character has been formed.

If he does as well as he is capable, we have no doubt of your experiencing the reward of your care over him."

For the several following years, Mr. Lawrence was deeply engaged in business; and the firm of which he was the senior partner became interested in domestic manufactures, which, with the aid of other capitalists, afterwards grew into so much importance, until now it has become one of the great interests of the country. Apart from all selfish motives, he early became one of the strongest advocates for the protection of American industry, believing that the first duty of a government is to advance the interests of its own citizens, when it can be accomplished with justice to others; and in opposition to the system of free trade, which, however plausible in theory, he considered prejudicial to the true interests of our own people. He was conscientious in these opinions; and, in their support, corresponded largely with some of the leading statesmen at Washington, as well as with prominent opponents at the South, who combatted his opinions while they respected the motives by which he was actuated. He tested his sincerity, by embarking a large proportion of his property in these enterprises; and, to the last, entertained the belief that the climate, the soil, and the habits of the people, rendered domestic manufactures one of the permanent and abiding interests of New England. During seasons of high political excitement and sectional strife, he wrote to various friends at the South, urging them to discard all local prejudices, and to enter with the North into manly competition in all those branches of domestic industry which would tend, not only to enrich, but also to improve the moral and intellectual character of their people. He watched, with increasing interest, the progress of Lowell and other manufacturing districts, and was ever ready to lend a helping hand to any scheme which tended to advance their welfare. Churches, hospitals, libraries, in these growing communities, had in him a warm and earnest advocate; and it was always with honest pride that he pointed out to the intelligent foreigner the moral condition of the operative here, when compared with that of the same class in other countries.

On the 1st of January, in each year, Mr. Lawrence was in the habit of noting down, in a small memorandum-book, an accurate account of all his property, in order that he might have a clear view of his own affairs, and also as a guide to his executors in the settlement of his estate, in case of his death. This annual statement commences in 1814, and, with the exception of 1819, when he was in great affliction on account of the death of his wife, is continued every year until that of his own death, in 1852. In this little volume the following memorandum occurs, dated January 1, 1826:

"I have been extensively engaged in business during the last two years, and have added much to my worldly possessions; but have come to the same conclusions in regard to them that I did in

1818. I feel distressed in mind that the resolutions then made have not been more effectual in keeping me from this *overen-gagedness* in business. . I now find myself so engrossed with its cares, as to occupy my thoughts, waking or sleeping, to a degree entirely disproportioned to its importance. The quiet and comfort of home are broken in upon by the anxiety arising from the losses and mischances of a business so extensive as ours; and, above all, that communion which ought ever to be kept free between man and his Maker is interrupted by the incessant calls of the multifarious pursuits of our establishment."

After noting down several rules for curtailing his affairs, he continues :

"Property acquired at such sacrifices as I have been obliged to make the past year costs more than it's worth; and the anxiety in protecting it is the extreme of folly."

1st of January, 1827. — "The principles of business laid down a year ago have been very nearly practised upon. Our responsibilities and anxieties have greatly diminished, as also have the accustomed profits of business; but there is sufficient remaining for the reward of our labor to impose on us increased responsibilities and duties, as agents who must at last render an account. God grant that mine be found correct!"

CHAPTER XI.

REFLECTIONS. BUNKER HILL MONUMENT. — LETTERS.

1st of January, 1828. — AFTER an account of his affairs, he remarks :

"The amount of property is great for a young man under forty-two years of age, who came to this town when he was twenty-one years old with no other possessions than a common country education, a sincere love for his own family, and habits of industry, economy, and sobriety. Under God, it is these same self-denying habits, and a desire I always had to please, so far as I could without sinful compliance, that I can now look back upon and see as the true ground of my success. I have many things to reproach myself with; but among them is not idling away my time, or spending money for such things as are improper. My property imposes upon me many duties, which can only be known to my Maker. May a sense of these duties be constantly impressed upon my mind; and, by a constant discharge of them, God grant me the happiness at last of hearing the joyful sound, 'Well done, good and faithful servant, enter thou into the joy of thy Lord!' Amen. Amen."

Previous to this date, but few private letters written by Mr. Lawrence were preserved. From that time, however, many volumes have been collected, a greater part of them addressed to his children. Out of a very large correspondence with them and with friends, such selections will be made as are thought most interesting, and most worthy to be preserved by his family and their descendants. The nature of this correspondence is such, involving many personal matters of transient interest that often scraps of letters only can be given; and, although it will be the aim of the editor to give an outline of the life of the author of these letters, it will be his object to allow him to speak for himself, and to reveal his own sentiments and character, rather than to follow out, from year to year, the details of his personal history. This correspondence commences with a series of letters extending through several years, and addressed to his eldest son, who was, during that time, at school in France and Spain.

"BOSTON, November 11, 1828.

"I trust that you will have had favoring gales and a pleasant passage, and will be safely landed at Havre within twenty days after sailing. You will see things so different from what you have been accustomed to, that you may think the French are far before or behind us in the arts of life, and formation of society. But you must remember that what is best for one people may be the worst for another; and that it is true wisdom to study the character of the people among whom you are, before adopting their manners, habits, or feelings, and carrying them to another people. I wish to see you, as long as you live, a well-bred, upright *Yankee*. Brother Jonathan should never forget his self-respect, nor should he be impertinent in claiming more for his country or himself than is due; but on no account should he speak ungraciously of his country or its friends abroad, whatever may be said by others. Lafayette in France is not what he is here; and, whatever may be said of him there, he is an ardent friend of the United States; and I will venture to say, if you introduce yourself to him as a grandson of one of his old Yankee officers, he will treat you with the kindness of a father. You must visit La Grange, and G. will go with you. He will not recollect your grandfather, or any of us. But tell him that your father and three uncles were introduced to him here in the State House; that they are much engaged in forwarding the Bunker Hill Monument; and, if ever he return to this country, it will be the pride of your father to lead him to the top of it."

Among Mr. Lawrence's papers, this is the first allusion to the Bunker Hill Monument, in the erection of which he afterwards took so prominent a part, and to which he most liberally contributed both time and money. From early associations, perhaps from the accounts received from his father, who was present during the battle, his mind became strongly interested in the project of erecting a monument, and particularly in that of reserving the whole battle-ground for the use of the public forever. He had been chosen one of the Building Committee of the Board of Directors in October, 1825, in company with Dr. John C. Warren, General H. A. S. Dearborn, George Blake, and William Sullivan. From this time until the completion of the monument, the object occupied a prominent place in his thoughts; and allusion to his efforts in its behalf during the succeeding years will, from time to time, be introduced.

On December 13, 1828, he thus alludes to the death of an invalid daughter six years of age :

"She was taken with lung fever on the 4th, and died, after much suffering and distress, on the 8th. Nothing seemed to relieve her at all; and I was thankful when the dear child ceased to suffer, and was taken to the bosom of her Saviour, where sickness and suffering will no more reach her, and the imperfections of her earthly tenement will be corrected, and her mind and spirit will be allowed to expand and grow to their full stature in Christ. In his hands I most joyfully leave her, hoping that I may rejoin her with the other children whom it has pleased God to give me."

(TO HIS SON.)
"December 29.

"My thoughts are often led to contemplate the condition of my children in every variety of situation, more especially in sickness, since the death of dear M. Although I do not allow myself to indulge in melancholy or fearful forebodings, I cannot but feel the deepest solicitude that their minds and principles should be so strengthened and stayed upon their God and Saviour as to give them all needed support in a time of such trial and suffering. You are so situated as perhaps not to recall so frequently to your mind as may be necessary the principles in which you have been educated. But let me, in the absence of these objects, remind you that God is ever present, and sees the inmost thoughts; and, while he allows every one to act freely, he gives to such as earnestly and honestly desire to do right all needed strength and encouragement to do it. Therefore, my dear son, do not cheat yourself by doing what you suspect *may* be wrong. You are as much accountable to your Maker for an enlightened exercise of your conscience, as you would be to me to use due diligence in taking care of a bag of money which I might send by you to Mr. W. If you were to throw it upon deck, or into the bottom of the coach, you would certainly be culpable; but, if you packed it carefully in your trunk, and placed the trunk in the usual situation, it would be using common care. So in the exercise of your conscience: if you refuse to examine whether an action is right or wrong, you voluntarily defraud yourself of the guide provided by the Almighty. If you do wrong, you have no better excuse than he who had done so willingly and wilfully. It is the sincere desire that will be accepted."

To his second son, then at school in Andover, he writes :

"I received your note yesterday, and was prepared to hear your cash fell short, as a dollar-bill was found in your chamber on the morning you left home. You now see the benefit of keeping accounts, as you would not have been sure about this loss without having added up your account. Get the habit firmly fixed of putting down every cent you receive and every cent you expend. In this way you will acquire some knowledge of the relative value of things, and a habit of judging and of care which will be of use to you during all your life. Among the numerous people who have failed in business within my knowledge, a prominent cause has been a want of system in their affairs, by which to know when their expenses and losses exceeded their profits. This habit is as necessary for professional men as for a merchant; because, in their business, there are numerous ways to make little savings, if they find their income too small, which they would not adopt without looking at the detail of all their expenses. It is the habit of consideration I wish you to acquire; and the habit of being accurate will have an influence upon your whole character in life."

(TO HIS SON IN FRANCE.)
". April 28, 1829.

"I beseech you to consider well the advantages you enjoy, and to avail yourself of your opportunities to give your manners a little more ease and polish; for, you may depend upon it, manners are highly important in your intercourse with the world. Good principles, good temper, and good manners, will carry a man through the world much better than he can get along with the absence of either. The most important is good principles. Without these, the best manners, although, for a time, very acceptable, cannot sustain a person in trying situations.

"If you live to attain the age of thirty, the interim will appear but a span; and yet at that time you will be in the full force of manhood. To look forward to that period, it seems very long; and it is long enough to make great improvement. Do not omit the opportunity to acquire a character and habits that will continue to improve during the remainder of life. At its close, the reflection that you have thus done will be a support and stay worth more than any sacrifice you may ever feel called on to make in acquiring these habits."

(TO THE SAME.)
"June 7, 1829.

"I was forcibly reminded, on entering our tomb last evening, of the inroads which death has made in our family since 1811, at the period when I purchased it. How soon any of us who survive may mingle our dust with theirs, is only known to Omniscience; but, at longest, it can be in his view but a moment, a mere point of time. How important, then, to us who can use this mere point for our everlasting good, that we should do it, and not squander it as a thing without value! Think upon this, my son; and do not merely admit the thought into your mind and drive it out by vain imaginations, but give it an abiding and practical use. To set a just value upon time, and to make a just use of it, deprives no one of any rational pleasure: on the contrary, it encourages temperance in the enjoyment of all the good things which a good Providence has placed within our reach, and thankfulness for all opportunities of bestowing happiness on our fellow-beings. Thus you have an opportunity of making me and your other friends happy, by diligence in your studies, temperance, truth, integrity, and purity of life and conversation. I may not write to you again for a number of weeks, as I shall commence a journey to Canada in a few days. You will get an account of the journey from some of the party."

CHAPTER XII.

JOURNEY TO CANADA. — LETTERS. — DIARY. — CHARITIES.

MR. LAWRENCE, with a large party, left Boston on the 13th of June, and passed through Vermont, across the Green Mountains, to Montreal and Quebec. Compared with these days of railroad facilities, the journey was slow. It was performed very leisurely in hired private vehicles, and seems to have been much enjoyed. He gives a glowing account of the beauty of the country through which he passed, as well as his impressions of the condition of the population.

From Quebec the party proceeded to Niagara Falls, and returned through the State of New York to Boston, " greatly improved in health and spirits." This, with one other visit to Canada several years before, was the only occasion on which Mr. Lawrence ever left the territory of the United States; for, though sometimes tempted, in after years, to visit the Old World, his occupations and long-continued feeble health prevented his doing so.

(TO HIS SON.)

"July 27.

"If, in an endeavor to do right, we fall short, we shall still be in the way of duty; and that is first to be looked at. We must keep in mind that we are to render an account of the use of those talents which are committed to us; and we are to be judged by unerring Wisdom, which can distinguish all the motives of action, as well as weigh the actions. As our stewardship has been faithful or otherwise, will be the sentence pronounced upon us. Give this your best thoughts, for it is a consideration of vast importance."

"August 27.

"Bring home no foreign fancies which are inapplicable to our state of society. It is very common for our young men to come home and appear quite ridiculous in attempting to introduce their foreign fashions. It should be always kept in mind that the state of society is widely different here from that in Europe; and our comfort and character require it should long remain so. Those who strive to introduce many of the European habits and fashions, by displacing our own, do a serious injury to the republic, and deserve censure. An idle person, with good powers of mind, becomes torpid and inactive after a few years of indulgence, and is incapable of making any high effort; highly important it is, then, to avoid this enemy of mental and moral improvement. I have no wish that you pursue trade. I would rather see you on a farm, or studying any profession."

"October 16.

"It should always be your aim so to conduct yourself that those whom you value most in the world would approve your conduct, if all your actions were laid bare to their inspection; and thus you will be pretty sure that He who sees the motive of all our actions will accept the good designed, though it fall short in its accomplishment. You are young, and are placed in a situation of great peril, and are perhaps sometimes tempted to do things which you would not do if you knew yourself under the eye of your guardian. The blandishments of a beautiful city may lead you to forget that you are always surrounded, supported, and seen, by that best Guardian."

"December 27.

"I suppose Christmas is observed with great pomp in France. It is a day which our Puritan forefathers, in their separation from the Church of England, endeavored to blot out from the days of religious festivals; and this because it was observed with so much pomp by the Romish Church. In this, as well as in many other things, they were as unreasonable as though they had said they would not eat bread because the Roman Catholics do. I hope and trust the time is not far distant when Christmas will be observed by the descendants of the Puritans with all suitable respect, as the first and highest holiday of Christians; combining all the feelings and views of New England Thanksgiving with all the other feelings appropriate to it."

"January 31, 1830.

"You have seen, perhaps, that the Directors of the Bunker Hill Monument Association have applied to the Legislature for a lottery. I am extremely sorry for it. I opposed the measure in all its stages, and feel mortified that they have done so. They cannot get it, and I desire that General Lafayette may understand this; and, if he will write us a few lines during the coming year, it will help us in getting forward a subscription. When our citizens shall have had one year of successful business, they will be ready to give the means to finish the monument. My feelings are deeply interested in it, believing it highly valuable as a nucleus for the affections of the people in after time; and, if my life be spared and my success continue, I will never cease my efforts until it be completed."

Further details will be given in this volume to show how nobly Mr. Lawrence persevered in the resolution thus deliberately formed; and, though he was destined to witness many fruitless efforts, he had the satisfaction at last of seeing the completion of the monument, and from its summit of pointing out the details of the battle to the son of one of the British generals in command* on that eventful day.

On the same page with the estimate of his property for the year 1830, he writes:

"With a view to know the amount of my expenditures for objects other than the support of my family, I have, for the year 1829, kept a particular account of such other expenses as come under the denomination of charities, and appropriations for the benefit of others not of my own household, for many of whom I feel under the same obligation as for my own family."

This memorandum was commenced on the 1st of January, 1829, and is continued until December 30, 1852, the last day of his life. It contains a complete statement of his charities during that whole period, including not only what he contributed in money, but also all other donations, in the shape of

---

* Lord Prudhoe, now Duke of Northumberland.

clothing materials, books, provisions, &c. His custom was to note down at cost the value of the donation, after it had been despatched; whether in the shape of a book, a turkey, or one of his immense bundles of varieties to some poor country minister's family, as large, as he says in addressing one, "as a small haycock." Two rooms in his house, and sometimes three, were used principally for the reception of useful articles for distribution. There, when stormy weather or ill health prevented him from taking his usual drive, he was in the habit of passing hours in selecting and packing up articles which he considered suitable to the wants of those whom he wished to aid. On such days, his coachman's services were put in requisition to pack and tie up "the small haycocks;" and many an illness was the result of over-exertion and fatigue in supplying the wants of his poorer brethren. These packages were selected according to the wants of the recipients, and a memorandum made of the contents. In one case, he notifies Professor ——, of —— College, that he has sent by railroad "a barrel and a bundle of books, with broadcloth and pantaloon stuffs, with odds and ends for poor students when they go out to keep school in the winter." Another, for the president of a college at the West, one piece of silk and worsted, for three dresses; one piece of plaid, for "M. and mamma;" a lot of pretty books; a piece of lignum-vitæ from the Navy Yard, as a text for the support of the navy; and various items for the children : value, twenty-five dollars.

To a professor in a college in a remote region he sends a package containing " dressing-gown, vest, hat, slippers, jack-knife, scissors, pins, neck-handkerchiefs, pantaloons, cloth for coat, 'History of Groton,' lot of pamphlets," &c.

Most of the packages forwarded contained substantial articles for domestic use, and were often accompanied by a note containing from five to fifty dollars in money.

The distribution of books was another mode of usefulness to which Mr. Lawrence attached much importance.

In his daily drives, his carriage was well stored with useful volumes, which he scattered among persons of all classes and ages as he had opportunity.

These books were generally of a religious character, while others of a miscellaneous nature were purchased in large numbers, and sent to institutions, or individuals in remote parts of the country.

He purchased largely the very useful as well as tasteful volumes of the American Tract Society and the Sunday-School Union. An agent of the latter society writes: "I had almost felt intimately acquainted with him, as nearly every pleasant day he visited the depository to fill the front seat of his coach with books for distribution."

Old and young, rich and poor, shared equally in these distributions; and he rarely allowed an occasion to pass unimproved when he thought an influence could be exerted by the gift of an appropriate volume.

While waiting one day in his carriage with a friend, in one of the principal thoroughfares of the city, he beckoned to a genteelly-dressed young man who was passing, and handed him a book. Upon being asked whether the young man was an acquaintance, he replied :

"No, he is not; but you remember where it is written, 'Cast thy bread upon the waters, for thou shalt find it after many days.'"

"A barrel of books" is no uncommon item found in his record of articles almost daily forwarded to one and another of his distant beneficiaries.

CHAPTER XIII.

CORRESPONDENCE WITH MR. WEBSTER. — LETTERS.

(TO HIS SON.)

"February 5, 1830.

"BE sure and visit La Grange before you return; say to General Lafayette that the Bunker Hill Monument will *certainly be finished*, and that the foolish project of a lottery has been abandoned. If, in the course of Providence, I should be taken away, I hope my children will feel it a duty to continue the efforts that are made in this work, which I have had so much at heart, and have labored so much for."

To his son, then at school at Versailles, he writes on Feb. 26, 1830:

"After hearing from you again, I can judge better what to advise respecting your going into Spain. At all events, let no hope of going, or seeing, or doing anything else, prevent your using the present time for improving yourself in whatever you find to do. My greatest fear is, that you may form a wrong judgment of what constitutes your true respectability, happiness, and usefulness. To a youth just entering on the scenes of life, the roses on the wayside appear without thorns; but, in the eagerness to snatch them, many find, to their sorrow, that all which appears so fair is not in possession what it was in prospect, and that beneath the rose there is a thorn that sometimes wounds like a serpent's bite. Let not appearances deceive you; for, when once you have strayed, the second temptation is more likely to be fallen into than the first."

"March 6 1830.

"We are all in New England deeply interested by Mr. Webster's late grand speech in the Senate, vindicating New England men and New England measures from reproach heaped upon them by the South; it was his most powerful effort, and you will see the American papers are full of it. You should read the whole debate between him and Mr. Hayne of South Carolina; you will find much to instruct and interest you, and much of what you ought to know. Mr. Webster never stood so high in this country as at this moment; and I doubt if there be any man, either in Europe or America, his superior. The doctrines upon the Constitution in this speech should be read as a text-book by all our youth."

After reading the great speech of Mr. Webster, Mr Lawrence addressed to that gentleman a letter, expressing his admiration of the manner in which New England had been vindicated, and also his own personal feelings of gratitude for the proud stand thus taken.

Mr. Webster replied as follows:

"WASHINGTON, March 8, 1830.

"DEAR SIR: I thank you very sincerely for your very kind and friendly letter. The sacrifices made in being here, and the mortifications sometimes experienced, are amply compensated by the consciousness that my friends at home feel that I have done

some little service to our New England. I pray you to remember me with very true regard to Mrs. Lawrence, and believe me
"Very faithfully and gratefully yours,
"DANIEL WEBSTER.
"To AMOS LAWRENCE, Esq."

EXTRACTS OF LETTERS TO HIS SON.

"April 13, 1830.

"You may feel very sure that any study which keeps your mind engaged will be likely to strengthen it; and that, if you leave your mind inactive, it will run to waste. Your arm is strengthened by wielding a broadsword, or even a foil. Your legs by various gymnastic exercises, and the organs of sight and hearing by careful and systematic use, are greatly improved; even the finger is trained, by the absence of sight, to perform almost the service of the eye. All this shows how natural it is for all the powers to grow stronger by use. You needed not these examples to convince you; but my desire to have you estimate your advantages properly induces me to write upon them very often. Every American youth owes his country his best talents and services, and should devote them to the country's welfare. In doing that, you will promote not only your own welfare, but your highest enjoyment.

"The duty of an American citizen, at this period of the world, is that of a responsible agent; and he should endeavor to transmit to the next age the institutions of our country uninjured and improved. We hope, in your next letter, to hear something more of General Lafayette. The old gentleman is most warm in his affection for Americans. May he live long to encourage and bless by his example the good of all countries! In contemplating a life like his, who can say that compensation even here is not fully made for all the anguish and suffering he has formerly endured? Long life does not consist in many years; but in the period being filled with good services to our fellow-beings. He whose life ends at thirty may have done much, while he who has reached the age of one hundred may have done little. With the Almighty, a thousand years are a moment; and he will therefore give no credit to any talents not used to his glory; which use is the same thing as promoting, by all means in our power, the welfare and happiness of the beings among whom we are placed."

"May 7, 1830.

"I have been pretty steady at my business, without working hard, or having anxious feelings about it. It is well to have an agreeable pursuit to employ the mind and body. I think that I can work for the next six years with as good a relish as ever I did; but I make labor a pleasure. I have just passed into my forty-fifth year, you know. At my age, I hope you will feel as vigorous and youthful as I now do. A temperate use of the good things of life, and a freedom from anxious cares, tend, as much as anything, to keep off old age."

"June 17, 1830.

"To-day completes fifty-five years since the glorious battle of Bunker Hill, and five years since the nation's guest assisted at the laying of the corner-stone of the monument which is to commemorate to all future times the events which followed that battle. If it should please God to remove me before this structure is completed, I hope to remember it in my will, and that my sons will live to see it finished. But what I deem of more consequence is to retain for posterity the battle-field, now in the possession of the Bunker Hill Monument Association. The Association is in debt, and a part of the land may pass out of its possession; but I hope, if it do, there will be spirit enough among individuals to purchase it and restore it again; for I would rather the whole work should not be resumed for twenty years, than resume it by parting with the land. I name this to you now, that you may have a distinct intimation of my wishes to keep the land open for our children's children to the end of time."

"July 17, 1830.

"Temptation, if successfully resisted, strengthens the character; but it should always be avoided. 'Lead us not into temptation' are words of deep meaning, and should always carry with them corresponding desires of obedience. At a large meeting of merchants and others held ten days ago, it was resolved to make an effort to prevent the licensing of such numbers of soda-shops, retailers of spirits, and the like, which have, in my opinion, done more than anything else to debase and ruin the youth of our city. It is a gross perversion of our privileges to waste and destroy ourselves in this way. God has given us a good land and many blessings. We misuse them, and make them minister to our vices. We shall be called to a strict account. Every good citizen owes it to his God and his country to stop, as far as he can, this moral desolation. Let me see you, on your return, an advocate of good order and good morals. * * *

"Our old neighbor the sea-serpent was more than usually accommodating the day after we left Portsmouth. He exhibited himself to a great number of people who were at Hampton Beach last Saturday. They had a full view of his snakeship from the shore. He was so civil as to raise his head about four feet, and look into a boat, where were three men, who thought it the wisest way to retreat to their cabin. His length is supposed to be about one hundred feet, his head the size of a ten-gallon cask, and his body, in the largest part, about the size of a barrel. I have never had any more doubt respecting the existence of this animal, since he was seen here eleven years ago, than I have had of the existence of Bonaparte. The evidence was as strong to my mind of the one as of the other. I had never seen either; but I was as well satisfied of the existence of both, as I should have been had I seen both. And yet the idea of the sea-serpent's existence has been scouted and ridiculed."

"September 25.

"The events of the late French Revolution have reached us up to the 17th August. The consideration of them is animating, and speaks in almost more than human language. We are poor, frail, and mortal beings; but there is something elevating in the thought of a whole people acting as with the mind and the aim of one man, a part which allies man to a higher order of beings. I confess it makes me feel a sort of veneration for them; and trust that no extravagance will occur to mar the glory and the dignity of this enterprise. Our beloved old hero, too, acting as the guiding and presiding genius of this wonderful event! May God prosper them, and make it to the French people what it is capable of being, if they make a right use of it! I hope that you have been careful to see and learn everything, and that you will preserve the information you obtain in such a form as to recall the events to your mind a long time hence. We are all very well and very busy, and in fine spirits, here in the old town of Boston. Those who fell behind last year have some of them placed themselves in the rear rank, and are again on duty. Others are laid up, unfit for duty; and the places of all are supplied with fresh troops. We now present as happy and as busy a community as you would desire to see."

CHAPTER XIV.

TESTIMONIAL TO MR. WEBSTER. — DANGEROUS ILLNESS. — LETTERS.

DURING the autumn of 1830, in order to testify in a more marked manner his appreciation of Mr. Webster's distinguished services in the Senate of the United States, Mr. Lawrence presented to that gentleman a service of silver plate, accompanied by the following note :

"HON. DANIEL WEBSTER. "BOSTON, October 23, 1830.

"DEAR SIR: Permit me to request your acceptance of the accompanying small service of plate, as a testimony of my gratitude for your services to the country in your late efforts in the Senate; especially for your vindication of the character of Massachusetts and of New England.

"From your friend and fellow-citizen,
"AMOS LAWRENCE.

"P. S. — If by any emblem or inscription on any piece of this service, referring to the circumstances of which this is a memorial, the whole will be made more acceptable, I shall be glad to have you designate what it shall be, and permit me the opportunity of adding it."

To which Mr. Webster replied, on the same evening, as follows:

"SUMMER-STREET, October 23, 1830.

"MY DEAR SIR: I cannot well express my sense of your kindness, manifested in the present of plate, which I have received this evening. I know that, from you, this token of respect is sincere; and I shall ever value it, and be happy in leaving it to my children, as a most gratifying evidence of your friendship. The only thing that can add to its value is your permission that it may be made to bear an inscription expressive of the donation.

"I am, dear sir, with unfeigned esteem,

"Your friend and obedient servant,

"DANIEL WEBSTER.

"AMOS LAWRENCE, Esq."

(TO HIS SON.)

"BOSTON, January 16, 1831.

"Our local affairs are very delightful in this state and city. We have no violent political animosities; and the prosperity of the people is very great. In our city, in particular, the people have not had greater prosperity for twenty years. There is a general industry and talent in our population, that is calculated to produce striking results upon their character. In your reflections upon your course, you may settle it as a principle, that no man can attain any valuable influence or character among us, who does not labor with whatever talents he has to increase the sum of human improvement and happiness. An idler, who feels that he has no responsibilities, but is contriving to get rid of time without being useful to any one, whatever be his fortune, can find no comfort in staying here. We have not enough such to make up a society. We are literally all working-men; and the attempt to get up a 'Working-men's party' is a libel upon the whole population, as it implies that there are among us large numbers who are not working-men. He is a working-man whose mind is employed, whether in making researches into the meaning of hieroglyphics or in demonstrating any invention in the arts, just as much as he who cuts down the forests, or holds the plough, or swings the sledge-hammer. Therefore let it be the sentiment of your heart to use all the talents and powers you may possess in the advancement of the moral and political influence of New England. New England, I say; for here is to be the stronghold of liberty, and the seat of influence to the vast multitude of millions who are to people this republic."

At the period when the preceding letter was written, the manufacturing interests had become of vast importance in this community; and the house of which Mr. Lawrence was the senior partner had identified itself with many of the great manufacturing corporations already created, or then in progress. With such pecuniary interests at stake, and with a sense of responsibility for the success of these enterprises, which had been projected on a scale and plan hitherto unknown, it may be supposed that his mind and energies were fully taxed, and that he could be fairly ranked among the working-men alluded to. While in the full tide of active life, and, as it were, at the crowning point of a successful career, the hand of Providence was laid upon him to remove him, for the rest of his days, from this sphere of honor and activity to the chamber of the invalid, and the comparatively tame and obscure walks of domestic life. Ever after this, his life hung upon a thread; and its very uncertainty, far from causing him to despond and rest from future effort, seemed only to excite the desire to work while the day lasted. The discipline thus acquired, instead of consigning him to the inglorious obscurity of a sick chamber, was the means of his entering upon that career of active philanthropy which is now the great source of whatever distinction there may be attached to his memory. His business life was ended; and, though he was enabled to advise with others, and give sometimes a direction to the course of affairs, he assumed no responsibility, and had virtually retired from the field.

On the 1st of June, 1831, the weather being very warm, Mr. Lawrence, while engaged in the business of his counting-room, drank moderately of cold water, and, soon after, was seized with a violent and alarming illness. The functions of the stomach seemed to have been destroyed; and, for many days, there remained but small hope of his recovery. Much sympathy was expressed by his friends and the public, and in such a manner as to afford gratification to his family, as well as surprise to himself when sufficiently recovered to be informed of it. He had not yet learned the place which he had earned, in the estimation of those around him, as a merchant and a citizen; and it was, not improbably, a stimulus to merit, by his future course, the high encomiums which were then lavished upon him.

Mr. Lawrence announced his sickness to his son, then in Spain, in the following letter, dated

"BOSTON, June 27, 1831.

"I desire to bless God for being again permitted to address you in this way. On the 1st day of this month, I was seized with a violent illness, which caused both myself and my friends almost to despair of my life. But, by the blessing of God, the remedies proved efficacious; and I am still in the land of the living, with a comfortable prospect of acquiring my usual health, although, thus far, not allowed to leave my chamber. In that dread hour when I thought that the next perhaps would be my last on earth, — my thoughts resting upon my God and Saviour, then upon the past scenes of my life, then upon my dear children, — the belief that their minds are well directed, and that they will prove blessings to society, and fulfil, in some good degree, the design of Providence in placing them here, was a balm to my spirits that proved more favorable to my recovery than any of the other remedies. May you never forget that every man is individually responsible for his actions, and must be held accountable for his opportunities! Thus he who has ten talents will receive a proportionate reward, if he makes a right use of them; and he who receives one will be punished, if he hides it in a napkin."

"June 29, 1831

"MY DEAR AND EVER-HONORED MOTHER: Through the divine goodness, I am once more enabled to address you by letter, after having passed through a sickness alarming to my friends, although to myself a comparatively quiet one. I cannot in words express my grateful sense of God's goodness in thus carrying me, as it were, in his hand, and lighting the way by the brightness of his countenance. During that period in which I considered my recovery as hardly probable, my mind was calm; and, while in review of the past I found many things to lament, and in contemplation of the future much to fear, but more to hope, I could find no other words in which to express my thoughts than the words of the publican, 'God be merciful to me a sinner!' All the small distinctions of sects and forms dwindled into air, thin air, and seemed to me even more worthless than ever. The cares and anxieties of the world did not disturb me, believing it to be of small moment whether I should be taken now or spared a few years longer. With returning health and strength, different prospects open, and different feelings take the place of those which were then so, appropriate; and the social feelings and sympathies have their full share in their hold upon me. * * * *

"From your ever-loving and dutiful son, A. L."

(TO HIS SON.)

"July 14.

"I have been constantly gaining since my last to you, and, with constant care, hope to acquire my usual health. I am, however, admonished, by the two attacks I have experienced within a month, that the continuance of my life for any considerable period will be very likely to depend upon a rigid prudence in my labor and living. The recovery from this last sickness is almost like being restored to life; and I hope the span that may be allowed me may be employed in better service than any period of my past life. We are placed here to be disciplined for another and higher state; and whatever happens to us makes a part of this discipline. In this view, we ought never to murmur, but to consider, when ills befall us, how we can make them subserve our highest good. What I am more desirous than anything else for you is, that you may feel that you are accountable for all your talents, and that you may so use them as to have an approving conscience, and the final recompense of a faithful servant at last. The period of trial is short; but the consequences are never-ending. How important to each individual, then,— to you and to me,— that we use aright the period assigned us!"

CHAPTER XV.

JOURNEY TO NEW HAMPSHIRE.— LETTERS. — RESIGNS OFFICE OF TRUSTEE AT HOSPITAL. — LETTERS.

A FEW days after the date of the preceding letter, a change was thought desirable for the improvement of Mr. Lawrence's health; and he accordingly, with Mrs. L., went to Portsmouth, New Hampshire, and remained a week with his friend and brother-in-law, the late Hon. Jeremiah Mason. From thence he proceeded to visit friends in Amherst, New Hampshire, where he was attacked by a severe rheumatic fever, which confined him for several weeks; and it was with great difficulty that he succeeded in reaching home about the 20th of September, after an absence of nearly two months. On the 27th of September, he writes to his son:

"It is only within a few days that I have been able to be removed to my own house. I am now able to walk my chamber, and sit up half the day; and, by the best care in the world, I have a fair hope of again enjoying so much health as to feel that I may yet be of some use in the world. My bodily sufferings have been great during this last sickness; but my mind in general has been quiet. I seem to want nothing which this world can give to make me an enviably happy man, but your presence and a return of my health; but these last are wisely withheld. We are apt, in the abundance of the gift, to lose the recollection whence it came, and feel that by our own power we can go forward. Happy for us that we are thus made to feel that all we have is from God; this recurrence to the Source of all our blessings makes us better men. I do not expect to be able to leave the house before the next spring; and, in the mean time, must be subject to the casualties incident to a person in my situation."

On October 29, Mr. Lawrence, in a letter to the same son, expresses his gratitude for the enjoyment of life, "even in a sick chamber, as mine must be termed."

"I receive my friends here, and once only have walked abroad for a few minutes. I drive in a carriage every pleasant day, and I can truly say that my days pass in the full enjoyment of more than the average of comfort. My mind is as easy as it ever is, and as active as is safe for the body. I employed myself yesterday in looking over your letters since you left home three years ago, and was reminded by them that the fourth year of your absence has just commenced. Although a brief space since it is passed, an equal time, if we look forward, appears to be far distant. The question you will naturally ask yourself is, How has the time been spent? and from the answer you may gather much instruction for the future. If you have made the best use of this period, happy is it for you, as the habit of the useful application of your time will make its continuance more natural and easy

If you have misused and abused your opportunities, there is not a moment to be lost in retracing your steps, and making good, by future effort, what has been lost by want of it. In short, we can none of us know that a future will be allowed us to amend and to correct our previous misdoings and omissions; and it is not less the part of wisdom than of duty to be always up and doing, that whenever our Master comes we may be ready. I never was made so sensible before of the power of the mind over the body. It is a matter of surprise to some of my friends, who have known my constant habits of business for a quarter of a century, that I can find so much comfort and quiet in the confinement of my house, when I feel so well, and there are so many calls for my labors abroad. I hope to pursue such a discreet course as shall allow me to come forth in the spring with my poor frame so far renovated and restored as to enable me to take my place among the active laborers of the day, and do what little I may for the advancement and well-being of my generation. If, however, I should, by any accident or exposure, be again brought to a bed of pain and suffering, may God grant me a patient and submissive temper to bear whatever may be put upon me, with a full conviction that such chastisements will tend to my good, if I make a right use of them!"

The first of January, 1832, found Mr. Lawrence confined to his sick room, and unable, from bodily weakness, to drive out in the open air, as he had hitherto done. He writes to his son:

"I am reminded, by the new year, that another portion of time has passed, by which we are accustomed to measure in prospect the space that is allotted us here; and the reflections at the close of the old and the commencement of the new year are calculated, if we do not cheat ourselves, to make us better than we otherwise should be. I am enjoying myself highly under the close confinement of two parlor chambers, from which I have only travelled into the entry since November. I have lived pretty much as other prisoners of a different character live, as regards food; namely, on bread and water, or bread and coffee or cocoa. I have come to the conclusion that the man who lives on bread and water, if he have enough, is the genuine epicure, according to the original and true meaning. I am favored with the visits of more pretty and interesting ladies than any *layman* in the city, I believe. My rooms are quite a resort; and, old fellow as I am, I have the vanity to suppose I render myself quite agreeable to them."

On the same day, in a letter of sympathy to his sister-in-law, whose invalid son was about to leave for a long voyage, he writes:

"While my family are all absent at church, I am sitting alone, my mind going back to the beginning of the year just ended and forward through that just commenced; and, in view of both periods, I can see nothing but the unbounded goodness of our heavenly Father and best friend, in all that has been taken from me, as well as in all that is left to me. I can say, with sincerity, that I never have had so much to call forth my warmest and deepest gratitude for favors bestowed as at the present time. Among my sources of happiness is a settled conviction that, in chastening his children, God desires their good; and if his chastisements are thus viewed, we cannot receive them in any other light than as manifestations of his fatherly care and kindness. Although, at times, 'clouds and darkness are round about him,' we do certainly know, by the words of inspiration, 'that justice and judgment are the habitation of his throne,' and goodness and mercy the attributes of his character; and if it should please him further to try me with disease during the period of my probation, my prayer to him is that my mind and heart may remain stayed on him, and that I may practically illustrate those words of our blessed Saviour, 'Not my will, but thine be done.' It is quite possible that there may still be a few years of probation for me; but it is more probable that I may not remain here to the close of the present; but whether I remain longer or shorter is of little consequence, compared with the preparation or the dress in which I may be found when called away. It has seemed to me that the habit of mind we cultivate here will be that which will abide with us hereafter; and that heaven is as truly begun here as that the affections which make us love our friends grow stronger by use, and improve by cultivation. We are here in our infancy; the feelings cherished at this period grow with our growth, and, in the progress of time, will fit us for the highest enjoyments of the most distant future. I say, then, what sources of happiness are open to us, not only for the present, but for all future time! These hasty remarks are elicited on occasion of the separation so soon to take place from your son. I know full well the anxieties of a parent on such an occasion.

"His health cannot, of course, be certainly predicted; but you will have the comfort of knowing that you have done everything that the fondest parents could do in this particular, whatever effect the absence may have upon him.

"—— should feel that his obligations are increased, with his means and opportunities for improvement. If by travel he acquire a better education, and can make himself more useful on his return, he can no more divest himself of his increased duties, than he can divest himself of his duty to be honest. The account is to be rendered for the *use* of the talents, whether they be ten, or five, or one. If I have opportunity, I shall write a few lines to —— before he leaves. If I should not, I desire him to feel that I have great affection for him, and deep interest in his progress, and an ardent hope that his health, improvement, and knowledge, may be commensurate with the rare advantages he will enjoy for the acquisition of all.

"I know the tender feelings of your husband on all things touching his family or friends; and perhaps I may find opportunity to speak a word of comfort to him. But I know not what more to say than to reiterate the sentiment here expressed. Nature will have its way for a time, but I hope reason will be sufficient to make that time very short. Whatever time it may be, of this I feel confident, that, after the feelings have once subsided, —— will have all the sunshine and joy which the event is calculated to produce. He cannot know until he has realized the pleasure of hearing the absent ones speak, as it were, in his ear, from a distance of three thousand miles.

"May the best blessings of the Almighty rest on you and yours! From your ever affectionate A. L."

(TO HIS SON.)

"Sunday morning, Feb. 5, 1832.

"I have seated myself at my writing-desk, notwithstanding it is holy time, in the hope and belief that I am in the way of duty. This consecration of one day in seven to the duties of religion,— comprising, as these do, every duty,— and if they be well performed, to self-examination, is a glorious renovation of the world. Who that has witnessed the effects of this rest upon the moral and physical condition of a people, can doubt the wisdom of the appointment? Wherever we turn our eyes or our thoughts, if we only will be as honest and candid, in our estimate of the value of the provision made for us, as we ordinarily are in our estimate of the character and conduct of our fellow-men, we must be struck with admiration and gratitude to that merciful Father who has seen our wants, and provided for our comfort to an extent to which the care and provision of the best earthly parents for their children hardly gives the name of resemblance."

In speaking of some application for aid which he had received from a charitable institution, he writes to his son:

"Our people are liberally disposed, and contribute to most objects which present a fair claim to their aid. I think you will find great advantage in doing this part of your duty upon a system which you can adopt; thus, for instance, divide your expenses into ten parts, nine of which may be termed for what is considered necessary, making a liberal calculation for such as your situation would render proper, and one part applied for the promotion of objects not directly or legally claiming your support, but such as every good citizen would desire to have succeed. This, I think, you will find the most agreeable part of your expense; and, if you should be favored with an abundance of means later in life, you may enlarge your appropriations of this sort, so as to be equal to one tenth of your income. Neither yourself nor those who depend upon you will ever feel the poorer. I assume that you have plenty, in thus fixing the proportion. I believe the rule might be profitably adopted by many who have small means; for they would save more by method than they would be required to pay.

"To-morrow completes a hundred years since the birth of Washington. The day will be celebrated, from one end of the country to the other, with suitable demonstrations of respect, by processions, orations, and religious ceremonies, according to the feelings of the people who join in it. I think the spectacle will be a grand one, of a whole people brought together to commemorate the birth of one of their fellow-mortals, who by his virtues and his talents has made his memory immortal, and whose precepts and example are calculated to secure happiness to the countless millions of his fellow-beings who are to people this vast empire through all future time. It is permitted to few to have open to them such a field as Washington had; but no one since the Christian era has filled his sphere so gloriously. We are jogging along, in political, theological and commercial affairs, very much as usual."

During the month of January, Mr. Lawrence, on account of ill health, resigned his seat in the Board of Trustees of the Massachusetts General Hospital, in which he had served for several years. This duty had always been one of unmingled pleasure to him; and, by means of his visits there, and at the McLean Asylum for the Insane, under the management of the same board, he became conversant with a class of sufferers who had excited a great interest in his mind, and whom he often visited during the remainder of his life, to cheer them in their sadness, and to convey to them such little tokens of kindness as assured them of his interest and sympathy.

In a letter to his second son, at Andover, he writes, Apri. 21 :

"You will be glad to hear I have got along very well through the wet, cold weather of the week, and am looking forward with cheerful hope to the sunny days to come. If it were not for my faculty of turning present disappointments to future pleasures in prospect, I should run down in spirits. I have always indulged myself in castle-building; but have generally taken care so to build as to be in no danger of their falling on my head, so that when I have gone as far with one as is safe, if it does not promise well, I transfer my labor to another, and thus am always supplied with objects. The last one finished was commenced last May, and it is one I delight to think of. It was then I determined to get your Uncle Mason* here. N. thought it a castle without foundation, but the result shows otherwise.

"I send some of W.'s late letters, by which you perceive he is not idle; the thought of the dear fellow makes the tears start. God in mercy grant him a safe return, fully impressed with his obligations as a man and a Christian! That I am now living in the enjoyment of so much health, surrounded by so many blessings, is overpowering to my feelings. What shall I render unto God for all these benefits? I feel my unworthiness, and devoutly pray him that I may never lose sight of the great end of my being; and that, whenever it shall please him to call me hence, I may be found in the company of the redeemed through the merits and mediation of the Son of his love. If there is any one thing I would impress on your mind more strongly than another, it is to give good heed to the religious impressions with which you

---

* Hon. Jeremiah Mason, of Portsmouth, New Hampshire who passed the rest of his life in Boston.

may be imbued; and, at a future day, these may prove a foundation that will support you when all other supports would fail. The youthful imagination frequently magnifies objects at a distance; experience is an able teacher, and detects, too late, perhaps, the fraud upon youth. Be wise in time, and avoid this fraud."

A few days later, he writes to the same son, on the subject of systematic charity:

"It is one of my privileges, not less than one of my duties, to be able thus to administer to the comfort of a circle of very dear friends. I hope you will one day have the delightful consciousness of using a portion of your means in a way to give you as much pleasure as I now experience. Your wants may be brought within a very moderate compass; and I hope you will never feel yourself at liberty to waste on yourself such means, as, by system and right principles, may be beneficially applied to the good of those around you. Providence has given us unerring principles to guide us in our duties of this sort. Our first duty is to those of our own household, then extending to kindred, friends, neighbors (and the term 'neighbor' may, in its broadest sense, take in the whole human family), citizens of our state, then of our country, then of the other countries of the world."

In another letter, written soon after the preceding, he speaks of certain principles of business which governed him in early life, and adds:

"The secret of the whole matter was, that we had formed the habit of promptly acting, thus taking the *top of the tide;* while the habit of some others was to delay until about *half-tide,* thus getting on the flats; while we were all the time prepared for action, and ready to put into any port that promised well. I wish, by all these remarks, to impress upon you the necessity of qualifying yourself to support yourself. The best education that I can secure shall be yours, and such facilities for usefulness as may be in my power shall be rendered; but no food to pamper idleness or wickedness will I ever supply willingly to any connection, however near. I trust I have none who will ever misuse so basely anything that may come to them as a blessing. This letter, you may think, has an undue proportion of advice. 'Line upon line, precept upon precept,' is recommended by one wiser than I am."

(TO HIS DAUGHTER.)
"Sunday morn.

"MY DEAR DAUGHTER: In the quiet of this morning, my mind naturally rests on those objects nearest and dearest to me; and you, my child, are among the first.

"The family are all at church, but the weather is not such as to permit my going; and the season by them employed in the service of the sanctuary will by me be employed in communicating with you.

"You have now arrived at an age when the mind and heart are most susceptible of impressions for weal or woe; and the direction which may be given to them is what no parent can view with indifference, or pass over without incurring the guilt of being unfaithful in his duties. My earnest desire for you is, that you may fully appreciate your opportunities and responsibilities, and so use them that you may acquire a reasonable hope that you may secure the object for which we are placed here. The probation is short, but long enough to do all that is required of us, if faithfully used; the consequences are never-ending.

"These simple views are such as any child of your age can comprehend, and should be made as familiar to your mind as the every-day duties of life. If the mind, from early days, be thus accustomed to look upon life as a school of preparation for higher services, then the changes and adversities to which we are all liable can only be viewed as necessary discipline to fit us for those higher services, and as such be considered as applied for our good, however painful they may seem at first. There is no truth better settled than this: that all the discipline of our heavenly Parent, if rightly used, will eventuate in our good. How, then, can we murmur and repine at his dealings with us? This conduct only shows our weakness and folly, and illustrates the better care of us than we should take of ourselves.

"We are in the condition of the sick man, who sometimes craves that which, if given him by his friend, would cause his certain death; but he is not aware at the time that it is withheld for his good. The importance, then, of cultivating a right understanding of the things of which our duties and our happiness are composed, is second to no object which can employ the mind; for, with this knowledge, we must suppose that no one can be so lost to his own interest as not to feel that in the performance of these duties is to result the possession of those riches which are promised to the faithful by our Father in heaven, through the Son of his love. In the preparation which awaits you, do not stop at the things which are seen, but look to those which are unseen. These views, perhaps, may be profitably pondered long after I have been gathered to my fathers.

"The tenure of my life seems very frail; still it may continue longer than the lives of my children; but, whenever it shall please God to call me hence, I hope to feel resigned to his will, and to leave behind me such an influence as shall help forward the timid and faint-hearted in the path of duty; and particularly on you, my child, do I urge these views. They debar you from no real or reasonable pleasure; they speak to you, in strong language, to enjoy all those blessings which a bountiful Parent has scattered in your path with unsparing plenty, and admonish you that to enjoy is not to abuse them; when abused, they cease to be enjoyed."

CHAPTER XVI.

DAILY EXERCISE. — REGIMEN. — IMPROVING HEALTH. — LETTERS

DURING the summer and autumn of 1832, Mr. Lawrence's health and strength were so much improved, that he was enabled to take exercise on horseback; and almost daily he took long rides, sometimes alone, sometimes with a friend, about the environs of the city. This habit he was enabled to continue, with some intermissions, for two or three years, through summer and winter. The effect of the exercise amidst the beautiful scenery of the environs of Boston, of which he was an enthusiastic admirer, was most beneficial to his health, and, it is believed, was a great means of prolonging his life. Whenever he could do so, he secured the company of a friend, and kept a horse expressly for the purpose. As the ride was taken in the morning, when his business acquaintances were occupied, his most usual companion was some one of the city clergy, whom he secured for the occasion, or one of his sons. No denominational distinctions seemed to regulate his choice on these occasions. His own beloved pastor and friend, the Rev. Dr. Lothrop,

Rev. Drs. Stone and Greenwood, and Father Taylor, the seamen's chaplain, were often his companions. Occasionally a stray merchant or lawyer was engaged; and, as was sometimes the case where they had not been much accustomed to the exercise, a long trot of many miles in the sun, or in the face of a keen winter north-wester, would severely tax their own strength, while they wondered how so frail a figure as that of Mr. Lawrence could possess so much endurance. With all this apparent energy and strength, he was extremely liable to illness, which would come when least expected, and confine him for days to his house. An item of bad news, some annoying incident, a little anxiety, or a slight cold, would, as it were, paralyze his digestive functions, and reduce his strength to the lowest point. It was this extreme sensitiveness which unfitted him to engage in the general current of business, and which compelled him to keep aloof from participation in commercial affairs, and to adopt that peculiar system in diet and living which he adhered to for the remainder of his life. This system limited him to the use of certain kinds of food, which, from time to time, was slightly modified, as was thought expedient. This food was of the most simple kind, and was taken in small quantities, after being weighed in a balance, which always stood before him upon his writing-table. To secure perfect quiet during his meals, and also that he might not be tempted to over step the bounds of prudence, a certain amount was sent to him in his chamber, from which he took what was allowed. The amount of liquid was also weighed; and so rigid was he in this system of diet, that, for the last sixteen years of his life, he sat down at no meal with his family. The amount of food taken varied, of course, with his strength and condition. In a letter to his friend, President Hopkins, of Williams College, he says:

"If your young folks want to know the meaning of epicureanism, tell them to take some bits of coarse bread (one ounce and a little more), soak them in three gills of coarse-meal gruel, and make their dinner of them and nothing else; beginning very hungry, and leaving off more hungry. The food is delicious, and such as no modern epicureanism can equal."

For a considerable period, he kept a regular diet-table, in which he noted down the quantity of solid and liquid food taken during the twenty-four hours. One of his memorandum-books, labelled "Record of Diet and Discipline for 1839 and 1840," contains accurate records of this sort.

In October, 1832, in writing to his son in the country, he alludes to this improvement in his health and strength:

"We are all doing as well as usual here, myself among them doing better than usual. My little 'Doctor'[*] does wonders for

[*] The name of his horse.

me. I ride so much, and so advantageously, that I do not know but I shall be bold enough, by and by, to ride to B—— and back in a day, but shall hardly dare do so until I have practised a little more in this neighborhood.

"I want you to analyze more closely the tendency of principles, associations, and conduct, and strive to adopt such as will make it easier for you to go right than go wrong. The moral taste, like the natural, is vitiated by abuse. Gluttony, tobacco, and intoxicating drink, are not less dangerous to the latter, than loose principles, bad associations, and profligate conduct, are to the former. Look well to all these things."

The year 1833 opened with bright and cheering prospects; for, with Mr. Lawrence's increasing strength and improved health, there seemed a strong ground of hope that he might yet recover all his powers, and once more take his place among his former business associates.

He writes at this time to his son at Andover:

"I am as light as a feather this morning, and feel as if I could mount upon a zephyr, and ride upon its back to A——; but I am admonished to be careful when my spirits are thus buoyant, lest I come down to the torpor of the insect, which is shut up by the frost. Extremes are apt to follow, unless I take great care. Last Sabbath, I kept my bed, most of the day, with a poor turn. Brother A. said, on Saturday, he knew I was going to have one, for I talked *right on.*"

In March, he writes

"The season is coming forward now so as to allow me the use of the roads around Roxbury and Dorchester. My 'Doctor looks so altered by a two hours' canter, that his own mother would hardly know him at first sight. We continue excellent friends; and I think he has never used me better than during the last few days. We both 'feel our oats' and our youth. I feel like sweet twenty-five; and he, I judge, like vigorous seven."

On April 28, he writes to a young friend:

"When you get married, do not expect a higher degree of perfection than is consistent with mortality in your wife. If you do, you will be disappointed. Be careful, and do not choose upon a theory either. I dislike much of the nonsense and quackery that is dignified with the name of intellectual among people. Old-fashioned common sense is a deal better. * * * *

"There was a part of Boston which used to be visited by young men out of curiosity when I first came here, into which I never set foot for the whole time I remained a single man. I avoided it, because I not only wished to keep clear of the temptations common in that part, but to avoid the appearance of evil. I never regretted it; and I would advise all young men to strengthen their good resolutions by reflection, and to plant deep and strong the principles of right, and to avoid temptation, as time gives them strength to stand against it."

On December 23, he writes to his wife, who had been summoned to the bedside of a dying relative:

"Your absence makes a great blank in the family; and I feel that I must be very careful lest any little accident should make me feel of a *deep blue* while you are away. Confidence is a great matter, not only in curing, but in preventing disease, whether of the body or the mind; and I have somehow got the notion that I am more safe when you* are looking after me than when you are not, and that any trouble is sooner cured when you are present than when you are not. This is, I suppose, the true charm which some people have faith in to keep off their ills. I have been forcibly reminded of the passage of time, by reviewing the scenes of the last three years, and am deeply sensible of the mercies that have been extended to me. What little I do is a poor return: may a better spirit prompt and guide my future services! What few I have rendered are estimated by my brethren beyond their value, and of course tend to flatter my self-love. This should not be; and I ought to see myself as I am seen by that eye that never sleeps. The situation I occupy is one that I would not exchange, if I had the power, with any man living: it is full of agreeable incidents, and free from the toils and anxieties frequently attendant on a high state of prosperity; and is, beside, free from that jealousy, or from any other cause of uneasiness, so common among the ardent and successful in this world's race."

To his daughter, who was on a visit at Washington, he writes:

"Boston, May 18th, 1834. Sunday evening.

"My dear Child: The contrast in the weather to-day with

---

* The editor, in justice to his own feelings, will here remark, that he believes the continuation of Mr. Lawrence's life, after he became a confirmed invalid, was, under Providence, in a great measure due to the care and faithful attentions of his wife. For more than twenty years, and during his frequent seasons of languor and sickness, she submitted to many sacrifices, and bestowed a degree of care and watchfulness such as affection alone could have enabled her to render.

what it has been most of the time since you left home, is as great as is usual between a bleak November day and the soft air of June. To-day it is beautiful, but on Wednesday it snowed, hailed, and rained, and I am told, indeed, that a few miles beyond Amherst the snow fell four inches in depth. You have reason to be thankful that you have been in a milder climate, and, at the same time, are seeing all the wonders that open upon you in the new world on which you have entered.

"I shall be expecting a letter from you within a day or two; there can be no want of materials where so many new objects are constantly presenting themselves, and there is a pleasure in receiving them just as they appear to you; so you need not be afraid to place before me the first sketches, precisely as you catch them.

"To-day I suppose you are in Philadelphia, and, if so, I hope you have attended a Friends' meeting. The manner of worship and the appearance of the people are different from anything you have seen; and the influence of this sect upon the taste and manners of the people is very striking, particularly in the matter of their dress. It is said that you can judge something of the character of a lady from her dress. Without deeming it an essential, I think it of some consequence. This strikes the eye only, and may deceive; how much more important that the dress of the heart and mind and affections be right, and that no deception be found there! I do most earnestly pray God that every opportunity may be improved by you, my dear S., to adorn yourself with all those graces that shall not only charm the eye, but also with those that shall win the affections of those whose affection you would prize, and more especially that you will secure the approval of our best Friend

* * * * * *

"*Monday afternoon, May* 19. — I have received your charming letter, dated on Thursday last. It is just the thing, a simple narrative of facts; and you will find plenty of materials of this sort, as I stated to you before. I have been in the saddle to-day nearly five hours with your Uncle W. and Father Taylor, and am very tired, but shall get refreshed by a night's rest.

"The day is beautiful, finer than any we have had since you left home. We went to Mount Auburn, and it appears very lovely; how much better than the dreary resting-places for the dead so common in New England, overgrown with thistles, and the graves hardly designated by a rude stone! Our Puritan forefathers mistook very much, I think, in making the place of deposit for our mortal remains so forbidding in appearance to the living. A better taste is growing among us. It may become a matter of ostentation (we are so apt to go to extremes), to build sepulchres and monuments to hold our bodies, that will speak to our shame when we are no longer subjects of trial; when, in short, we shall have gone to our account. If these monuments could speak to their living owners, and induce them to labor to merit, while they may, a good word from the future lookers on, then they would be valuable indeed. As it is, I have no fault to find; it is decidedly better than the old fashion of making these tenements look as dreary as anything in this world can look."

To the same he writes, a few days later:

"Tell —— that I saw little —— this morning. She is the sweetest little creature that ever lived, and I find myself smiling whenever I think of the dear child in health. Sympathy is a powerful agent in illustrating through the countenance the feelings within. I believe my face is as arrant a tell-tale as ever was worn; and whenever I think of those I love, under happy circumstances, I am happy, too. So you may judge how much I enjoy in the belief that you are enjoying so much, and doing so well, in this journey."

On February 8, 1835, he writes to a young friend:

"Take care that fancy does not beguile you of your understanding in making your choice: a mere picture is not all that is needful in the up and down hills of life. The arrangements of the household and the sick room have more in them to fasten upon the heart than all the beauties and honors of the mere gala days, however successfully shown off. Be careful, when you pick, to get a heart, a soul, and a body; not a show of a body that has mere vitality. All this comes in *by the ears;* but it is in,— I will not blot it out."

March 16, he writes to his sister.

"I have had so much call for my sympathy, assistance, and advice, among my brethren in trade, that I have little inclination or spirit to write social or family letters since my last; but, in all this turmoil and trouble (and it really is as disastrous as a siege or a famine to the country), I have kept up a good heart, and have been able to view the work of destruction with as much composure as the nature of the case will allow. Whatever effects it shall produce on my property, I shall submit to, as the inevitable destruction that comes without any fault of my own, of course without any self-reproaches; but for the authors I feel a just indignation. As regards the pecuniary distress among us, it is subsiding: there have been fewer failures than were anticipated; but there have been numbers on the brink, who have been saved by the help of friends. A few persons have done great service in helping those who could not help themselves; and the consequences will be felt here for years to come in the credit and standing of many worthy people, who must otherwise have been broken down. Brother A. has had a load of care and responsibility much too severe for him, and has now agreed to throw off a part of the business as soon as the present pressure is past."

April 29, he writes:

"I am busy these days, but have no very important duties, except riding with the ministers and the young ladies."

Again, a few days later:

"I am completely on one side, while I appear to be quite busy in putting in an oar now and then."

To his daughter, on her eighteenth birth-day, he writes:

"Boston, May 23, 1835.

"My dear S.: You have been much in my mind to-day, and now that I am sitting alone this evening, I place myself at your writing-desk to communicate with you, and thus impart some portion of those feelings of interest and affection which a return of this day brings more strongly into play. Eighteen years of your life are now passed, and the events of this period have been deeply interesting to me, and have made such impressions on you, and have left such marks of progress, I hope, in the divine life, as will insure your onward and upward course, until you shall join that dear one whose home has been in heaven for nearly the whole period of your life. When I look upon you, or think of your appearance, the image of your mother is before me, and then I feel that deep solicitude that your mind and heart may be imbued with those heavenly influences that gave a grace and charm to all she did.

"There is no substitute for those traits, and you may feel entire confidence that a practical use of them in prosperity will prove the best security against the changes which adversity brings about. If I were to select for you the richest portion which a fond father could choose, it would be that you might have a mind and a heart to perform all those duties which your station and condition in life require, upon the true Christian principle of using your one or more talents, and thus, at the day of account, receive the cheering sound of the Master's voice.

"What treasure will compare with this? The charms of life are captivating to the imagination, but there are none more calculated to add to our joys here than elevated Christian principles, however they may be branded by the mere worldling as 'cold, unsocial,' and the like. You see how important it is to form a just estimate of the value of these different objects. When a mistake is made here, the consequences may be never-ending. Our danger is in cheating ourselves, by leaving undone those things our conscience tells us we ought to do, and doing others that it tells us we ought not to do.

"I have thought, for some time past, my dear child, that your mind was laboring under the influence of religious truth, and I have been made most comfortable in this belief. Cultivate those feelings, and study to make your example good to others, as well as safe for yourself. Our time here is short, but it is long enough to accomplish the work we are sent to perform, and the consequences will be on our own heads if we omit or neglect to do it."

(TO THE SAME.)

"GROTON, August 9, 1835.

"DEAR S.: I have been talking with your grandmother, for the last hour, upon the events of her early days, and I feel (as I always do when I contrast our present condition with the past) that we, as a whole people, and as individuals, have more reasons for gratitude and obedience to our heavenly Father than have ever before been placed before any people; and it seems to me we are more likely to disregard them than any other people I have any knowledge of. The fact is, we are so prosperous that we seem to forget the source of our prosperity, and take it as a matter of course that the character and conduct of a people cannot influence their condition. We are ready to say of an individual when he has been reckless and extravagant, that he has brought destruction on himself. Why, then, may not a whole people be judged by the same standard? Our great danger arises from false principles. We never act above the standard we adopt; and if our standard be so low as to authorize the gratification of the basest passions, how natural that our tastes become conformed to this standard!

"These reflections arose in my mind by hearing from my mother the stories of the 'times that tried men's souls;' how she was separated from her husband immediately after her marriage, when he joined the army in Rhode Island; how, after a battle, his mother said to her 'she did not know but Sam was killed;' how she fell instantly upon the floor, and how, within a day or two, after a separation of eight months, she was rejoiced to see her husband safe and sound (although at the time alluded to he had been in great peril, having been saved from captivity by the desperate efforts of a company of blacks, and by the fleetness and force of his fine charger); and how, by confidence in the justness of the cause and the aid of the Almighty, they trusted they should get through the contest, and be permitted to enjoy the fruits of their own labor in their own way. And now, what proportion of the people do you suppose refer to the aid of the Almighty, or to his justice or judgment as a motive to their actions, or how far does his fear or his love influence their conduct? These questions are more easily asked than answered; but they fill the mind with mournful forebodings of the necessary consequences to any people of forgetting God and departing from his love. You and I, and every individual, have it in our power to keep off in some degree this fatal consummation. Let us, therefore, examine well ourselves, and strive to be numbered among those faithful stewards who, at their Master's coming, shall be placed among the happy company who enter the joy of their Lord.

"This morning is one of those delightful quiet Sabbaths that seem to be like the rest of the saints above. We are all soon to be on our way to public worship. * * * *

(TO HIS MOTHER.)

"Aug. 16, 1835.

"MY DEAR AND HONORED MOTHER: My mind turns back to you almost as frequently as its powers are brought into separate action, and always with an interest that animates and quickens my pulse; for, under God, it is by your good influence and teachings that I am prepared to enjoy those blessings which he has so richly scattered in my path in all my onward progress in life. How could it be otherwise than that your image should be with me, unless I should prove wholly unworthy of you? Your journey is so much of it performed, that those objects which interested you greatly in its early stages have lost their charms; and well it is that they have; for they now would prove *clogs* in the way; and it is to your children, to your Saviour, and your God, that your mind and heart now turn as the natural sources of pleasure. Each of these, I trust, in their proper place and degree, supply all your wants. The cheering promise that has encouraged you when your powers were the highest, will not fail you when the weight of years and infirmities have made it more necessary to your comfort to get over the few remaining spans of the journey. To God I commend you; and pray him to make the path light, and your way confiding and joyful, until you shall reach that home prepared for the faithful."

In a letter to his sister, dated Oct. 25, he further alludes to his mother, as follows

"My thoughts this morning have been much engaged with my early home. I conclude it best to embody them in part, and send them forward to add (if they may) a token of gratitude and thankfulness to that dear one who is left to us, for her care of our early days, and her Christian instruction and example to her children, grandchildren, and great-grandchildren; each generation of whom, I trust, will be made better in some of its members by her. It is more natural, when in our weakness and want, to turn our thoughts to those whom they have been accustomed to look to for assistance; and thus to me the impression of the blessing I enjoy in having such a home as mine is, and the blessing I early enjoyed of having such a home as mine was under my father's roof, say to my heart: 'All these increase thy responsibilities, and for their use thou must account.' I have had one of my slight ill turns within the last two days, that has brought back all these feelings with increased force; and I look upon these as gentle monitors, calculated to make me estimate more fully my blessings and my duties. Frequently as I am admonished of the frail tenure by which I hold my life, I am negligent and careless in the performance of those high and every-day duties which I should never lose sight of for an hour. I have also such buoyancy of spirits, that life seems to me a very, very great blessing, and I do at times strive to make it useful to those around me."

CHAPTER XVII.

REFLECTIONS. — VISIT TO WASHINGTON. — VISIT TO RAINSFORD ISLAND. — VIEWS OF DEATH. — REFLECTIONS.

FROM memorandum-book of property, December 31, 1835 :

"My expenses have been —— thousand dollars this year; of which about one half went for persons and objects that make me feel that it has been well expended, and is better used than to remain in my possession. God grant that I may have the disposition to use these talents in such manner as to receive at last the joyful sound of ' Well done ! ' "

On March 29, 1836, Mr. Lawrence writes :

" My anxiety for a day or two about little things kept me from the enjoyment of those bright scenes that are so common to me when not oppressed by any of these *may be* events. My nerves are in such a shattered state, that I am quite unfit to encounter the responsibilities incident to my station, and I am ashamed of myself thus to expose my weakness."

During the spring, Mr. Lawrence's health was so feeble, and his nervous system so shattered, that a journey was recommended ; and, in the month of

May, in company with his friend and pastor, the Rev Dr. Lothrop, he paid a visit to his brother Abbott, at Washington, then the representative in Congress for Boston. During this journey, he experienced a severe illness, and was shortly joined by Mrs. Lawrence. The visit to Washington extended through several weeks: and, although his health remained feeble and the weather unfavorable, he seems to have been alive to objects around him, and interested in what was going forward in the halls of Congress as well as in the society of the capital. He speaks of visits to the houses of Congress, and pleasant rides on horseback, "with hosts of agreeable companions ready to sally forth when the weather shall permit." He also takes a survey of the general state of society in Washington, with an occasional allusion to some particular personage. He writes:

"It used to be said that Washington and the Springs were the places for matrimonial speculations. I feel a natural dislike to a lady being brought out as an extraordinary affair, having all perfections, and having refused *forty-nine* offers, and still being on the carpet. It shows that she is either very silly herself, or has very silly friends, or both. Good strong common sense is worth more than forty-nine offers, with any quantity of slaves, or bank-notes, or lands, without it. * * * * *

"I have passed two hours in the Representatives' Hall and Senate Chamber to-day. I heard the usual sparring, and confess myself greatly interested in it. I could learn nothing of the merits of any of the questions; but I had a preference, such as one feels in seeing two dogs fight, that one should beat. It was very agreeable to me to see and hear those various distinguished characters, and goes to demonstrate the common saying, that some objects appear smaller by our getting nearer to them."

During this absence, one of his family remaining at home had experienced a light attack of varioloid; and, according to the law then in force, was obliged to be transported to the Quarantine Hospital, situated in Boston Harbor. Soon after Mr. Lawrence's return from the South, he paid a visit to Rainsford Island, on the invitation of Dr. J. V. C. Smith, then Quarantine Physician, and there passed some weeks very pleasantly, riding about the island on his horse, and watching, from the shores, the sea-views, which, with the passing ships, here afford an endless variety.

In August, he returned to his own house in Boston; and, on the 21st, writes to his sister as follows:

"The scenery in front, side, and rear, and all within, is unrivalled, except by the charms of the dear old home of my mother and sister; in short, it seems to me that no two spots combine so many charms as my early and present homes; and they impress me more fully now by my being so well as to enjoy not only natural scenery, but the social intercourse with loved ones, that more than compensate for anything I may have lost by sickness and suffering. I yesterday was on horseback nearly three hours, but did not ride more than ten miles; and, in that distance, I went over some scenes that I felt unwilling to leave, especially some of the old works on and near Dorchester Heights; for they appeared more interesting than ever before, from the circumstance of your showing me that mass of original letters from Washington, Hancock, Samuel Adams, and various other revolutionary characters, to General Ward; some of them touching the occupation of these heights sixty years ago, and some of them alluding to scenes which have scarcely been noticed in the published histories of those days. All go to show, however, the whole souls of those men to have been engaged in their work; and, further, how vain it is for us of this day, who are ambitious of distinction, to found it on any other basis than uprightness of character, purity of life, and the active performance of all those duties included in 'the doing justly, loving mercy, and walking humbly.' How few of us remember this! I hardly know when I have been more forcibly impressed with a plain truth than I was yesterday, while sitting alone on horseback, on the top of the redoubt on Dorchester Heights, and the considerations of the past, the present, and the future, were the subject of my thoughts, connecting the men of those days with the present, and the men of these days with the future. The evidence is irresistible, that there is a downhill tendency in the character of the people, which, in sixty years more, will make us more corrupt than any other enlightened nation so young as ours, unless we are checked by adversity and suffering. But this is not what I intended to write about, so I will go to something else. The old revolutionary documents, memorials of our father, never appeared to me so interesting as now; and those I now return to you will be carefully preserved, and such others as you may find, added to them. I would give a great sum of money, if by it I could get all the documents I used to see when I was a child, and which we thought of so little value that we did not preserve them with that care which sh have been used in a family which cherishes such deep feelings of respect and affection for parents."

The year 1837 will be remembered as one of great pecuniary embarrassment and distress in the commercial world. Mr. Lawrence alludes to it as follows, on May 13

"The violent pecuniary revulsion that has been anticipated for more than a year has at length overtaken this country, and is more severe than our worst fears. In addition to the failure of people to pay their debts, in all sections of the country, for the last two months, the banks, from Baltimore to Boston, and probably throughout the Union, as fast as the intelligence spreads, have suspended specie payment, and will not probably resume again very soon."

On December 17 of the same year, he writes to his mother as follows

"This day completes thirty years since my commencing business, with the hope of acquiring no very definite amount of property, or having in my mind any anticipation of ever enjoying a tithe of that consideration my friends and the public are disposed to award me at this time. In looking back to that period, and reviewing the events as they come along, I can see the good hand of God in all my experience; and acknowledge, with deep humiliation, my want of gratitude and proper return for all his mercies. May each day I live impress me more deeply with a sense of duty, and find me better prepared to answer his call, and account for my stewardship! The changes in our family have been perhaps no greater than usual in other families in that period, excepting in the matter of the eminent success that has attended our efforts of a worldly nature. This worldly success is the great cause of our danger in its uses, and may prove a snare, unless we strive to keep constantly in mind, that to whom much is given, of him will much be required. I feel my own deficiencies, and lament them; but am encouraged and rewarded by the enjoyment, in a high degree, of all my well-meant efforts for the good of those around me. In short, I feel as though I can still do a little to advance the cause of human happiness while I remain here. My maxim is, that I ought to 'work while the day lasts; for the night of death will soon overtake me, when I can no more work.' I continue to mend in strength, and feel at times the buoyancy of early days. It is now raining in torrents, keeping us all within doors. I have been at work with gimblet, saw, fore-plane, and hammer, thus securing a good share of exercise without leaving my chamber."

"*January* 1, 1838.— Bless the Lord, O my soul! and forget not all his benefits; for he has restored my life twice during the past year, when I was apparently dead, and has permitted me to live, and see and enjoy much, and has surrounded me with blessings that call for thankfulness. The possession of my mind, the intercourse with beloved friends, the opportunity of performing some labor as his steward (although imperfectly done), all call upon me for thanksgiving and praise. The violent revulsion in the business of the country during the past year has been ruinous to many; but, so far as my own interests are concerned, has been less than I anticipated. My property remains much as it was a year ago. Something beyond my income has been disposed of; and I have no debts against me, either as a partner in the firm or individually. Everything is in a better form for settlement than at any former period, and I hope to feel ready to depart whenever called."

The following is copied from an account-book, presented at the commencement of the year to his youngest son, then twelve years of age:

"MY DEAR SON: I give you this little book, that you may write in it how much money you receive, and how you use it. It is of much importance, in forming your early character, to have correct habits, and a strict regard to truth in all you do. For this purpose, I advise you never to cheat yourself by making a false entry in this book. If you spend money for an object you would not willingly have known, you will be more likely to avoid doing the same thing again if you call it by its right name here, remembering always that there is *One* who cannot be deceived, and that *He* requires his children to render an account of all their doings at last. I pray God so to guide and direct you that, when your stewardship here is ended, he may say to you that the talents intrusted to your care have been faithfully employed.
"Your affectionate father, A. L."

In transmitting to his sister a letter received from Baltimore, from a mutual friend, he writes, on March 12, in a postscript:

"This morning seems almost like a foretaste of heaven. The sun shines bright, the air is soft; I am comfortable, and expect a pleasant drive in the neighborhood. It is indeed brilliant, beautiful, and interesting to me, beyond any former experience of my life. I am the happiest man alive, and yet would willingly exchange worlds this day, if it be the good pleasure of our best Friend and Father in heaven."

The extract quoted above will give an idea of that state of mind in which Mr. Lawrence was often found by his friends, and which he unceasingly strove to cultivate. He could not always exult in the same buoyant and almost rapturous feelings here expressed; for, with his feeble frame and extreme susceptibility to outward influences, to believe such was the case would be to suppose him more than mortal. The willingness to exchange worlds was, however, a constant frame of mind; and the daily probability of such an event he always kept in view. The work of each day was performed with the feeling that it might be his last; and there is, throughout his correspondence and diary, frequent allusion to the uncertain tenure by which he held life, and his determination to work while the day lasted. If a matter was to be attended to, of great or little importance, whether the founding a professorship, signing a will, or paying a household bill, all was done at the earliest moment, with the habitual remark, "I may not be here to-morrow to do it."

In the same cheerful spirit, he writes to his son a few days after his marriage, and then on a journey to Virginia:

"The whole scene here on Thursday last was so delightful

that I hardly knew whether I was on the earth, or floating between earth and heaven. I have been exalted ever since, and the group of happy friends will be a sunny spot in your no less than in their remembrance."

To his sister he writes, Dec. 22 :

"It is thirty-one years this week since I commenced business on my own account, and the prospects were as gloomy at that period for its successful pursuit as at any time since; but I never had any doubt or misgiving as to my success, for I then had no more wants than my means would justify. The habits then formed, and since confirmed and strengthened by use, have been the foundation of my good name, good fortune, and present happy condition. At that time (when you know I used to visit you as often as I could, by riding in the night until I sometimes encroached upon the earliest hour of the Sabbath before reaching my beloved home, to be at my business at the dawn of day on Monday morning), my gains were more than my expenses; thus strengthening and encouraging me in the steady pursuit of those objects I had in view as a beginner. From that time to this, I am not aware of ever desiring or acquiring any great amount by a single operation, or of taking any part of the property of any other man and mingling it with my own, where I had the legal right to do so. I have had such uniform success as to make my fidelity a matter of deep concern to myself; and my prayer to God is, that I may be found to have acted a uniform part, and receive the joyful 'Well done,' which is substantial wealth, that no man can take away. If my experience could be made available by my successors, I sometimes feel that it would be a guaranty that they would keep in the best path; but, as they are to be fitted by discipline for the journey, it is perhaps a vain thing for me to allow any doubts to rest upon my mind that *that* discipline is not for their highest good. The pleasures of memory have never been more highly enjoyed than during the period of my last sickness. They have solaced my pains, and supported me through numerous fainting fits, growing out of the surgical treatment I have endured. I would ask you, my dear sister, if a merciful Parent has not stretched forth his hand almost visibly to support me through this trying scene, by scattering in my path these flowers and fruits so freely as almost to make me forget bodily pains; and bless him for what is past, and trust that what is future will be the means of making me a better man."

"*December* 31, 1838.— The business of the year now brought to a close has been unexpectedly productive, and the prospects of continued success are very flattering. At the commencement of the year, my life seemed a flickering light, with small hope of its continuance through the winter; but a merciful Providence has permitted a brighter view, and my happiness through the year has been superior to that of any year of my life."

After enumerating some domestic events which had contributed to this result, he adds:

"My own health is so far restored as to allow me the enjoyment of everything around me in perfection. May God in mercy keep me mindful of my duties, and prepared to surrender my account at any moment he may call me hence!"

CHAPTER XVIII.

BROTHER'S DEATH. — LETTERS. — GIFTS. — LETTERS. — DIARY. — APPLICANTS FOR AID. — REFLECTIONS. — LETTER FROM REV DR. STONE. — DIARY.

IF, at the close of the last year, Mr. Lawrence could say that "his happiness had been superior to that of any year of his life," it could not be said that its successor was one of unmingled brightness. The unbroken band of brothers who had marched thus far hand in hand, united by a common bond of sympathy and affection, sustaining each other in all trials, and rejoicing together in their common prosperity, was about to be sundered. Since their earliest days, they had had but one interest, and, residing near each other after leaving their early home, had been in the habit of most constant and intimate intercourse. Many of their friends will well remember seeing four, and sometimes five, of them, on Sunday evening, after service, walking together abreast, arm in arm; and have been tempted to exclaim, "Behold how good and pleasant a thing it is for brethren to dwell together in unity." They had more than obeyed their father's injunction "not to fall out by the way, for a three-fold cord is not quickly broken." With them, it had been a five-fold cord; and, amidst all the perplexities of business, the management of important interests, and the various vicissitudes of domestic life, no strand had been broken until severed by the ruthless hand of death. The eldest brother, Luther, had been educated at Harvard College; had studied law with the Hon. Timothy Bigelow, then of Groton, afterwards of Medford, whose sister he subsequently married; and had commenced the practice of his profession in his native town. There he met with good success, and, for many years, represented the town in the House of Representatives, of which he was chosen Speaker for the session of 1821 and 1822. He was induced by his brothers, who had become largely interested in the new town of Lowell, to remove thither; and he accordingly took up his residence there in 1831, having accepted the presidency of the bank which had been lately established. In 1838, he had been elected Mayor of the city, and had given himself up to the pressing duties incident to the office in a new and growing community. While holding this office, he, on the 17th of April, 1839, accompanied an old friend and connection, who was on a visit at Lowell, to inspect the works of the Middlesex Manufacturing Company, recently erected by his brothers. In passing rapidly through one of the rooms, he made a misstep, and was precipitated many feet into a wheel-pit, causing almost instant death

This sad event was deeply felt by Mr. Lawrence, as well as by all who knew and appreciated the character of the deceased. In a letter to his sisters, dated April 22, he says:

"I should have addressed a word of comfort to you before this. That he should be taken, and I left, is beyond my *ken*, and is a mystery which will be cleared up hereafter. I do, however, know *now* that all is right, and better ordered than we could have done it. We *must* submit, and *should be* resigned. Brother L.'s death may, perhaps, be more efficient in instructing us in the path of duty than would have been his life; and the whole community around is admonished by this event in a way that I have rarely seen so marked. The homage to his character is a legacy to his children of more value than all the gold of the mint. Shall we, then, repine at his separation from us? Surely not. He has fulfilled his mission, and is taken home, with all his powers fresh and perfect, and with the character of having used these powers for the best and highest good of all around him. We shall all soon be called away, and should make his departure the signal to be also ready. This is the anniversary of my birth, and has been marked by many circumstances of peculiar interest."

On the same date, he writes to a connection, who was about to take possession of his house on that day for the first time after his marriage:

"I intended speaking a word in your ear before your leaving us for your own fireside and home, but have concluded to take this mode of doing it; and it is to say, that you possess a jewel in your wife, above price, which should be worn in such an atmosphere as will increase its purity and value the longer you possess it; and that is around the family altar. That you intend to establish it, I have no doubt; but, as to the precise time, you may not be fixed. What time so good as the present time, when the first evening of possession of this paradise on earth (a house and home of your own with such a wife), to make that offering to the Father of mercies which ascends to his throne as sweet incense from his children? It is the nutriment and efficient producing power of the best principles and the best fruits of our nature. Be wise in time, and strive to secure these, that you may go on from one degree to another, until you shall have reached our Father's house, and shall hear the cheering 'Well done!' promised to such as have used their talents without abusing them. My blessing attend you!"

(TO HIS DAUGHTER.)

"Monday evening.

"DEAR S.: The admonition of the last week comes home to me in a way not to be neglected, and I hope to keep in mind that, in my best days, I am as likely to be called off, as in these days of anxious care, when pressed down with pain and weakness, and surrounded by those dear ones who look upon every emotion with deep solicitude. On comparing myself now with myself a year ago, I have much to animate and cheer in the increased strength of body and renewed powers, by which I can enjoy life; but I have also much to speak to the heart, and to tell me to be constantly ready to be called off without previous note of preparation. May I never lose sight, for a single hour, of the tenure by which I hold the privilege of seeing the dear ones settled so happily! It is more than I had reason to anticipate.

"May you, dear child, never lose sight of the end for which your privileges are made so ample, nor forego the happiness of

BIRTH PLACE AT GROTON

doing the best in your power at every stage of your journey, so that whenever you may be called hence, you may feel that you are ready, and that your work is done. It will not do for me to rely upon my every-day firmness to secure me against attacks of the kind last experienced. I do most fervently desire to be kept in mind of my exposure, and never for an hour forget that it may be my last."

Several passages in Mr. Lawrence's letters will show the attachment which he felt towards the place of his birth, connected as it was with so many associations and memories of the past. The old house, with the great elm in front and its welcome shade; the green meadow, stretching for a mile along a gentle declivity to the river; the range of mountains in the west, just distant enough to afford that tinge of blue which adds an indescribable charm to every landscape; the graceful undulations of the hills on the east, with the quiet village sleeping at their base, all seemed in his mind so associated with the loved inmates of his early home, that he ever contemplated the picture with delight.

On June 4, in a letter to his sisters, he writes:

"R. leaves us this morning, on his way to the old homestead, which, to my mind's eye, has all the charms of the most lovely associations of early days, with all the real beauty of those splendid descriptions given by the prophets of the holy city. I would earnestly impress all my children with a deep sense of the beauty and benefit of cherishing and cultivating a respect and affection for this dear spot, and for those more dear objects that have served to make it what it really is to all us children."

In a letter to his son, whose visit is alluded to above, he says:

"The beautiful scenery from Gibbet Hill, in Groton, and from the road from our old mansion south for a mile, towards the Wachusett and the Monadnock Mountains, comes next, in point of beauty, to my taste, to these views around the Boston Common. Be careful to do all things as you will wish you had done, that you may look back upon this visit with pleasure, and forward to another visit with increased relish. Remember that in the best performance of all your duties lies the highest enjoyment of all your pleasures. Those pleasures that flow from plans and doings that your conscience condemns are to be shunned as the net of the wicked one. When once entangled, the desire and effort to be released grow weaker, till, at length, conscience is put asleep, and the sleep of death comes over the soul. Be careful, therefore, to avoid evil, and not only so, but to avoid all appearance of evil. In this way, you will grow up with principles and fixed habits that will secure you against the ills of life, and supply a foretaste of the enjoyments of a better life to come."

During a visit which he made to his early home a few months subsequent to the date of the preceding extract, he writes to his daughter:

"I was very tired on arriving here last evening, but a quiet sleep has brought me into my best state.

"This morning has allowed me to ride for two hours, and I have enjoyed everything and everybody here to the utmost.

Groton is beautiful beyond any other place I have ever seen; but perhaps I am in the situation of old Mr. ——, whose opinion of his wife's beauty, when questioned of its accuracy, was justified by the declaration that the person must have his eyes to look through.

"The whole country is full of charms; nothing seems wanting to impress upon the heart the goodness of that Parent who seeks by all means to bring us nearer to himself.

"This visit has been full of interest, and it is a source of unfeigned thanksgiving that it has been permitted to me."

Mr. Lawrence always took great delight in sending to friends and relatives, little and great, mementoes of his affection; and a great deal of time was spent in penning and reading the letters and notes which such transactions called forth. He had a rare faculty of adapting his gift to the peculiar necessities or tastes of the recipient; and, whether the matter treated of was a check for thousands or a bouquet of flowers, equal pleasure seemed to be given and received. In sending a gift of the former description, he notices the commencement of the year 1840 as follows:

"January 1.

"DEAR S.: W. will prize the enclosed more highly from your hand; for he will have proof that a good wife brings many blessings, that he never would know the value of but for you. May you experience many returns of the 'new year,' and each more happy than the past!"

In a letter to his second son, then on a visit to Europe, he writes, under date of March 5, 1840:

"We are all curious to know what impressions your visit to France and Italy produces, and still more what impressions a careful overlooking of our fatherland makes upon you. There is much food for reflection, and abundant material for the exercise of your powers of observation, in every league of the '*fast-anchored isle*,' especially in the scenes so beautifully portrayed in many of the books we have access to. In fact, I have an extensive collection of materials to renew your travels and observations, and shall value them more highly when you point out this or that seat or castle or abbey, which has arrested your notice. But the best scenes will be those in which the living souls of the present day are engaged. The habits and tastes of the people of England have doubtless much changed since the *Spectator* days; but, in many important particulars, I should hope they had not. Some thirty years ago, I had a good specimen of the feelings and principles of a great variety of people, embracing almost all classes, from the year 1774 to 1776, in a multitude of letters that had accumulated in the post-office in this town, under Tuthill Hubbart. After his death, his house was pulled down; and, among the strange things found in it, were bushels of letters, of which I was permitted to take what I pleased. These letters showed a deeper religious feeling in the writers of those days, from England, Ireland, and Scotland, than I have seen in any miscellaneous collections of a later date. If that deep-toned piety which pervaded them has not been extinguished by the Jacobinism and freethinking of later days, happy for the people and the government! But I fear it has, in some great measure, been blotted out or obscured, as there seems to be a spirit of reckless adventure in politics and religion not contemplated seventy years ago. How far our experience in self-government in this country is going to advance the cause of good government, and the ultimate happiness of man, is yet a problem. Our principles are of the most elevating character; our practices under them, of the most debasing; and, if we continue in this way another generation, there will not be virtue enough in active use to save the forms of our government. We may hope that a better heart may be given us."

In a letter to his son-in-law, the Rev. Charles Mason, who was at that time in company with his own son on a visit to England, he writes on June 28th, 1840:

"I intended to defer writing until to-morrow morning; but the beauty of the western scenery and sunset is so striking, that I am strongly impelled to tell you that, much as you see, and highly as you enjoy the scenes of old England, there is nothing there more beautiful and sublime than this very scene from my chamber windows. It seems as though nature never was so beautifully dressed at this time of the year as at present. The season has been unusually favorable for the foliage, fruits, and flowers; and all around bears evidence of that goodness that never rests, and in my own person I feel that I am enjoying in a month what ought to content me for a year."

The foregoing extract is selected from among many others of a similar nature, as an illustration of Mr. Lawrence's appreciation of the beauties of natural scenery.

Towards the close of the day, his favorite seat was at a window, from which he could witness the glories of the setting sun, and, still later, the fading beauties of the twilight. Nature to him was no sealed volume; and with her, in all her phases, he loved to commune.

The gorgeous hues of the western sky, the changing tints of the autumnal foliage, and the smiling features of the landscape, were in his mind typical of the more resplendent beauties of the future world. He writes:

"To-day is one of those holy spring days which make us feel that, with right principles and conduct, we may enjoy a foretaste of that beautiful home we all long for. I have been over the Roxbury and Dorchester hills, which are a transcript of the beautiful scenery around Jerusalem. Mount Zion seemed before me, and by stretching my arms, I could almost fly upon its sides."

He loved to think that the spirits of the departed may be permitted to hover around, and minister to those whom they have once loved on earth; and sometimes, as he viewed nature in her softer moods, he would imagine himself as holding communion with former cherished objects of affection. He writes to a friend:

"Dear S. and R. speak in words without sounds, through every breeze and in every flower, and in the fragrance of every perfume from the field or the trees."

And again:

"Is there anything in Scripture to discourage the belief that the spirits of departed friends are still ministering spirits to such as are left here, and that a recognition and reünion will follow when we are called off? I believe fully in this happy reünion; and it is, next to the example of the beloved, the most animating feeling that prompts me through this wearisome journey."

To a friend who had invited him to pay her a visit at her residence in the country, he writes:

"N—— says I am like a child in the matter of the visit, and would be as much disappointed if it should not be accomplished; and I must admit that I am guilty of this weakness. There are so many loved ones on the old spot, so many lessons to be reviewed, and so many friends 'passed on,' whose spirits surround and fill the place with the peculiar halo and charm of the good angels (those ministering spirits in whose company we may ever find comfort, if we will think so). I say, with all these things, can I be blamed for being a child in this matter? You will all say No, and will love me the better for it."

On the anniversary of his commencing his business, Dec. 17, Mr. Lawrence, as usual, reviews his past life and mercies, and adds:

"My daily aspirations are for wisdom and integrity to do what is required of me; but the excuses for omissions, and the hidden promptings of pride or selfishness in the sins of commission, take away all confidence that all is done as it should be

I am in the enjoyment of as much as belongs to our condition here. Wife, children, and friends, those three little blessings that were spared to us after the fall, impart enjoyment that makes my home as near a heaven on earth as is allowed to mortals.

"*Dec.* 23. — This morning has been clear and beautiful, and I have enjoyed it highly. Have been sleigh-riding with Chancellor Kent. Went over to Bunker Hill Monument, and around by the river-side to Charlestown Neck, and had a regular old-fashioned talk with him. He gave me an account of the scenes which occurred where he was studying, in Connecticut, when the news came of the Lexington fight. As we parted, he promised to come again in the spring, take another ride, and resume the conversation. He leaves for New York at three o'clock, and is as bright and lively as a boy, though seventy-eight years old. The old gentleman attends to all his own affairs, had walked around the city this morning some miles, been to the Providence Railroad Dépôt for his ticket, overlooked divers bookstores, and so forth. He is very interesting, and has all the simplicity of a child."

About this time, also, Mr. Lawrence seems to have had pleasant intercourse with the Chevalier Hulsemann, the Austrian Minister, so well known by his correspondence with Mr. Webster when the latter was Secretary of State. The minister was on a visit to Boston, and, from the correspondence which ensued, seems to have conceived a high regard for Mr. Lawrence, expressed in very kind and courteous terms; and this regard seems to have been fully reciprocated.

"*April* 1, 1841. — S. N., of T., an apprentice on board the United States ship 'Columbus,' in this harbor, thirteen years old, whom I picked up intoxicated in Beacon-street a month ago, and to whom I gave some books, with request to call and see me when on shore, came to-day, and appears very well. Gave him a Testament and some good counsel.

"*June* 6. — G. M. called to sell a lot of sermons called the ——, which he said he caused to be published to do good; he repeated it so often that I doubted him. He seems to me a *wooden nutmeg* fellow, although he has the Rev. Mr. ——'s certificate."

The preceding entry is given here merely as a sample of many such which are found in Mr. Lawrence's diary. Few who have not had the like experience can estimate the annoyance to which his reputation for benevolence and well-doing subjected him, in the shape of applications for aid in every imaginable form. His perceptions were naturally acute; and a long experience and intercourse with men enabled him to form, at a single glance, a pretty fair estimate of the merits of the applicant. He may sometimes have judged precipitately, and perhaps harshly; but, when he discovered that he had done so, no one could have been more ready to confess his fault and make reparation. A few years after this time, the annoyance became so serious, from the number and character of the applicants, that he felt obliged, on account of ill-health, to deny himself to all, unless personally known to him, or accredited by some one in whose statement he had confidence. Further than this, he was confirmed in his decision by actual abuse which had occasionally been administered to him by disappointed candidates for charitable aid. He kept upon his table a small memorandum-book, in which he recorded the names of those who sought aid, with their business, and often their age, the age and number of their children, sometimes facts in their past history, and any other information which could enable him to form an opinion of their claim upon him for assistance. He sometimes indulges also in somewhat quaint remarks respecting those who apply, or the manner in which they have presented their application.

To the Rev. Robert Turnbull, a Baptist clergyman then settled in Boston, and who had sent to Mr. Lawrence a copy of his work entitled "Claims of Jesus," he writes under date of Nov. 2:

"REV. AND DEAR SIR: I thank you for the little volume so kindly presented, and deem it the duty of all the friends of the Saviour to do what they can to stop the flood of infidelity and atheism that threatens such waste and devastation among us. However we may seem to be, I trust many may be found, in the ranks of my Unitarian friends, who admit the 'claims of Jesus' in their most elevated character, and who repudiate the doctrine of those who sink him to the level of a mere human teacher, as subversive of his authority and as nullifying his teachings. We take the record, and what is clearly declared; we do not go behind, even though we do not clearly comprehend it. It gives me pleasure to learn you are so well recovered from the injury you received from the overturn of your carriage near my house.

"With great respect, believe me truly yours,   A. L."

"*January*, 1842. — This year opens with renewed calls upon me to bless God for his mercies throughout its course. My family circle has not been broken by the death of any one of our whole number, and my own health has been better for the last half-year than for five years before. I have not had occasion to call a physician through the year. My brothers A. and W. have been dangerously sick, but are happily recovered; and both feel, I believe, that their hold on life is not as firm as they have felt it to be in former years. My dear children are growing up around me to bless and comfort me; and all I need is a right understanding of my duties, and a sincere purpose to fulfil them. I hope to have the will to continue them in as faithful a manner as heretofore, to say the least."

Among the traits in Mr. Lawrence's character was that enlarged spirit of Christian feeling which enabled him to appreciate goodness in others, without reference to sect or denomination. This spirit of universal brotherhood was not in him a matter of mere theory, but was carried out in the practice of daily life, and was the means of cementing many and lasting friendships, especially among the clergy of various denominations around him. It may not be uninteresting in future years, for those now in childhood, for whom this volume has been prepared, to be reminded of the strong feeling of sympathy and affection which their grandfather entertained for the Rev. John S. Stone, D.D., once the Rector of St. Paul's Church, in Boston, and now the Rector of St. Paul's, in Brookline, Mass. The following is an extract from a letter written by that gentleman from Brooklyn, N. Y., during the year 1842, with a memorandum endorsed by Mr. Lawrence, dated October, 1847, in which he says:

"This letter was very interesting to me when received. I kept it in my pocket-book with one from Judge Story, which he had requested me to keep for my children. While son —— was in Europe, I did not expect to live but a short time, and sent him the two letters, as the proper person to keep them for the use of his children."

The letter commences by strong expressions of affection and regard, over which Mr. Lawrence's modesty had induced him to paste a slip of paper, endorsed as follows: "Personal matters between the writer and myself, covered up here, and not to be read by any of the friends to whom I may show this letter." The letter continues as follows:

"Shall I ever forget the happy moments, hours, days, I may say weeks, which I have spent in riding with you, and chatting, as we rode, of all things as we passed them, till I seemed to myself to be living in the by-gone days of Boston and its neighborhood; and all its old families, houses, names, and anecdotes, became as familiar to my mind as the stories of my boyhood? Can I forget it all? I trow not. These things are all blended in with the beautiful scenery through which we used to ride, and associated with those graver lessons and reflections which you used to give me; insomuch that the picture which my memory retains of nature, society, history, and feeling, truth, friendship, and religion, and in which Boston and the living friends there are comprehended, has become imperishable. It never can fade out of my mind. It is a picture in which man has done much, friendship more, religion most, and God all; for religion is his, and friendship is from him, and man is his creature, and the green earth and glorious heavens are his home. There are many, very many, objects in this picture, which I contemplate with special delight; and few which give me pain, or which I would not have had there, had the whole ordering of its composition been left to me. Indeed, had this whole ordering been left to me, it may well be doubted whether, as a whole, it would have contained half of the beautiful and blessed things which it now contains. Taking it as it is, therefore, I am well content to receive it, hang it up in the choicest apartment of my memory, and keep it clean and in good order for use." * * *

As an illustration of the pleasant intercourse alluded to above, among Mr. Lawrence's papers is found another most friendly letter from the Rev. Henry Ware, jun., dated a few days afterwards, with the following endorsement:

"I went on Friday to Mr. Ware's house, and had a free, full, and deeply-interesting conversation upon the appointment of his successor; and was delighted to find him with the same views I have upon the necessity of removing the theological department from Cambridge."

Dec. 2, Mr. Lawrence alludes to the probability of his own death taking place in the manner in which it actually occurred ten years afterwards, as follows :

"Yesterday I was very well, and have been so for some time past. Experienced a severe ill turn this morning at five o'clock, more so than for years. This check brings me back to the reflection that, when I feel the best, I am most likely to experience one of my ill turns; some one of which will probably end my journey in this life. God grant me due preparation for the next!"

CHAPTER XIX.

REFLECTIONS.—LETTERS.—ACCOUNT OF EFFORTS TO COMPLETE BUNKER HILL MONUMENT.

IN the memorandum-book of property for 1843 is found the usual estimate and list of expenditures; after which Mr. Lawrence writes as follows:

"My outlay for other objects than my own family, for the last fourteen years, has been —— dollars, which sum I esteem better invested than if in bond and mortgage in the city; and I have reason to believe many have been comforted and assisted by it, and its influence will be good on those who follow me. God grant me grace to be faithful to my trust!"

To Hon. R. C. Winthrop, Member of Congress, at Washington, enclosing a letter from a young colored man:

"BOSTON, Feb. 15, 1843.

"DEAR SIR: This young man, as you will observe by his style, is well educated; and the circumstances he states, I have no doubt, are true. He applied to me, about two years since, for employment in writing or other business, to obtain means for further education; and I interested myself to secure to him what was required. A few months since, he started from here to go to Jamaica, to commence the practice of law, and was supplied by those who had taken an interest in him with a library suited to his wants. He received his early education in Indiana; and his parents were once slaves. He is a handsome colored fellow, better-mannered, better-looking, and more to be respected, than many young gentlemen who move in the higher walks of life, either in Carolina or Massachusetts. Now, I should like to know, if he should be admitted as an attorney to practice in our courts, and should take passage for Jamaica, and put into Charleston, would he be imprisoned, as is now the practice in regard to our black sailors? I feel a much stronger desire to see your report upon this subject of imprisoning our colored people, after the unfair course taken by the majority of your house to smother it; and I hope still to see it in print before the adjournment. I would further remark, that N. T. is a member of Grace Church in this city, I believe, under the care of Rev. T. M. Clark; and would, doubtless, bear affliction, if it should ever be his fortune to be afflicted by being imprisoned because his skin is dark, with a spirit becoming his profession. With great respect and esteem, believe me very truly yours, AMOS LAWRENCE."

(TO HIS SISTER.)

"BOSTON, April 19, 1843.

"DEAR SISTER M.: When I heard a gun this morning, I was immediately transported back in imagination to the 19th of April, 1775, when our grandmother retreated from her house on the roadside in Concord, with her family, to keep out of the way of the 'regulars;' and that day and its scenes, as described, came back upon me with a force which kept me awake in considering whether the gun was fired to recall the facts to the people of this day; and, if recalled, whether we can profit by the events which followed. I found, however, on receiving my newspapers, that the gun was not for commemoration of Lexington and Concord, but to announce the arrival of the British steamer from Liverpool. The news by this steamer is of no more than common interest; and the intercourse is now so easy and rapid, that the interest felt to learn what is passing in Europe is not much greater than we used to feel on Call's stage-coach arriving at Groton from Boston once a week, fifty years ago. The changes within my own recollection are such as almost to make me distrust my own senses; and many of the changes are at the cost of much good. The downhill tendency in the standard of character is a bad sign, and threatens the prostration of our political fabric. Built as it is on the virtue and intelligence of the people, every waste of these endangers the stability of the whole structure."

"*April* 24. — I resume, though not in the same train of thought, which is slept off. My birth-day has passed since then; and I am now in my fifty-eighth year. This is the birth-day of our father, who would have been eighty-nine if living; and this week on Saturday will also complete thirty-six years since I left home to spend a few months in this city, preparatory to my commencing business in Groton. Here I have continued; and the consequences to our family seem to have stamped upon us such marks as make us objects of influence, for good or evil, to a much greater extent than if I had returned to commence my business career in my native town. I view in this a hand pointing upward,—' Seek me and ye shall find,'— and a caution to us to use without abusing the good things intrusted to us. How hard it is for those in prosperity to bring home to their feelings their dependence, their abuse of their privileges, their desires for objects wholly disproportionate to their value, their anxiety about trifles, while they are so utterly careless and indifferent about those of the highest moment! How we strive unceasingly to secure objects that can, at best, give us but a slight reward, and, in many cases, if attained to the full extent of our hopes, only serve to sharpen our appetite for more; thus demonstrating the benevolence of our heavenly Father in removing these obstacles to our progress in the ways and works of godliness! How important, then, for us to see a Father's hand in the disappointments, not less than in the success, of our plans! I now speak practically of those anxieties which I feel and condemn myself for, in looking forward to the condition of my family. This is all wrong; and I pray God to pardon me the want of faith this feeling implies.

"I have thought much of your account of Mrs. N. going out, on the Sabbath after her husband's death, with her nine children. I remember her, and many others of my youthful schoolmates, with interest and regard. Please say so to her. And now, dear M., as the clouds seem thinner, I may hope to secure a little run, and shall take the post-office in my way; so must bid you adieu."

(TO GENERAL ———.)

"May 5, 1843.

"MY DEAR OLD GENERAL: Our anticipated drive to-day is not to be: the weather settles it that I must keep house; and, to indemnify myself for the disappointment, will you allow me to feel that I have not gone too far in requesting you to receive the enclosed check? I am spared here for some object, and do not feel that to hoard money is that object. While I am in the receipt of an income so ample, I find it sometimes troublesome to invest exactly to my mind. In the present case, the hope that you may, by using this, add something to your enjoyment, makes me feel that it is one of my best investments; and for the reason that your proverbial good-will cannot refuse me such a boon, I have made this request. My heart yearns strongly toward the old-fashioned John Jay school in politics and morals; and, when I have an opportunity to minister in any way to one of the early members, it is a pleasure that sweetens my days as they pass."

On the letter written in reply to the above, Mr. Lawrence has endorsed:

"This letter from old General ――, now eighty-eight years old, and blind, is an acknowledgment of some little kindnesses I was enabled to render through the hand of Judge Story. It has afforded me more pleasure than it could have done either the Judge or the General. I am sure the good old man's feelings were gratified; and I am thankful that I could comfort him."

On the 17th of June, 1843, took place the celebration in honor of the completion of the Bunker Hill Monument; an event which was regarded with no ordinary emotions by Mr. Lawrence, after so many years of effort and expectation. His only regret was that the whole battle-field could not have been preserved, and have remained, to use his own words, "a field-preacher for posterity." Eleven years before this, he had written to his son in Europe:

"If we be true to ourselves, our city is destined to be the Athens of America, and the hallowed spots in our neighborhood to be the objects of interest throughout all future time. In this view, I would never permit a foot of the battle-field of Bunker Hill to be alienated; but keep it for your great-great-grandchildren, as a legacy of patriotism worth more than their portion of it, if covered with gold by measure. Until you are older, I do not expect you to feel as I do on this subject."

This would seem to be the proper place to mention a few facts in regard to Mr. Lawrence's agency in securing the completion of the monument. It has already been mentioned that he was one of the earliest friends of the project to erect a monument, and, in 1825, had been placed upon the Standing Committee of Directors, with full powers to manage the affairs of the Association. In September, 1831, in a letter to his friend, Dr. J. C. Warren, who himself had been one of the warmest and most efficient advocates of the measure, he proposed to subscribe five thousand dollars, on condition that fifty thousand dollars should be raised within one year. The following passage occurs in that letter:

"I think it inexpedient to allude to the sale of the land on Bunker Hill, as a resource for paying the debt, except in case of extreme necessity; and, at this time, I should personally sooner vote to sell ten acres of the Common, in front of my house, to pay the city debt (of Boston), than vote to sell the ten acres on Bunker Hill, until it shall appear that our citizens will not contribute the means of saving it."

The proposition thus made was not responded to by the public.* As early as December, 1830, he had made provision by his will, in case of his own death,

---

* For a history of the Bunker Hill Monument, see an article in collections of "Maine Historical Society," vol. iii., by Professor Packard, of Bowdoin College.

to secure the battle-field, liquidate the debts of the corporation, and complete the monument. These provisions were superseded by another will, executed April 1, 1833, after his health had failed, so as to forbid active participation in affairs. An extract from this document will show the views of the testator:

"I am of opinion that the land owned by the Bunker Hill Monument Association, in Charlestown, will be of great value to posterity, if left as public ground. The spot is the most interesting in the country; and it seems to me it is calculated to impress the feelings of those who come after us with gratitude to the people of this generation, if we preserve it to them. The whole field contains about fifteen acres; and, in the hope of preserving it entire, either as the property of the State, of this city, or of any other competent body, and with the further view of insuring the completion of the monument, which now stands as a reproach to us, I have set apart a larger share of my property than would be necessary, had not the subject been presented to the public in such a manner as to discourage future attempts at raising the necessary funds by voluntary contribution."

The amount thus devised for the monument, in case that amount should not be raised in other ways, was fifty thousand dollars. In June, 1832, before the annual meeting of the Bunker Hill Monument Association, the same offer of five thousand dollars, as first named, was renewed, with an urgent appeal for the preservation of the land, and completion of the monument. A movement followed this appeal, but was not successful. In April, 1833, Mr. Lawrence proposed to the Massachusetts Charitable Mechanic Association to attempt the raising of fifty thousand dollars, to be secured within three months, for completing the monument and preserving the field; accompanying the proposition was an offer of five thousand dollars, or ten per cent. on any less sum that might be raised, as a donation to the Association. A public meeting was held in Faneuil Hall in response to this proposition, at which Hon. Edward Everett made a most powerful appeal, which produced so great an effect upon his auditors that the object was considered as accomplished. The effort was again unsuccessful. Early in 1839, Mr. Lawrence addressed a letter to George Darracott, Esq., President of the Mechanic Association, in which, after expressing regret that his feeble and precarious health would not permit him to make personal application to the citizens of Boston, he adds:

"The next best thing I can do is to give money. The Monument Association owes a debt. To discharge the debt, finish the monument, surround it with a handsome iron fence, and otherwise ornament the ground as it deserves, will require forty thousand dollars more than it now has. If the Association will collect thirty thousand dollars the present year, and pay off the debt, I will give to the Charitable Mechanic Association ten thousand dollars to enable it to complete the work in a manner which our fathers would have done, had they been here to direct it."

A further donation of ten thousand dollars was made by Judah Touro, Esq., of New Orleans; five thousand dollars were received from other sources; and this, with thirty thousand dollars received at the great fair held in Quincy Hall, September, 1840, afforded the means of completing the monument according to the original design. Thus was consummated a work which had been very near to Mr. Lawrence's heart, and which had cost him many a sleepless night, as well as days of toil and perplexity. To his associates in this work too much credit cannot be awarded, discouraged, as they often were, by indifference, and even censure. Their names will be handed down for centuries, in connection with a monument, which, while it commemorates a nation's freedom, teaches also a practical lesson of the perseverance and energy of man.

The following is an extract from a newspaper published about the time the monument was completed, giving an account of a festival held in commemoration of the event:

"The president remarked, that, among the benefactors to whom the Association had been particularly indebted for the means of completing the monument, two, whose names were written on a scroll at the other end of the hall, were Amos Lawrence and Judah Touro, each of whom had made a donation of ten thousand dollars. He thought it proper they should be remembered at the festive board, and gave the following:

"Amos and Judah! venerated names!
Patriarch and prophet press their equal claims;
Like generous coursers, running neck and neck,
Each aids the work by giving it a check.
Christian and Jew, they carry out a plan;
For, though of different faith, each is in heart a man."

CHAPTER XX.

INTEREST IN MOUNT AUBURN. — REV. DR. SHARP. — LETTER FROM BISHOP McILVAINE. — LETTER FROM JUDGE STORY.

AFTER the establishment of the cemetery at Mount Auburn, Mr. Lawrence had taken a deep interest in its progress, as well as in every plan for its gradual improvement and embellishment. In connection with his brothers, he had purchased a large space, which had been enclosed by a permanent granite wall and iron railing. To this spot he habitually resorted, containing, as it did, the remains of some of the dearest earthly objects of his affection, and destined, as it was, to be the final resting-place of not only himself, but of the various branches of his family. When this enclosure had been finished, it became an object with him to gather around him in death those whom he had loved and honored in life. In this way, he had been instrumental in causing to be removed to a burial-lot adjoining his own the remains of the Rev. J. S. Buckminster, the former minister of Brattle-street Church; and had also presented another lot to his friend and pastor, the Rev. Dr. Lothrop. Another friend, whose grave he wished to have near his own, was the Rev. Daniel Sharp, D.D., minister of the Charles-street Baptist Church, in Boston. There were few in Boston who were not familiar with the appearance of this venerable clergyman, as he daily appeared in the streets; and fewer still who had not learned to appreciate the truly catholic and Christian spirit which animated him in his intercourse with men of all sects and parties. Mr. Lawrence had early entertained a great esteem for his character; and this esteem had become mutual, and had ripened into the closest intimacy and friendship. On receiving a deed of a lot at Mount Auburn, Dr. Sharp writes as follows:

"Boston, August 23, 1843.

"MY DEAR SIR: I cannot find words with which to express my sense of your unexpected and considerate kindness, in providing so beautiful a resting-place in Mount Auburn for me and my loved ones. It is soothing to me to anticipate that my grave will be so near your own. May the Almighty, in his infinite mercy, grant, that, when the trumpet shall sound, and the dead shall awake, we may both rise together, to be forever with the Lord! If the proximity of my last place of repose to ministers of another denomination shall teach candor, charity, and peace, I enjoy the sweet consciousness that this will be in harmony with the object of my life.   Yours, gratefully,

"DANIEL SHARP.

"AMOS LAWRENCE, Esq."

The enlarged Christian spirit which formed so prominent a trait in Mr. Lawrence's character, and which enabled him to appreciate goodness wherever it could be found, without reference to nation, sect, or color, may be further illustrated by the following note of acknowledgment, received about the same time with the preceding, from Bishop McIlvaine, of the Protestant Episcopal Church in Ohio, who was then on a visit to Boston to procure funds in aid of Kenyon College:

" Wednesday evening.

" MY DEAR SIR: I have just received your very kind and grateful letter, with its cheering enclosure of a hundred dollars towards an object which engrosses me much just now. Thank you, dear sir, most truly, for your kindness, and the *first fruits* of Boston, for I came only to-day. I trust the ingathering will not dispossess the first ripe sheaf. Coming from one not of my own church, it is the more kind and grateful. O, sir! if God shall so bless my present effort as to send me home with the sum I seek, I shall know a freedom of mind from care and anxiety such as I have not experienced for many years, during which our present crisis has been anticipated. I shall have great pleasure in riding with you, according to your note to Mr. R. To-morrow will probably be a day of more leisure to me than any other while I shall be in Boston.

" Yours, very truly and respectfully,
" CHARLES P. MCILVAINE."

(TO ONE OF HIS PARTNERS.)

" December 18, 1843.

" DEAR MR. PARKER: I am *puffed up* (with ague), but not in a manner to gratify my pride, as I am housed, and denied the sight of most of those who call, but not the privilege of reading their papers, and spending money. In short, I have more use for money when in the house than when able to be abroad. If you will tell Brother Sharp * his beautiful bills find an exceedingly ready use, I shall be glad of one hundred in ones and twos, two hundred in fives, and three hundred in tens and twenties; say six hundred dollars, just to keep me along till the end of the month. The calls are frequent and striking. 'Do with thy might what thy hand findeth to do; for the night cometh, when no man can work.' God grant me the blessing of being ready to answer the call, whether it be at noon or at midnight!"

Twelve days after, he writes to the same gentleman for another supply; the sum already received not having been sufficient apparently to carry him through the year:

"December 30, 1843.

"'The good there is in riches lieth altogether in their use, like the woman's box of ointment; if it be not broken and the contents poured out for the refreshment of Jesus Christ, in his distressed members, they lose their worth; the covetous man may therefore truly write upon his rusting heaps, "These are good for nothing." He is not rich who lays up much, but he who lays out much; for it is all one not to have, as not to use. I will therefore be the richer by charitable laying out, while the worldling will be poorer by his covetous hoarding up.'

"Here is the embodiment of a volume, and whoever wrote it deserves the thanks of good men. I would fain be rich, according as he defines riches; but *possession, possession, is the devil*, as the old Frenchman at —— said to George Cabot. This devil

---

* For more than forty years Teller in Massachusetts Bank.

I would try to cast out; you will therefore please send me twelve hundred dollars, which may do something for the comfort of those who have seen better days. Your friend, A. L.

"To C. H. PARKER, Esq."

The following letter from Judge Story was received at about the time the preceding letter was written; but no memorandum is found by which to ascertain the occasion which called it forth. It may be that he had been made the channel, as was the case a few months before, of some donation to a third person; a mode which Mr. Lawrence often adopted when he felt a delicacy in proffering direct aid to some one whose sensitiveness might be wounded in receiving assistance from a comparative stranger:

"CAMBRIDGE, Saturday noon.

"MY DEAR SIR: I have this moment finished reading your letter and its enclosures, which did not reach me until this noon, and I can scarcely describe to you how deeply I have been affected by them. I almost feel that you are too much oppressed by the constant calls for charitable purposes, and that your liberal and conscientious spirit is tasked to its utmost extent. 'The poor have ye always with you' is a Christian truth; and I know not, in the whole circle of my friends, any one who realizes it so fully, and acts upon it so nobly, as yourself. God, my dear sir, will reward you for all your goodness; man never can. And yet the gratitude of the many whom you relieve, their prayers for your happiness, their consciousness of your expanded benevolence, is of itself a treasure of inestimable value. It is a source of consolation, which you would not exchange for any earthly boon of equal value. Wealth is to you an enlightened trust, for the benefit of your race. You administer it so gracefully, as well as so justly, that I can only regret that your means are not ten times as great. Gracious Heavens! What a contrast is your life to that of some wealthy men, who have lived many years, and have yet to learn how to give, or, as you beautifully expressed it the other day, who have yet to learn to be their own executors! My heart is so full of you, and of the whole matter, that I would fain pour out my thoughts at large to you; for you understand *me*, and I can sympathize with *you*. But just now I am full of all sorts of business, and without a moment to spare, having many judicial opinions to prepare in the few remaining days before I go to Washington; and, withal, having Mrs. S. very ill, in respect to whom, I feel a deep anxiety. But, wherever I am, I pray you to believe that you are always in my thoughts, with the warmest affection and dearest remembrance. And, if this hasty scrawl is not too slight for such a matter, pray preserve it among your papers, that your children may know what I thought of their father, when you and I shall be both in our graves.

"I am most truly and faithfully your obliged friend,
"JOSEPH STORY.
"AMOS LAWRENCE, Esq.

"P. S. — I have sent the letter and its accompaniments to Mr. ——. Think of ——. Think of those rich men in ——, who have never dreamed of the duties of charity. Cast a view to their own posterity. How striking a memento is the very case of ——, presented in his own letters, of the instability of human fortune!"

Mr. Lawrence closes the year 1843 by a review of his temporal affairs, and by fresh resolutions of fidelity to his trusts. He then gives an estimate of his income and expenditures, showing a somewhat large excess of the latter, though, as he says, from the state of the times, not to the detriment of his property.

(TO THE MECHANIC APPRENTICES' LIBRARY ASSOCIATION.)

"My young Friends: It cheers and comforts me to learn of your well-doing, and encourages me to offer a word of counsel, as prosperity is often more dangerous in its time than adversity. Now is your seed-time. See to it that it is good; for 'whatsoever a man soweth, that shall he also reap.' The integrity, intelligence, and elevated bearing, of the Boston mechanics, have been and are a property for each citizen of great value; inasmuch as the good name of our beloved city is a common property, that every citizen has an interest in, and should help to preserve. At your time of life, habits are formed that grow with your years. Avoid rum and tobacco, in all forms, unless prescribed as a medicine; and I will promise you better contracts, heavier purses, happier families, and a more youthful and vigorous old age, by thus avoiding the beginning of evil. God speed you, my young friends, in all your good works! With the enclosed, I pray you to accept the felicitations of the season.

"Amos Lawrence."

CHAPTER XXI.

ACQUAINTANCE WITH PRESIDENT HOPKINS. — LETTERS. — AFFECTION FOR BRATTLE-STREET CHURCH. — DEATH OF MRS. APPLETON — LETTERS. — AMESBURY CO.

AT the commencement of the year 1844, President Hopkins, of Williams College, delivered a course of lectures on the "Evidences of Christianity," before the Lowell Institute, in Boston. Mr. Lawrence had previously seen him, and had thought that he detected, in some features of his face, a resemblance to the family of his first wife. In allusion to this acquaintance, he writes to his son about this period:

"President H. has the family look of your mother enough to belong to them; and it was in consequence of that resemblance, when I was first introduced to him many years ago, that I inquired his origin, and found him to be of the same stock."

The acquaintance was renewed, and an intimacy ensued, which was not only the cause of much happiness to Mr. Lawrence through the remainder of his life, but was also the means of directing his attention to the wants of Williams College, of which he eventually became the greatest benefactor. An active and constant correspondence followed this acquaintance, and was so much prized by Mr. Lawrence that he had most of the letters copied, thereby filling several volumes, from which extracts will from time to time be made. In one of his first letters to that gentleman, dated May 11, he says:

"If, by the consecration of my earthly possessions to some extent, I can make the Christian character practically more lovely, and illustrate, in my own case, that the higher enjoyments here are promoted by the free use of the good things intrusted to me, what so good use can I make of them? I feel that my stewardship is a very imperfect one, and that the use of these good things might be extended profitably to myself; and, since I have known how much good the little donation did your college, I feel ashamed of myself it had not been larger,— at any rate, sufficient to have cleared the debt."

To the same gentleman, who had informed Mr. Lawrence that an accident had befallen a plaster bust of himself, he writes, under date of May 16:

"DEAR PRESIDENT: You know the phrase 'Such a man's head is full of notions' has a meaning that we all understand to be not to his credit for discretion, whatever else may be said of him. As I propose throwing in a caveat against this general meaning, I proceed to state my case. And, firstly, President H. is made debtor to the Western Railroad Corporation for the transportation of a barrel to Pittsfield. The bill is receipted, so that you can have the barrel to-morrow by sending for it; which barrel contains neither biscuit nor flour, but the clay image of your friend. In the head are divers notions that my hand fell upon as I was preparing it for the jaunt; and, when the head was filled with things new and old, I was careful to secure the region under the shoulders, especially on the *left side*, and near the heart, by placing there that part of a lady's dress which designates a government that we men are unwilling openly to acknowledge, but is, withal, very conservative. Within its folds I wrapped up very securely 'Pilgrim's Progress,' and stuffed the empty space between my shoulders, and near my heart, *brim full.* I hope my young friend will find a motive and a moral in the image and in the book, to cheer him on in his pilgrimage of life."

"*July* 22, 1844. — Sixty-seven years ago this day, my mother, now living, was married; and, while standing up for the ceremony, the alarm-bell rang, calling all soldiers to their posts. My father left her within the hour, and repaired to Cambridge; but the colonel, in consideration of the circumstances, allowed him to return to Groton to his wife, and to join his regiment within three days at Rhode Island. This he did, spending but a few hours with his wife; and she saw nothing more of him until the last day of the year, when he made her a visit. I have ordered a thousand dollars paid to the Massachusetts General Hospital, to aid in enlarging its wings, and to commemorate this event. The girls of this day know nothing of the privations and trials of their grandmothers."

On the same day with the above entry in his diary occurs another, in which he alludes to assistance afforded to some young persons in Brattle-street Church, — "sons of Brattle-street, and, as such, assisted by me." Mr. Lawrence's early religious associations were connected with this church, where, it is believed, he attended from the first Sunday after his coming to Boston. With such associations, and connected as they were with the most endeared recollections of those who had worshipped there with him in early days, all that pertained to this venerable church possessed a strong and abiding interest. In this connection is quoted the beautiful testimony of his pastor, the Rev. Dr. Lothrop, furnished in the funeral sermon delivered by him, where he speaks of Mr. Lawrence's love for the church, as well as of his religious character:

"The prominent feature in Mr. Lawrence's life and character, its inspiration and its guide, was religion,— religious faith, affection, and hope. He loved God, and therefore he loved all God's creatures. He believed in Christ as the Messiah and Saviour of the world, and therefore found peace and strength in his soul, amid all the perils, duties, and sorrows of life. His religious opinions lay distinct and clear in his own mind. They were the result of careful reading and of serious reflection, and were marked by a profound reverence for the Sacred Scriptures, and the divine authority of Jesus Christ. A constant worshipper here during the forty-six years of his residence in this city, for more than forty years of this period a communicant, and for more than ten a deacon of this church,— resigning the office, at length, because of his invalid state of health,— he had strong attachments to this house of God. 'Our venerable church,' he says in one of his notes to me, 'has in it deeply impressive, improving, instructive, and interesting associations, going back to the early days of my worshipping there; and the prayers of my friends and fellow-worshippers of three generations, in part now belonging there, come in aid of my weakness in time of need; and no other spot, but that home where I was first taught my prayers, and this my domestic fireside, where my children have been taught theirs, has the same interest as our own old Brattle-square Church.'"

To an old business friend and acquaintance, Joshua Aubin, Esq., the agent of the Amesbury Company, who had from the beginning been associated with him in this first and favorite manufacturing enterprise in which he had engaged, he writes on September 18, after receiving a quantity of manufactured articles for distribution among the poor:

"You are brought very near to me on such a day as this (when I am shut up in the house), by your work as well as by your words.

"Now, as to your last consignment, I have derived, and expect to derive, as much comfort and enjoyment from it as I ordinarily should from a cash dividend on my shares. In truth, I am able to employ these *odds and ends* to such uses and for such persons as will make me feel as though I were spared here for some use.

"For instance, I had a call from a most respectable friend (president of one of the best colleges in the West) last week, who agreed to come again this week to do some shopping as soon as he got some money for preaching on Sunday, and look over my stock of goods.

"I intend making him up a good parcel of your work, and, depend on it, it is good seed, and will take root at the West. He says that they have no money, but plenty of corn, and beef, and pork. Corn pays for growing at ten cents a bushel, and will not bring that in cash; and ten bushels will not pay for a calico gown, or a flannel petticoat.

"With his large family of children, don't you think these *odds and ends* will come as a blessing? Besides, he is an old-fashioned Massachusetts Whig; loves the old Bay State as well as ever the Jews loved their State, and is, through his college, exercising an influence in —— that no body of men in that State can do; and will, in the end, bring them into regular line, as to education and elevation of character. Send me some of your flannels to give to Madam —— for her family of one or two hundred children in the Children's Friend Society.

" —— will give them over to these poor little destitute, unclad creatures. They are taken and saved by this interesting society.

"A rainy day like this is the very time for me to work among my household goods. Many a poor minister and his family, and many a needy student at school or college, fare the better for your spinning and weaving.

"I am living in my chamber, and on very close allowance. Every day to me is a day of glorious anticipations, if I am free from bodily suffering, and if my mind is free."

On another occasion he writes to the same gentleman:

"I have your letter and package; the cold of this morning will make the articles doubly acceptable to the shivering and sick poor among us. J. C.'s case is one for sympathy and relief. Engage to supply him a hundred dollars, which I will hand to you when you visit me; and tell the poor fellow to keep in good heart, for our merciful Father afflicts in love, and thus I trust that this will prove a stepping-stone to the mansions of bliss. I shall never cease to remember with interest the veterans of the A. F. Co. How are my friends B. and others of early days? Also, how is old father F. ? Does he need my warm outside coat, when I get supplied with a better?

"After your call upon me a few weeks since, I went back in memory to scenes of olden times, which had an interest that you can sympathize in, and which I intended to express to you before this; but I have had one of those admonitory ill turns since, that kept me under the eye of the doctor for a number of days.

"In reviewing my beginnings in manufacturing, under your recommendation and care, almost a quarter of a century ago, I can see the men, the machines, the wheel-pit, and the speed-gauge, and especially I can see our old friend W. lying on the bottom of the pit, lamp in hand, with his best coat on, eying the wheels and cogs as an astronomer makes observations in an observatory. All these scenes are as fresh in my memory as though seen but yesterday.

"Do you remember C. B., the brother of J. and G. B.? All three of whom were business men here at the time you were, and all were unfortunate. C. tried his hand in ——, and did not succeed there; returned to this country, and settled on a tract of land in ——, where he has been hard at work for ten years, and has maintained his family. His wife died a few months since. One after another of his family sickened, and he became somewhat straitened, and knew not what to do. He wrote to an old business friend, who was his debtor, and who had failed, had paid a part only, and was discharged thirty years ago, and who has since been prosperous. He stated his case, and asked me to say a good word for him. That person sent one half, and I sent the other half, the day before Thanksgiving. It will reach him on Monday next, and will make his eyes glisten with joy.

"Remember me to Capt. —— and J. C., and B., and any other of the veterans."

Sept. 23, Mr. Lawrence receives from an old debtor, once a clerk in his establishment, a check for five hundred dollars, which a sense of justice had induced him to send, though the debt of some thousands had been long since legally discharged. On receiving it, he writes, in a memorandum at the bottom of the letter received, to his brother and partner:

"DEAR ABBOTT: I have the money. J. D. was always a person of truth. I take the statement as true; but I had no recollection of the thing till recalled by his statement. What say you to putting this money into the life office, in trust for his sister? Your affectionate brother, AMOS."

"MEMORANDUM. *November* 23. — Done, and policy sent to the sister."

There are but few men, distinguished in public or private life, who are burdened with an undue amount of praise from their contemporaries; and yet this was the case with Mr. Lawrence, who was often chagrined, after some deed of charity, or some written expression of sympathy, to see it emblazoned, with superadded colors, in the public prints. Some one had enclosed to him a newspaper from another city, which contained a most labored and flattering notice of the kind referred to, to which he writes the following reply:

"September, 1844.

"Dear —— : I received the paper last evening, and have read and re-read it with deep interest and attention. However true it may be, it is not calculated to promote the ultimate good of any of us; for we are all inclined to think full well enough of ourselves; and such puffs should be left for our obituaries. Truth is not always to be pushed forward; and its advocates may sometimes retard it by injudicious urging. Such is the danger in the present case. The writer appears to be a young man who has received favors, and is laboring to repay them or secure more. He has told the truth; but, as I before said, neither you nor I, nor any one of our families, are improved or benefited in any degree by it. God grant us to be humble, diligent, and faithful to the end of our journey, that we may then receive his approval, and be placed among the good of all nations and times!"

On the 29th of October, Mrs. Appleton, his sister-in-law, and widow of the Rev. Jesse Appleton, D.D., formerly President of Bowdoin College, died at his house, after a lingering illness. In a letter to his son, after describing her character and peaceful death, he says:

"With such a life and such hopes, who can view the change as any other than putting away the fugitive and restless pleasures of an hour for the quiet and fixed enjoyments of eternity? Let us, then, my dear children, not look upon the separation of a few short years as a calamity to be dreaded, should we not meet here again in any other way than as we now meet. While I am here, every joy and enjoyment you experience, and give us an account of, is not less so to us than if we were with you to partake, as we have done of all such heretofore; and, in this source of enjoyment, few people have such ample stores. Three families of children and grandchildren within my daily walk,— is not this enough for any man? And here I would impress upon my grandsons the importance of looking carefully to their steps. The difference between going just right and a little wrong in the commencement of the journey of life, is the difference between their finding a happy home or a miserable slough at the end of the journey. Teach them to avoid tobacco and intoxicating drink, and all temptations that can lead them into evil, as it is easier to prevent than to remedy a fault. 'An ounce of prevention is worth a pound of cure.' I was going on to say that, according to my estimate of men and things, I would not change conditions with Louis Philippe if I could by a wish, rich as he is in the matter of good children. I have a great liking for him, and a sincere respect for his family, as they are reported to me; but I trust that mine will not be tried by the temptations of great worldly grandeur, but that they will be found faithful stewards of the talents intrusted to them. Bring up your boys to do their work first, and enjoy their play afterwards. Begin early to teach them habits of order, a proper economy, and exact accountability in their affairs. This simple rule of making a child, after he is twelve years old, keep an exact account of all that he wears, uses, or expends, in any and every way, would save more suffering to families than can fairly be estimated by those who have not observed its operation.

"And now, to change the subject," he writes Nov. 15, "we have got through the elections, and are humbled as Americans. The questions affecting our local labor, produce, and pecuniary interests, are of small moment, compared with that of annexing

Texas to this Union. I wrote a brief note yesterday to our friend Chapman, late Mayor of the city, and a member of the Whig Committee, which speaks the language of my heart. It was as follows:

"'MY DEAR SIR: The result of the election in Massachusetts is matter of devout and grateful feelings to every good citizen, and, so far as pride is allowable, is a subject of pride to every citizen, whatever his politics; for, wherever he goes, and carries the evidence of belonging to the old Bay State, he may be sure of the respect of all parties. This glorious result has not been wrought "without works;" and for it we, the people, are greatly indebted to your committee. So far as may be needed, I trust you will find no backwardness on our part in putting matters right. I bless God for sparing my life to this time; and I humbly beseech him to crown your labors with success in future. If Texas can be kept off, there will be hope for our government. All other questions are insignificant in comparison with this. The damning sin of adding it to this nation to extend slavery will be as certain to destroy us as death is to overtake us. The false step, once taken, cannot be retraced, and will be to the people who occupy what rum is to the toper. It eats up and uproots the very foundation on which Christian nations are based, and will make us the scorn of all Christendom. Let us work, then, in a Christian spirit, as we would for our individual salvation, to prevent this sad calamity befalling us.'"

CHAPTER XXII.

DEATH OF HIS DAUGHTER. — LETTERS. — DONATION TO WILLIAMS COLLEGE. — BENEFICENCE. — LETTERS.

On the 29th of November, Mr. Lawrence addressed to his son a most joyous letter, announcing the birth of twin-grand daughters, and the comfortable health of his daughter, the wife of the Rev. Charles Mason, Rector of St. Peter's Church, at Salem, Massachusetts. The letter is filled with the most devout expressions of gratitude at the event, and cheering anticipations for the future, and yet with some feelings of uneasiness lest the strength of his daughter should not be sufficient to sustain her in these trying circumstances. He adds:

"Why, then, should I worry myself about what I cannot help, and practically distrust that goodness that sustains and cheers and enlivens my days?"

The fears expressed were too soon and sadly realized; the powers of her constitution had been too severely taxed, nature gave way, and, four days afterwards, she ceased to live. Mr. Lawrence announced the death of this cherished and only daughter in the following letter:

"Boston, December 14, 1844.

"My dear Son: The joyous event I mentioned of S.'s twins has in it sad memorials of the uncertainty of all joys, excepting those arising from the happiness of friends whose journey is ended, and whose joys are commencing. Long life does not consist in many years, but in the use of the years allowed us; so that many a man who has seen his four-score has, for all the purposes of life, not lived at all. And, again, others, who have impressed distinct marks, and have been called away before twenty-eight years have passed over them, may have lived long lives, and have been objects of grateful interest to multitudes who hardly spoke to them while living. Such has been the case with our hearts' love and desire, Susan Mason. The giving birth to those two babes, either of whom would have been her pride and delight, was more than she could recruit from. The exhaustion and faintness at the time were great, but not alarming; and the joy of our hearts for a season seemed unmixed. After three days, the alarm for her safety had taken stronger hold of her other friends than of myself; and, at the time I wrote you last, I felt strong confidence in her recovery. On Sunday evening, at seven o'clock, a great change came over her, that precluded all hope, and she was told by C. how it was. She seemed prepared for it, was clear in her mind, and, with what little strength she had, sent messages of love. 'Give love to my father, and tell him I hope we shall meet in heaven,' was her graphic and characteristic message; and then she desired C. to lead and guide her thoughts in prayer, which he continued to do for as many as six times, until within the last half-hour of her life. At three o'clock on Monday morning, the 2d instant, her pure spirit passed out of its earthly tenement to its heavenly home, where our Father has called her to be secured from the trials and pains and exposures to which she was here liable. It is a merciful Father, who knows better than we do what is for our good. What is now mysterious will be made plain at the right time, for 'He doeth all things well.' Shall we, then, my dear children, doubt him in this? Surely not. S. was ripe for heaven, and, as a good scholar, has passed on in advance of her beloved ones; but beckons us on, to be reünited, and become joint heirs with her of those treasures provided for those who are found worthy. We are now to think of her as on the other side of Jordan, before the same altar that we worship at, without any of the alloy that mixes in ours; she praising, and we praying, and all hoping an interest in the Beloved that shall make all things seem less than nothing in comparison with this. We have had the sympathy of friends; and the circumstances have brought to light new friends, that make us feel our work here is not done. I feel called two ways at once: S. beckoning me to come up; the little ones appealing to the inmost recesses of my heart to stay, and lead them, with an old grandfather's fondest, strongest, tenderest emotions, as the embodiment of my child. Her remains are placed at the head of her mother's; and those two young mothers, thus placed, will speak to their kindred with an eloquence that words cannot. I try to say, in these renewed tokens of a Father's discipline, 'Thy will be done,' and to look more carefully after my tendency to have some idol growing upon me that is inconsistent with that first place *he* requires; and I further try to keep in mind, that, if I loved S. much, *he* loved her more, and has provided against the changes she was exposed to under the best care I could render. Let us praise God for her long life in a few years, and profit by the example she has left. The people of her own church are deeply afflicted, and not until her death were any of us aware of the strong hold she had upon them. Some touching incidents have occurred, which are a better monument to her memory than any marble that can be reared. * * * *

"This morning opens most splendidly, and beautifully illustrates, in the appearance of the sky, that glorious eternity so much cherished in the mind of the believer.

"With sincerest affection, your father, A. L."

"TREMONT-STREET, Tuesday morning.

"DEAR PARTNERS: The weather is such as to keep me housed to-day, and it is important to me to have something to think of beside myself. The sense of loss will press upon me more than I desire it, without the other side of the account. All is ordered in wisdom and in mercy; and we pay a poor tribute to our Father and best Friend in distrusting him. I do most sincerely hope that I may say, from the heart, 'Thy will be done.' Please send me a thousand dollars by G., in small bills, thus enabling me to fill up the time to some practical purpose. It is a painful thought to me that I shall see my beloved daughter no more on earth; but it is a happy one to think of joining her in heaven. Yours, ever, A. L.

"A. & A. LAWRENCE & Co."

On the last day of 1844, a date now to be remembered by his friends as that on which his own departure took place, eight years later, he writes to his children in France:

"This last day of the year seems to have in it such tokens and emblems as are calculated to comfort and encourage the youthful pilgrim, just in his vigor, not less than the old one, near the end of his journey; for the sun in the heavens, the hills in the west, and the ocean on the east, all speak, in tones not to be mistaken, 'Be of good courage,' 'Work while it is day,' and receive, without murmuring, the discipline a Father applies; for he knows what is best for his children. Whether he plants thorns in the path, or afflicts them in any way, he does all for their good. Thus, my dear children, are we to view the removal of our beloved S. This year had been one of unusual prosperity and enjoyment, from the first day to the present month; and all seemed so lovely here that there was danger of our feeling too much reliance on these temporals. The gem in the centre has been removed, to show us the tenure by which we held the others."

At the opening of the year 1845, Mr. Lawrence, after noting in his property-book the usual annual details, makes the following reflections:

"The business of the past year has been eminently successful, and the increased value of many of the investments large. In view of these trusts, how shall we appear when the Master calls? I would earnestly strive to keep constantly in mind the fact that he *will* call, and that speedily, upon each and all of us; and that, when he calls, the question will be, How have you used these? not How much have you hoarded?"

With the new year, he set himself at work with renewed zeal to carry into effect his good resolutions. One of the first results was a donation of ten thousand dollars to Williams College, which he enters upon his book with the following memorandum:

"I am so well satisfied with the appropriations heretofore made for the advancement and improvement of Williams College that I desire to make further investment in the same, to the amount of ten thousand dollars. In case any new professorship is established in the college, I should be gratified to have it called the Hopkins Professorship, entertaining, as I do, the most entire confidence and respect for its distinguished President."

Nearly every day, at this period, bears some record of his charities; and among others was a considerable donation to a Baptist college, in another State, enclosed to a Baptist clergyman in Boston, with a check of fifty dollars for himself, to enable him to take a journey for recruiting his health and strength, of which he was much in need. Soon after Mr. Lawrence's death, an article appeared in an influential religious publication giving an estimate of the amount of his charities, and also stating that his pocket-book had written upon it a text of Scripture, calculated to remind him of his duties in the distribution of his wealth. The text was said to be, "What shall it profit a man if he gain the whole world, and lose his own soul?"

After making diligent search, the editor of this volume, rather to correct the statement in regard to the amount of his charities than for any other object, contradicted the assertion, and also expressed the opinion that Mr. Lawrence needed no such memorial as this to remind him of his duties; for the law of charity was too deeply graven on his heart to require the insertion of the text in the manner described. Some time afterward, an old pocket-book was found, which had not probably been in use for many years, but which contained the text alluded to, inscribed in ink, though faded from the lapse of time and constant use. It may have been useful to him in early years, before he engaged systematically in the work of charity; but, during the latter years of his life, if we can judge from his writings, as well as from his daily actions, his sense of accountability was extreme, if there can be an extreme in the zealous performance of one's duty in this respect.

If the class of politicians alluded to in the following extract could have foreseen the course of events with the same sagacity, it might have saved them from much uncertainty, and have been of service in their career:

"We are in a poor way, politically, in this country. This practice of taking up demagogues for high office is no way to perpetuate liberty. The new party of Native Americans is likely to go forward, and will break up the Whig party, and where it will stop is to be learned."

"*March* 1.— Spring opens upon us this morning with a frowning face; the whole heaven is veiled, and the horizon dark and lowering."

"*May* 7.— My venerated mother finished her earthly course last Friday, with the setting sun, which was emblematic of her end. She was such a woman as I am thankful to have descended from. Many interesting circumstances connected with her life, before and after her marriage (in July, 1777), are worth recording. She was in her ninetieth year."

(TO HIS SON.)

"April 30.

"I began a record yesterday morning, referring to my position and duties thirty-eight years ago, when I left my father's house (one week after I was free), with less than twenty dollars in my possession. I came an unknown and unfriended young man, but feeling richer the morning after I came than I have ever felt since; so that I gave the man who came with me, in my father's chaise, a couple of dollars to save him from any expense, and insure him against loss, by his spending two days on the journey, for which he was glad of an excuse. Had he been as industrious and temperate and frugal, he would have left his wife and children independent, instead of leaving them poor and dependent. These contrasts, and the duties they impose, have pressed heavily upon my strength for a few days past; and, in endeavoring to place in a clear view my hopes and wishes, I became pressed down, and, since yesterday, have been upon my abstinence remedy. My wish has been to do a good work for our Athenæum and our Institution for Savings, by making it the interest of the Savings Institution to sell their building to the Athenæum, so that a handsome and convenient building may be erected while we are about it. To this end, I have offered to supply the beautiful temple built for the Washington Bank, rent free, for one year, or a longer period to the end of time, while used as a Savings Bank; intending, by this, to express to those who deposit their money there that I feel deeply interested in their welfare, and would earnestly impress upon them the importance of saving, and, when they become rich, of spending for the good of their fellow-mortals the surplus which a bountiful Father in heaven allows them to acquire. This surplus with me, at the present time, will be sufficient to allow me to speak with earnestness, sincerity, and power, to the tens of thousands of industrious *Thomases* and *Marthas*,* as well as to the young mechanics, or the youngsters who have had little sums deposited for their education. All these characters appreciate a kind act as fully as those who move in a different sphere in the world.

"7 P. M. — I have just learned that there is some difficulty not easily overcome in this removal of the Bank; and, after all, nothing may come out of my offer. If not, I shall have more spare means for something else."

The value of the building thus offered was about twenty thousand dollars. Owing to the difficulties alluded to in the preceding letter, the offer was declined, though the motive for the act was fully appreciated.

(TO A FRIEND.)

"MY DEAR FRIEND: I have this moment learned the death of your dear boy J. L., and am with you in spirit in this trying scene. Our Father adapts his discipline to our needs; and in this (although to our weak perception it may seem harsh discipline) he has a Father's love and care of and for you; and the time will come when all will be made clear to you. In this trust and confidence, I hope both your dear wife and self will be able to say from the heart, 'Thy will be done.' Our business in this world is to prepare for another; and, if we act wisely, we shall view aright the calls upon us to make this world our great object, by attaining its honors, its houses, its lands, its praises for generosity, disinterestedness, and divers other things that pass well

---

* Names of two faithful domestics.

among men. Where we hope to be welcomed, temptations are **not** needed. We pray, therefore, to be accepted, through the Beloved, and so make all things work together to help us safely through our course. Yours ever, A. L."

To the agent of a manufactory in which he was largely interested he writes:

"We must make a good thing out of this establishment, unless you ruin us by working on Sundays. Nothing but works of necessity should be done in holy time; and I am a firm believer in the doctrine that a blessing will more surely follow those exertions which are made with reference to our religious obligations, than upon those made without such reference. The more you can impress your people with a sense of religious obligation, the better they will serve you."

CHAPTER XXIII.

LETTER FROM DR. SHARP. — ILLNESS AND DEATH OF SON. — LETTERS. — AFFLICTIONS.

THE Rev. Dr. Sharp, of the Baptist denomination, who has been previously alluded to as a valued friend of Mr. Lawrence, had made a visit to England, the land of his birth, after an absence of forty years, and thus addresses him from Leeds, July 1 :

"I esteem it one of the happy events of my life that I have been made personally acquainted with you. Not certainly because of your kind benefactions to me and mine, but because I have enjoyed your conversation, and have been delighted with those manifestations of principle and conduct, which, let them grow under what Christian culture they may, I know how to honor, to acknowledge, and to love."

The same gentleman writes, shortly afterwards :

"I thank you for the kind manner in which you express yourself in regard to my occasional sermons. I never had any taste for controversy, nor for theological speculation ; although, as a Christian watchman, I have kept myself informed of the religious opinions that have been, and that are. I thank you, as does my dear wife, for your thoughtful concern of the sacred spot so dear both to my recollections and hopes. There, when life's journey is ended, I hope to rest by the side of those whose company and unfailing affection have gladdened so many of my years; and it has given me a subdued pleasure, when I have thought that my own bed of death would be so near that of the kind and gentle-hearted friend who provided me with mine. May all who shall repose near that interesting spot be imbued with a pure and loving Christian spirit, that, when the trumpet shall sound, and the dead shall arise, we may all rise together in glorious forms, to be forever with the Lord!"

(TO ONE OF HIS PARTNERS.)

"Tremont-street, September 30, 1845.

"DEAR MR. PARKER: I am buoyant and afloat again, and able to enjoy the good things you are so liberal in providing. The widow's box of ointment was broken before its value was learned. The sermon is significant and practical. I would be thankful to improve under its teaching. Will you send me two thousand dollars this morning in Mr. Sharp's clean money? thus allowing me the opportunity of expressing my gratitude to a merciful Father above, that he still permits me to administer the goods things he has intrusted to me. Dear R. had a quiet night, although he did not sleep much during the first part. This experience is, indeed, the most trying; but I hope to be able to say truly, 'Thy will be done.' Your friend,

"A. L.

"C. H. PARKER, Esq."

The trying experience alluded to was the serious illness of his youngest son, Robert, then a member of Harvard College. He had for some time been troubled by a cough, which had now become alarming, and excited the worst apprehensions of his friends. In relation to this sickness, he writes several letters to his son, from which the following extracts are made:

"October 15

"We are in great anguish of spirit on account of dear R. We are getting reconciled to parting with the dear child, and to feel that he has done for us what any parents might feel thankful for, by living a good life, and in nineteen years giving us no cause to wish any one of them blotted out. If now called away, he will have lived a long life in a few years, and will be spared the trials and sufferings that flesh is heir to, and will be gathered like early fruit, before the blight or frost or mildew has marked it."

"October 29.

"R. remains gradually failing with consumption, but without much suffering, and perfectly aware of his situation. He never appeared so lovely as he has on his sick bed; so that his happy spirit and resignation, without a complaint or a wish that anything had been done differently, keep us as happy as we can be under such a weight of apprehension that we may so soon part with him. He asked me yesterday what I should write to you about him. I told him I should say that he was very sick, and might never be any better; but that he might also be better if the great Physician saw best, as it is only for him to speak, and the disease would be cured. If he were taken before me, I told him, it would be, I hoped, to welcome me to the company of the loved ones of our kindred and friends who have gone before, and to the society of angels and just men made perfect, who compose the great congregation that are gathered there from all the world, that God's love, through Christ, has redeemed. God so loved the world that he gave his only-begotten Son to redeem it from sin; and his teachings should not be lost on us, while we have power to profit by them. In this spirit, we talked of the good men whose writings have an influence in helping on this good work; and especially we talked of Dr. Doddridge, and his 'Rise and Progress.'

"P. M.—I have been with M. to Brookline since writing the above. The falling leaves teach a beautiful lesson. The green leaf, the rose, the cypress, now enclosed to you, and all from your grounds, are instructive. These were cut within the last two hours."

"November 1.

"Dear R. had a trying day yesterday, and we thought might not continue through the night. He is still alive, and may continue some time; was conscious and clear in his mind after he revived yesterday; feels ready and willing and hoping to be with his Saviour."

"November 14.

"We toil for treasure through our years of active labor, and, when acquired, are anxious to have it well secured against the time when we or our children may have need of it; and we feel entire confidence in this security. We allow the common flurries of the world to pass by without disturbing our quiet or comfort essentially. What treasure of a temporal character is comparable with a child who is everything a Christian parent could desire, and who is just coming into mature life universally respected and beloved, and who is taken before any cloud or spot has touched him, and who has left bright and clear marks upon those who have come within his sphere of influence? Such was R. The green earth of Mount Auburn covers his mortal remains; the heavens above have his immortal; he was a ripe child of God, and I therefore feel that blessed assurance of entire security which adds another charm to that blessed company to which I hope, through mercy, to be admitted in our Father's own good time. This early death of our beloved youngest comes upon us as an additional lesson, necessary, without doubt, to prepare us for our last summons; and the reasons which now seem mysterious will be fully understood, and will show us that our good required this safe keeping of this treasure, so liable to be made our idol. R. had passed the dangerous period of his college life without blemish, and was only absent from prayers three times (which were for good cause), and had a settled purpose, from the beginning of his college life, so to conduct in all respects as to give his parents no cause for anxiety; and, for the last year, I have felt perfectly easy in regard to him. We have visited his grave to-day. The teachings there are such as speak to the heart with an eloquence that language cannot. Dear S. and R.! She the only daughter, he the only son of his mother! and both placed there since you left!"

"November 22.

"President H., in a letter a few days before I wrote to you, had this sentiment: 'The old oak, shorn of its green branches, is more liable to decay.' Applying this to the old oak fronting the graves of those loved ones who have passed on, the outspread branches of which make the spot more lovely, I was more deeply impressed than mere words could have impressed me. A few months after the death of S., a violent storm tore off a main limb of the old oak about midway between the ground and the top, in such way as to mar its beauty, and endanger its life. The limb fell upon the graves, but avoided the injury to the monuments which might have been expected. Since then, I noticed that some of the lower limbs cast a sort of blight or mildew upon the pure white of your mother's monument, and they required dressing. I desired the 'master' to do this, and also to come and heal the wound occasioned by the loss of this main limb on that side of the tree. The trimming out was done at once; the other was left undone until the request was renewed. On my visit there last week, I discovered, for the first time, that the wound had been healed, and the body of the tree appeared smooth, and of its natural color, and its health such as to give good hope that its other branches will spread out their shade more copiously than before. What a lesson was here! The appeal was to the heart; and, in my whole life, I remember none more eloquent. To-day I have been to Mount Auburn again; and the spot seems to be none other than the gate of heaven.'"

"December 22.

"Twenty-five years ago this morning, I came home from Plymouth, where I had spent the night previous, and heard Webster's great address. He has never done anything to surpass it; and it now is a model and a text for the youth of our country. The people who then were present are principally taken hence; and the consideration of how the time allowed has been spent, and how it now fares with us, is of deep interest. God in mercy grant us to act our part so as to meet his approval, when called to answer for the trust in our hands! I have thought of the emblem of the 'old oak,' till it has assumed a beauty almost beyond anything in nature; and, if I live to see the fresh leaves of spring spreading their covering over the head of the stranger or the friend who may stop under its shade, I will have a sketch of the spot painted, if the right person can be found. There is in the spot and scene a touching eloquence that language can scarcely communicate. The dear child's expressive look, and motion of his finger, when he said 'I am going up,' will abide with me while I live. The dealings of a Father with me have been marked, but ofttimes mysterious for a season. Now many things are clear; and all others will be, I trust, when I am fitted to know them."

(TO HIS GRANDSON.)

"BOSTON, December 30, 1845.

"MY DEAR F.: Your charming letter of 28th November reached me by last steamer, and showed, in a practical way, how important the lessons of childhood are to the proper performance of the duties of manhood. It carried me back to the time when my own mother taught me, and, from that period, forward through the early lessons inculcated upon your father, and especially to the time when he began to write me letters, which I always encouraged him in, and thus formed a habit which has been the best security for our home affections that can be devised when separated from those most dear to us. If the prayers and labors of your ancestors are answered by your good progress and good conduct in the use of the privileges you enjoy, you will come forth a better and more useful man than any of the generations preceding; for you enjoy advantages that none of us have enjoyed. My heart beats quicker and stronger whenever I think of you; and my prayers ascend for you at all hours, and through every scene connecting us. Last Saturday, I had the first sleigh-ride of the season. The day was beautiful; and there was just snow enough to make the sleigh run smoothly. I visited Mount Auburn; and the day and place, the 'old oak' standing in front of our graves leafless and apparently almost lifeless, spoke to me a language as intelligible as if utterance had been given in sounds. I thought of you, dear F., as my eldest grandson, and in a manner the representative of the family to future times, and asked myself whether I was doing all I ought to make you feel the force of your trusts. There lie the mortal parts of your dear aunt and uncle, both placed there since you left home; and the spirits of both, I trust, are now rejoicing with the multitude of the beloved ones, whose work here is well done, and whom the Saviour has bid to 'come unto him,' and through whom they hoped to be accepted. Dear R. seems to call to us to 'come up;' and, whether I ever see you again or not, I pray you never to forget that he was such an uncle as you might well feel anxious to copy in your conduct to your parents; for he had a settled principle to do nothing to cause his parents anxiety. So, if you see your young companions indulging in any evil practices which may lead to bad habits, avoid them; for prevention is better than remedy. When you stand near the 'old oak,' whether its branches are green with shady leaves, or dry from natural decay, let it speak to your conscience, 'Come up,' and receive the reward promised to the faithful.

"Ever your affectionate grandfather, A. L."

The year 1845 closed with many sad recollections; and nearly every letter written at this period dwells upon the mournful events which had marked its course. In one letter, he says, "Death has cut right and left in my family." In a little more than twelve months, ten of his own immediate family and near connections were removed, and most of them when least expected. Although bowed down, and penetrated with grief at each successive blow, there was a deep-seated principle in Mr. Lawrence's heart, which made him rise above them all, and receive each call in that spirit of submission which the Christian faith alone can give. His own sorrows seemed only to augment his sympathy for the woes of others, and to excite him to renewed efforts in the great cause of charity and truth, to which he had consecrated every talent he possessed. In this spirit he makes an entry in his memorandum-book on the first day of the opening year.

CHAPTER XXIV.

EXPENDITURES. — LETTERS. — DONATION FOR LIBRARY AT WILLIAMS COLLEGE. — VIEWS ON STUDY OF ANATOMY.

"*January* 1, 1846. — THE business of the past year has been very prosperous in our country; and my own duties seem more clearly pointed out than ever before. What am I left here for, and the young branches taken home? Is it not to teach me the danger of being unfaithful to my trusts? Dear R. taken! the delight of my eyes, a treasure secured! which explains better than in any other way what my Father sees me in need of. I hope to be faithful in applying some of my trusts to the uses God manifestly explains to me by his dealings. I repeat, 'Thy will be done.'"

That his trusts, so far as the use of his property was concerned, were faithfully performed, may be inferred from the fact that, in July, or at the termination of the half-year, in making up his estimate of income and expenditures, he remarks that the latter are nearly twenty thousand dollars in advance of the former.

Mr. Lawrence was often much disturbed by the publicity which attended his benevolent operations. There are, perhaps, thousands of the recipients of his favors now living, who alone are cognizant of his bounty towards themselves; but when a public institution became the subject of his liberality, the name of the donor could not so easily be concealed. The following letter will illustrate the mode which he sometimes was obliged to adopt to avoid that publicity; and it was his custom not unfrequently to contribute liberally to objects of charity through some person on whom he wished the credit of the donation to fall.

(TO PRESIDENT HOPKINS.)

"Boston, Jan. 26, 1846.

"My dear Friend: Since Saturday, I have thought much of the best mode of helping your college to a library building without getting into the newspapers, and have concluded that you had better assume the responsibility of building it; and, if anybody objects that you can't afford it, you may say you have friends whom you hope to have aid from; and I will be responsible to you for the cost to an amount not exceeding five thousand dollars; so that you may feel at liberty to prepare such a building as you will be satisfied with, and which will do credit to your taste and judgment fifty years hence. If I am taken before this is finished, which must be this year, my estate will be answerable, as I have made an entry in my book, stating the case. I had written a longer story, after you left me, on Saturday evening, but have laid it aside to hand you this, with best wishes, and that all may be done 'decently and in order.' I will pay a thousand or two dollars whenever it is wanted for the work.

"Your friend,   A. L."

Mr. Lawrence had read in the newspapers the

memorial to Congress of Mrs. Martha Gray, widow of Captain Robert Gray, the well-known navigator, who discovered, first entered, and gave its present name to the Columbia River. Captain Gray had been in the naval service of his country; and his widow, who had survived him for forty years, amidst many difficulties and struggles for support, petitioned for a pension, in consideration of the important discovery, and for the services rendered by her husband. Mr. Lawrence sent to Mrs. Gray a memorial of his regard, with the following note:

"As a token of respect to the widow of one whose name and fame make a part of the property of every American who has a true heart, will Mrs. Gray accept the accompanying trifle from one, who, though personally unknown, felt her memorial to Congress through every nerve, and will hope to be allowed the pleasure of paying his respects in person when his health permits."

About the same date, he says to President Hopkins:

"I am happily employed, these days, in administering upon my own earnings, and have hope of hearing soon from you and your good work. I am still on my good behavior, but have been able to chat a little with Mr. D., and administer to His Excellency Governor Briggs, who has had a severe trial of fever and ague. On Saturday he rode an hour with me, and returned with his face shortened considerably. I can only say to you that I believe I am left here to do something more to improve and help on the brethren and sons who have more mind and less money than I have; but the precise way to do it is not so clear to me as it may be by and by."

After receiving the proposed plan of the library which he had authorized to be built at Williams College, Mr. Lawrence writes to the same, on May 15 :

" I left off, after a brief note to you, three hours since, furnishing you a text on epicureanism to preach from, which I trust will find favor and use.

" What think you? Why, that I am interfering in your business. When I awoke this morning, thinks I to myself, My friend won't have elbow-room in the centre of his octagon ; and, as there is plenty of land to build upon, he may as well make his outside to outside fifty feet as forty-four feet, and thus give himself more space in the centre. The alcoves appear to me to be very nice; and, in the matter of expense, my young friend A. L. H. will see to that, to the tune of one or two thousand dollars. So you may feel yourself his representative in acting in this matter."

"*April* 22. — My birth-day! Three-score years old! My life, hanging by a thread for years, and apparently, at times, within a few hours of its close, still continued, while so many around in the prime of life and vigor have been called away ! "

(TO A FRIEND.)
" Tremont-street, April, 1846.

" MY FRIEND —— : I have arisen after my siesta, and, as the Quakers say, am moved by the spirit to speak. So you will give what I have to say the value you consider it worth. And, in the first place, I will say, that this period of the year is so full of deeply-interesting memories of the past, that I hardly know where to begin. From my earliest days, the story of the intelligence reaching Groton at ten o'clock on the 19th April, 1775, that the British were coming, was a most interesting one. My father mounted Gen. Prescott's horse, and rode, at a speed which young men even of the present day would think rapid, to the south end of the town, by Sandy Pond, and notified the minute-men to assemble at the centre of the town forthwith. He made a range of seven miles, calling on all the men, and was back at his father's house in forty minutes. At one o'clock, P. M., the company was in readiness to march, and under way to Concord to meet the British. They kept on until they reached Cambridge; but, before that, they had seen and heard all that had been done by the troops sent out to Concord. The plough was left in the field; and my grandfather, with his horse and wagon, brought provisions to his neighbors and his son shortly after. My grandmother on my mother's side, then living in Concord, has described to me over and over again the appearance of the British, as she first saw them coming over the hill from Lincoln, about two miles from the centre of Concord; the sun just rising; and the red coats, glittering muskets, and fearful array, so captivating to us in peace-times, appearing to her as the angel of destruction, to be loathed and hated. She therefore left her house with her children (the house was standing within the last thirty years, and may be now, near the turn to go through Bedford, half a mile or more this side of Concord meeting-house), and went through the fields, and over the hills, to a safe place of retreat. The British, you are aware, on their retreat, had a hard time of it. They were shot down like wild game, and left by the wayside to die or be taken up as it might happen. Three thus left within gun-shot of my grandmother's house were taken up, and died in the course of a very few hours. But what I am coming to is this: Lord Percy, you know, was sent out from Boston with a strong body of troops to protect those first sent out; and, but for this, the whole would have been destroyed or made prisoners. About three years ago, Lord Prudhoe, second son of Lord Percy, was here; and I had considerable delightful intercourse with him. He, as you may well suppose, was deeply interested in all that related to his father; and I met him in the library at Cambridge, where he was very observant of the order and arrangement, and especially of the curious old documents and books, so nicely arranged, touching the early history of the province. After leaving Cambridge, he went to Mr. Cushing's and Mr. Pratt's, at Watertown, and was much interested in all that we in this city are proud of. I had not strength to be devoted to him more than an hour or two at a time, having then some other strangers under my care, belonging to Gov. Colebrooke's family, Lady Colebrooke being a niece of Major André; so that I had only some half-dozen interviews with him, all of which were instructive and interesting."

The dissection of human bodies by medical students has always been a subject of deep-rooted prejudice in New England; and, even to this day, it exists in so great a degree that the facilities for this important and absolutely essential branch of instruction are not nearly as great as they should be, nor such as are afforded in the schools of other countries. When these difficulties shall be removed, and the prejudice allayed against the acquisition of a kind of knowledge which it is of the utmost interest to every one that the surgeon and physician shall receive, many young men will remain at home, and acquire that education which, with few exceptions, might be attained here as well as by a resort to foreign schools. In this prejudice Mr. Lawrence could not sympathize, as will be seen in the following extract of a letter to a friend

* * * * * *

"Many years ago, there was a great stir, on account of graves being robbed for subjects for dissection, and some laws were passed: the want became so pressing, that subjects were brought from a long distance, and in a very bad state. Dr. Warren was attending me, and said he had invited the Legislature, then in session, to attend a lecture in the Medical College. He told me he intended to explain the necessity of having fit subjects, he having been poisoned in his lecture to his students a few days before, and was then suffering from it. He invited me also to attend, which I did, and took with me my precious boy R. While lecturing, the doctor had a man's hand, which he had just taken·off at the hospital, brought in, nicely wrapped up in a wet cloth, by his son J. M. W., then a youngster. There were present about two hundred representatives; and, as soon as they saw the real hand, two or three fainted nearly away, and a half-dozen or more made their escape from the room. The scene was so striking, that I told Dr. Warren it was a pity that such a prejudice should exist; and, as I was desirous to be of use as far as in my power, and probably should be a good subject for him, I would gladly have him use me in the way to instruct the young men: but to take care of my remains, and have them consumed or buried, unless my bones were kept. I also told him that I desired very much to have this false feeling corrected, and perhaps my example might do something toward it. Some time afterwards, I spoke to —— upon the subject; but I found it gave pain, and the plan was given up.   *   *   *   A. L."

"Outward gains are ordinarily attended with inward losses. He indeed is rich in grace whose graces are not hindered by his riches."

In a letter, dated June 3, Mr. Lawrence bears testimony to the character and services of the late Louis Dwight, so long and favorably known as the zealous Secretary of the Massachusetts Prison Discipline Society:

"I have this moment had an interview with Louis Dwight, who leaves for Europe in two days. My labors and experience with him for nearly a quarter of a century enable me to testify to his ability, and unceasing efforts in the cause."

"*May* 27, 1846. — The following commentary* on the Lectures of the Rev. Dr. —— accompanied their return to me from one to whom I had loaned the volume. I have now no recollection who the person is; but the words are full, and to the point:

"'This sucking the marrow all out of our Bible, and leaving it as dry as a husk, pray what good to man, or honor to God, does that do? If we are going to fling away the old book from which ten thousand thousand men have drawn and are still draw-

---

* Supposed to be by Hon. Jeremiah Mason.

ing the life of their souls, then let us stand boldly up, and fling it away, cover and all; unless, indeed, a better way would be to save the boards and gilding, and make a family checker-board of it.' "

CHAPTER XXV.

DONATION TO LAWRENCE ACADEMY. — CORRESPONDENCE WITH R. G. PARKER. — SLEIGH-RIDES. — LETTERS. — AVERSION TO NOTORIETY. — CHILDREN'S HOSPITAL.

MR. LAWRENCE had always taken a deep interest in the academy at Groton, of which he, with all his brothers and sisters, had been members. The residence of his former master, James Brazer, Esq., with whom he lived when an apprentice, bordered on the academy grounds. It was a large, square, old-fashioned house, and easily convertible to some useful purpose, whenever the growing prosperity of the institution should require it. He accordingly purchased the estate; and, in July, 1846, presented it to the Board of Trustees by a deed, with the following preamble:

"To all persons to whom these presents shall come, I, Amos Lawrence, of the City of Boston, in the County of Suffolk, and Commonwealth of Massachusetts, Esquire, send greeting:

"Born and educated in Groton, in the County of Middlesex, in said Commonwealth, and deeply interested in the welfare of that town, and especially of the Lawrence Academy, established in it by my honored father, Samuel Lawrence, and his worthy associates, and grateful for the benefits which his and their descendants have derived from that institution, I am desirous to promote its future prosperity; trusting that those charged with the care and superintendence of it will ever strive zealously and faithfully to maintain it as a nursery of piety and sound learning."

This had been preceded by a donation of two thousand dollars, with smaller gifts, at various dates, of valuable books, a telescope, etc., besides the foundation of several free scholarships. The present prosperity of the academy is, however, mainly due to his brother, William Lawrence, who has been by far its greatest benefactor; having, in 1844, made a donation of ten thousand dollars, followed by another, in 1846, of five thousand, and, finally, by will, bequeathed to it the sum of twenty thousand. The following memoranda are copied from Mr. Lawrence's donation-book:

"*August* 20, 1847. — I have felt a deep interest in Groton Academy for a long time; and while brother L. was living, and its president, he had it in charge to do what should be best to secure its greatest usefulness, and, while perfecting these plans, he was suddenly taken from this world. Since then, I have kept on doing for it; which makes my outlay for the school about twenty thousand dollars. I had prepared ten thousand dollars more, which brother William has assumed, and has taken the school upon himself, to give it such facilities as will make it a very desirable place for young men to enter to get a good preparation for business or college life."

In an address[*] delivered at the jubilee celebration

[*] See account of Jubilee of Lawrence Academy.

of the Lawrence Academy, held in Groton, July 12, 1854, the Rev. James Means, a former preceptor of the Institution, thus speaks of the benefactions of the two brothers:

"It was my good fortune, after becoming the preceptor, in 1845, to have frequent intercourse with them in this particular regard,— the interests of the school. I shall never forget the impression made upon my mind by the depth of their feeling, and the strength of their attachment. They were both of them men of business; had been trained to business habits, and would not foolishly throw away the funds which God had intrusted to them as stewards. But it seemed to me then, as the event has proved, that they were willing to go as far as they could see their way clear before them to establish this school on a foundation that never should be shaken.

"There was a singular difference in the character of these two brothers, and there is a similar difference in the results of their benefactions. I have reason personally to know that they conferred frequently and earnestly respecting the parts which they should severally perform in upbuilding this school. There was an emulation; but there was no selfishness, there was no difference of opinion. Both loved the academy, both wished to bless it and make it a blessing; each desired to accommodate the feelings of the other, each was unwilling to interfere with the other, each was ready to do what the other declined. Out of more than forty-five thousand dollars provided for the academy by Mr. William Lawrence, forty thousand still remain in the hands of the trustees for purposes of instruction. Of the library Mr. Amos Lawrence says, in one of his letters: 'I trust it will be second to no other in the country except that of Cambridge, and that the place will become a favorite resort of students of all ages before another fifty years have passed away. When he presented a cabinet of medals, he writes, 'I present them to the Institution in the name of my grandsons, F. W. and A. L., in the hope and expectation of implanting among their early objects of regard this school, so dear to us brothers of the old race, and which was more dear to our honored father, who labored with his hands, and gave from his scanty means, in the beginning, much more in proportion than we are required to do, if we place it at the head of this class of institutions, by furnishing all it can want.'"

At the same celebration, the Hon. John P. Bigelow, president of the day, in his opening address, said:

"Charles Sprague, so loved and so honored as a man and a poet, was an intimate friend of the lamented William and Amos Lawrence. I invited him hither to-day. He cannot come, but sends a minstrel's tribute to their memory, from a harp, which, till now, has been silent for many years.

> 'These, these no marble columns need:
> Their monument is in the deed;
> A moral pyramid, to stand
> As long as wisdom lights the land.
> The granite pillar shall decay,
> The chisel's beauty pass away;
> But this shall last, in strength sublime,
> Unshaken through the storms of time.'"

On July 15, Mr. Lawrence made a considerable donation of books to the Johnson School for girls, accompanied by a note to R. G. Parker, Esq., the Principal, from which the following extract is taken:

"The sleigh-ride comes to me as though daguerreotyped, and I can hardly realize that I am here to enjoy still further the comfort that I then enjoyed. If the pupils of your school at that time were gratified, I was more than satisfied, and feel myself a debtor to your school of this day; and, in asking you to accept, for the use of the five hundred dear girls who attend upon your instruction, such of the books accompanying as you think proper for them, I only pay a debt which I feel to be justly due. The Johnson School is in my own district; and many a time, as I have passed it in my rides, have I enjoyed the appropriate animation and glee they have manifested in their gambols and sports during their intermission, and have felt as though I would gladly be among them to encourage them. Say to them, although personally unknown, I have looked on, and felt as though I wanted to put my hand upon their heads, and give them a word of counsel, encouragement, and my blessing. This is what I am left here for; and, when the Master calls, if I am only well enough prepared to pass examination, and receive the 'Well done' promised to such as are faithful, then I may feel that all things here are less than nothing in comparison to the riches of the future."

The allusion to the sleigh-ride was called forth by a note received from Mr. Parker a day or two before, in which that gentleman writes:

"As you have not the credit of a very good memory, so far as your own good actions are concerned, it will be proper that I should remind you that the occasion to which I refer was the time that the pupils of the Franklin School were about enjoying a sleigh-ride, from which pleasure a large number were excluded. On that occasion, as you were riding by, you were induced to inquire the reason of the exclusion of so many sad little faces; and, on learning that their inability to contribute to the expense of the excursion would cause them to be left behind, you very generously directed that all should be furnished with seats, and a draft made upon you for the additional expense."

To a fondness for children, there seemed to be united in Mr. Lawrence a constant desire to exert an influence upon the youthful mind; and rarely was the opportunity passed over, when, by a word of advice or encouragement, or the gift of an appropriate book, he thought he could effect his object. His person was well known to the boys and girls who passed him in the streets; and, in the winter season, his large, open sleigh might often be seen filled with his youthful friends, whom he had allowed to crowd in to the utmost capacity of his vehicle.

The acquaintances thus made would often, by his invitation, call to see him at his residence, and there would receive a kind notice, joined with such words of encouragement and advice as could not sometimes fail to have a lasting and beneficial influence.

"*August* 2. — 'Give an account of thy stewardship, for thou mayest be no longer steward.'— Luke 16 : 2.

"How ought this to be sounded in our ears! and how ought we to be influenced by the words! Surely there can be no double meaning here. The words are emphatic, clear, and of vast concern to every man. Let us profit by them while it is day, lest the night overtake us, when we can no longer do the work of the day."

On the 22d of August, Mr. Lawrence sent a cane to Governor Briggs, at Pittsfield, with the following inscription graven upon it:

FROM THE "OLD OAK" OF MOUNT AUBURN:
A Memento of Loved Ones gone before.
AMOS LAWRENCE TO GEORGE N. BRIGGS.
1846.

The cane was accompanied by the following note:

"MY DEAR FRIEND: Your letter of Monday last came, as all your letters do, just right as a comforter through a feeble week; for I have been confined to the house, and unable to speak above a whisper, most of the time, and am still not allowed to talk or work much. The corresponding week of the last year, when our precious R. was your guest, comes over my mind and heart, at all hours of the night and the day, in a manner I need not attempt to describe to *you;* and it is only distressing when I see the suffering of his dear mother. But we feel that he is now the guest of the Supreme Governor, whose care and kindness takes from him all that can interrupt his perfect happiness through all time; and this surely ought to satisfy us. The good opinion of good men you know how to value, and can therefore judge how much I prize yours. Acting upon the public mind for good as you do, the memorial from the old oak will not be without its use in your instruction and advice to the young, whose special improvement and safety you have so much at heart. The cane is a part of the same branch as that sent to President H., and came to me since

noon to-day. Accept it with assurances of continued and increased affection and respect. Most sincerely yours,
"A. L."

"*August* 28. — Called at —— shop, Washington-street, and there saw a nice-looking boy seventeen or eighteen years old, named T. S., to whom I gave a word of good counsel and encouragement. Shall look after him a little, as I like his manners."

"*August* 29. — A woman writes a figuring letter, calling herself S. M.; says she is sixty years old; has lost her sons, and wants help; came from New Hampshire. Also, N. T. wants aid to study, or something else. Also, a Mr. F., with a great share of hair on his face, gold ring, and chains, wants to travel for his health; has a wife and child. These three cases within twenty-four hours are very forbidding."

In a letter of advice to a young gentleman who was a stranger to him, but who through a mutual friend had asked his opinion on a matter of business, he writes, on Sept. 19th:

"Your letter of the 17th is a flattering token of confidence and respect, that I wish were better merited. Such as I am, I am at your service; *but there is nothing of me.* I have been stricken down within a few days, and am hardly able to stand up. A kind Father keeps me vigilant by striking without notice, and when least expected; and on some one of these occasions I am to close the account of my stewardship, and no matter when, if the accounts are right. I cannot advise you except in one particular: Do with your might what your hands find to do; spend no man's money but your own, and look carefully after little items that tempt you."

The notoriety attendant upon acts of beneficence which Mr. Lawrence instinctively shrunk from, and which so often deters the sensitive from the good acts which, without this penalty, they would gladly perform, was, as has before been stated, a subject of serious annoyance. This is illustrated by the following note, written to Mr. Parker, the Principal of the Johnson School for girls:

"October 2, 1846.

"I hope to send a few volumes to help forward the young guides of the mind and heart of the sons of New England, wherever they may be; for it is the mothers who act upon their sons more than all others. I hope to be felt as long as I am able to work, and am quite as vain as I ought to be of my name and fame, but am really afraid I shall wear out my welcome if my little paragraphs are printed so frequently in the newspapers. I gave some books last Monday, and saw them acknowledged yesterday in the newspaper, and since have received the letter from the children. Now, my dear sir, I merely want to say, that I hope you will not put me in the newspaper at present; and, when my work is done here, if you have anything to say about me that will not hurt my children and grandchildren, *say on*."

A few days afterwards, Mr. Lawrence received a letter from the parties to whom the books above alluded to had been sent, inquiring if he could suggest the name of some benevolent individual, to whom application might be made for aid in furthering the objects of the Association. He writes:

"In reply to yours of to-day, I know of no one, but must request that my name be not thrust forward, as though I was to be a byword for my vanity. I want to do good, but am sorry to be published, as in the recent case."

During the autumn of this year, Mr. Lawrence purchased the large building in Mason-street, which had, for many years, been used as the Medical School of Harvard College, with the intention of founding a charitable hospital for children. He had heard of the manner in which such institutions were conducted in France, and believed that a great benefit would be conferred on the poorer classes by caring for their sick children when their own poverty or occupations prevented their giving them that attention which could be secured in an institution of this kind. The great object was to secure the confidence of that class, and to overcome their repugnance to giving up their children to the care of others. The plan had not been tried in this country; though in France, where there exists a much larger and more needy population, the system was completely successful. Although but an experiment, Mr. Lawrence considered the results which might be obtained of sufficient magnitude to warrant the large outlays required. He viewed it not only as a mode of relieving sickness and suffering, but as a means of exercising a humanizing effect upon those who should come directly under its influence, as well as upon that class of persons generally for whose benefit it was designed. His heart was ever open to the cry of suffering; and he was equally ready to relieve it, whether it came from native or foreigner, bond or free. The building which had been purchased for the object, from its internal arrangement, and from its too confined position, was found less suitable than another, in the southerly part of the city, where an open view and ample grounds were more appropriate for the purpose; while there was no cause for that prejudice which, it was found, existed toward the project in the situation first thought of. With characteristic liberality, Mr. Lawrence offered the Medical College, now not required, to the Boston Society of Natural History at the cost, with a subscription from himself of five thousand dollars. The offer was accepted. An effort was made by the Society to raise by subscription the necessary funds; and the result was their possession of the beautiful building since occupied by their various collections in the different departments of natural history. The large house on Washington-street was soon put in complete repair, suitably furnished, provided with physicians and nurses, and opened as the Children's Infirmary, with accommodations for thirty patients. The following spring was marked by a great degree of mortality and suffering among the emigrant passengers, and consequently the beds were soon occupied by whole families of children, who arrived in the greatest state of destitution and misery. Many cases of ship-fever were admitted; so that several of the attendants were attacked by it, and the service became one of considerable danger. Many now living in comfort attribute the preservation of their life to the timely succor then furnished; and, had no other benefits followed, the good bestowed during the few weeks of spring would have compensated for the labor and cost. This institution continued in operation for about eighteen months, during which time some hundreds of patients were provided for. The prejudices of parents, which had been foreseen, were found to exist, but disappeared with the benefits received; and the whole experiment proved conclusively that such an institution may be sustained in this community with vast benefit to a large class of the suffering; and it is hoped that it may one day lead to an establishment of the kind on a larger scale, and with a more extensive organization and means of usefulness. In this experiment, it was found, from the limited number of beds, that the cost of each patient was much greater than if four times the number had been provided for, and so large that Mr. Lawrence decided that the same amount of money could be made to afford relief to much larger numbers of the same class of sufferers applied in some other way. He was a constant visitor at the Infirmary, and took a deep interest in many of the patients, whose varied history had been recited to him; and in after years, as he passed through the streets, many an eye would brighten as it caught a glimpse of the kind friend who had whispered words of consolation and hope in the lonely hours of sickness.

CHAPTER XXVI.

CAPTAIN A S. McKENZIE. — DIARY. — AID TO IRELAND. — MADAM PRESCOTT. — SIR WILLIAM COLEBROOKE.

(TO CAPT. ALEXANDER SLIDELL MCKENZIE, U. S. N.)

"November 2, 1846.

"MY DEAR SIR: I was exceedingly gratified by your kind remembrance of me, a few days since, in sending me a copy of your 'Life of Decatur,' which to its merits as a biography adds the charm of bringing before me my old friend Bainbridge, and the writer, whom I have felt a strong interest in ever since reading his 'Year in Spain;' for my son resided in the same family soon after you left, and made me acquainted with you before I had seen you. I am a 'minute-man' in life, but, while I remain here, shall always be glad to take you by the hand when you visit us. Whether we meet here is of less importance than that our work be done, and be said by the Master to be well done, when called off. Respectfully and faithfully yours,

"A. L."

"*December* 17. — Thirty-nine years have passed since my first entry in this book; and, in reviewing this period, I have abundant reason to bless God for his great mercies, and especially for continuing us four brothers, engaged as we have been in business, an unbroken band to this day, and for the success attending our labors. We have been blessed more than most men, and have the power, by our right use of these blessings, of benefiting our fellow-men. God grant that the spirits of our parents may be cheered in their heavenly home by our doing the work here that we ought to do! To my descendants I commend this memorial, with the prayer that they may each of them be better than I am." * * *

" Fifteen years hence, and the chief interest in us will be found in our Mount Auburn enclosure; and we ought to look well to the comment."

As an expression of the feeling here referred to, he purchased a gold box of beautiful workmanship, and forwarded it to his youngest brother, then a resident of Lowell, with the following inscription engraven upon it:

"BEHOLD, HOW GOOD AND HOW PLEASANT IT IS FOR BRETHREN TO DWELL TOGETHER IN UNITY!"
TO SAMUEL LAWRENCE,
FROM
HIS BROTHER AMOS.

"*December* 19. — Rode to-day to the Asylum for the Blind with Major Arthur Lawrence, of the Rifle Brigade, British Army, and had a very interesting visit. Dr. Howe very attentive; and Laura Bridgman and Oliver Caswell both appeared well."

"*December* 27. — Rev. Mr. Rogers said to-day, 'Gold is not the coin of heaven: if it had been, Christ would have been rich; but he was a poor man.'"

"*January* 1, 1847. — In July last, I had spent the advance of my income, but am thankful now to be able to state the case differently, being in the receipt of ample means to be a comfort to the needy."

From the various entries quoted in his Diary, it will be inferred that Mr. Lawrence's means for charitable distribution varied considerably in amount from year to year. To explain this difference, it may not be amiss to state here, that he had, from the first efforts to establish home manufactures in New England, taken a deep interest in their success, and had consequently invested a large proportion of his property in the various manufacturing corporations which had been built up in Lowell and other towns in Massachusetts and New Hampshire. The great fluctuations in this department of industry are known to every one; for, while the returns of one year would be ample, those of the next year would, from embarrassments in the commercial world, or from some other cause, be little or nothing.

"*January* 8. — T. R. and S. J., two Englishmen in the employ of J. C., mended our pump to-day. I gave them some books and a word of counsel, and hope to observe their progress."

"*February* 15. — T. J. called, and is to embark to-morrow, on his way to the war in Mexico. He asked me to give him money to buy a pistol, which I declined, as I could not wish them success in Mexico; but gave him some books, a Bible, and good counsel."

During the month of February, an appeal was made to the citizens of Boston in behalf of the famished population of Ireland, and resulted in the sending to that country a large quantity of food and clothing. Mr Lawrence contributed himself towards the object, and, as was often the case, endeavored to interest others equally with himself. On the 24th of that month, he addressed a note to J. A. Stearns, Esq., Principal of the Mather School, at South Boston, for the pupils of his school composing the Lawrence Association. This Association, comprising a large number of boys and girls, had been formed for moral and intellectual improvement, and had been named in honor of Mr. Lawrence, who had, from its commencement, taken a deep interest in its success, and had often contributed books and money when needed.

" Wednesday, March 2.

"MY FRIENDS: The value of the offering to suffering Ireland from our city will be enhanced by the numbers contributing, as the offering will do more good as an expression of sympathy than as a matter of relief. The spirit of dear R. seems to speak through your 'Oak Leaf,' * and to say, 'Let all who will of the Association subscribe a half-dollar each, and all others a quarter each, for their suffering brethren, and children of a common Father.' A. L.

P. S. — The purses were presents to me, and must be returned. One of them from the lady of Sir John Strachan, herself a descendant of one of our Boston girls; the two open-work ones from ladies in this city. Take from them what is required, and return the balance, if any be left. If more is required, let me know, as I do not know the amount in the purses. A. L."

One hundred and two members of the Association,

---

* A little newspaper published by the Association

and four hundred and thirty-eight other members of the school, in all five hundred and forty, availed themselves of the privilege thus offered them, and contributed the sum of one hundred and sixty dollars towards the object.

At the church in Brattle-street, a collection was taken in aid of the same object; and, among other contributions, was a twenty-dollar bank-note, with the following attached to it, probably by Mr. Lawrence:

"A ship of war to carry bread to the hungry and suffering, instead of powder and ball to inflict more suffering on our brethren,— children of the same Father,— is as it should be; and this is in aid of the plan."

Among the most respected and valued friends of Mr. Lawrence was the venerable Madam Prescott, widow of the late Judge William Prescott, and mother of the distinguished historian of "Ferdinand and Isabella." Years seemed rather to quicken her naturally warm sympathies for the distresses of others; and, at the age of more than four-score, she was to be daily seen on foot in the streets, actively engaged upon her errands of mercy. Mr. Lawrence had, the year before, found a small volume, entitled the "Comforts of Old Age," by Sir Thomas Bernard; and had sent it to several of his friends, principally those in advanced age, asking for some record of their experience. His note to Madam Prescott on this subject was as follows.

"March 8, 1847.

"DEAR MADAM PRESCOTT: I have been a long time anxious to receive a favor from you, and have felt diffident in asking it; but am now at the required state of resolution. The book I send you is so much in character with your own life, that my grandchildren, who love you, will read to their grandchildren your words, written by your own hand in this book, if you will but place them there. I must beg you, my excellent friend, to believe that I am desirous of securing for my descendants some of your precious encouragements in the discipline of life.

"Your friend,

"AMOS LAWRENCE."

The volume was returned with the following record:

"BOSTON, March 10, 1847.

"MY DEAR SIR: You ask me what are the comforts of old age. I answer, the retrospection of a well-spent life. The man who devotes himself to the cause of humanity, who clothes the naked, feeds the hungry, soothes the sorrows of the afflicted, and comforts the mourner,— whom each rising sun finds in the contemplation of some good deed, and each night closes with the assurance that it has been performed,— surely such a life must be the comfort of an old age. But where shall we find such a man? May I not be permitted to apply the character to my highly valued and respected friend, whose charities are boundless, and who daily dispenses blessings to all around him? May the enduring oak be emblematical of the continuance of your life! I depend much upon accompanying you to Mount Auburn, and to visit the spot which contains the precious relics of him whose life it is sweet to contemplate, and whose death has taught us how a Christian should die. The perusal of this little volume has increased my veneration and friendship for its owner.

"Respectfully and affectionately,

"C. G. PRESCOTT."

"MEM. *by A. L., May* 20, 1850.— Madam P., now much passed four-score years of age (born August 1, 1767), is as bright and active in body and mind as most ladies of fifty."

"*April* 10.— Mrs. T. called to ask aid for a poor widow, which I declined, by telling her I did not hear or read people's stories from necessity, and I could not inquire this evening. She claims to be acquainted with Rev. Mr. —— and Rev. Mr. ——. She gave me a severe lecture, and berated me soundly."

"*April* 19.— Mrs. C., of Lowell, asks me to loan her three hundred dollars to furnish a boarding-house for twelve young ladies at S., which I declined by mail this morning."

In reply to Sir William Colebrooke, Governor of New Brunswick, who requested Mr. Lawrence to notify certain poor people in the neighborhood of Boston that their deposits in the Frederickstown Savings' Bank, which had been previously withheld, would be paid by means of an appropriation for the purpose recently made by the Provincial Assembly, he writes:

"BOSTON, April 26, 1847.

"MY DEAR SIR WILLIAM: Your kind letter of the 8th instant reached me on the 13th, and is most welcome and grateful, in making me the medium of so much solid comfort to the numerous people whose earnings are thus restored to them through your unceasing and faithful labors. May God reward you, and enable you to enjoy through life the elevated satisfaction that follows such good works to those who can give you nothing but their prayers! It is alike creditable to your Provincial Government and those true principles which are the best riches of all free governments; and I hope may exercise some good influence upon our State Governments, which have done injustice to many poor persons who have given credit to their promises. I have caused your notice to be scattered broadcast, and trust that all who have any interest in the Frederickstown Savings' Bank will know that their money and interest are ready for them. Pray present me most affectionately to Lady Colebrooke and your daughters; and assure her we shall take more comfort than ever in showing her over our beautiful hills, that have health and joy in every breeze. My own health continues as good as when you were last here; and my family (who have not been taken hence) seem devoted to my comfort. What reason have we for devout thanksgiving, that our two countries are not at swords' points, and that the true feeling of our common ancestry is now sweeping over our land! We are in deep disgrace on account of this wicked Mexican business. What the end is to be can only be known to Infinite Wisdom; but one thing is certain,— no good can come to us from it.

"Again I pray you to be assured of my highest respect and regard, and am very faithfully yours,

"AMOS LAWRENCE."

CHAPTER XXVII.

MR. LAWRENCE AS AN APPLICANT. — LETTERS. — DIARY. — PRAYER AND MEDITATIONS. — LIBERALITY TO A CREDITOR. — LETTERS.

It was not uncommon for Mr. Lawrence, when a good work was in progress, to give not only his own means, but to lend a helping hand by soliciting contributions from others. The following note, addressed to a wealthy bachelor, is a specimen:

"Boston, June 11, 1847.

"My dear Sir: You will be surprised at this letter, coming as it does as a first; but I know, from my experience of your skill and talents as a business man, how pleasant it is to you to make good bargains and safe investments; and, although you are a bachelor, the early business habits you acquired are marked, and are to be carried forward till the footing up of the account, and the trial-balance presented to the Master at his coming. As I said before, you like safe investments, that shall be returned fourfold, if such can be made. Now, I am free to say to you, I know of such an one; and the promisor is a more secure one than A. & A. L. & Co., Uncle Sam, the Old Bay State, or bonds and mortgages in your own neighborhood. You ask, Then why not take it yourself? I answer, Because I have invested in advance in the same sort of stock in other quarters, but am willing to give my guaranty that you shall be satisfied that it is all I represent when you make your final settlement. It is this: Amherst College you know all about; and that is now in especial need of new instructors, and increased funds for their support. Twenty thousand dollars from you will place it on high ground, give a name to a professorship, make you feel happier and richer than you ever did in your life. What say you? — will you do it? The respect of good men will be of more value to you through your remaining days than any amount of increase, even if as vast as Girard's or Astor's. As I am a mere looker-on, you will take this, as I design it, as an expression of good-will to the college, no less than to you."

"MEM. by A. L. — Received an answer on the 16th, very good and kind, from Mr. ———."

In addition to the " very good answer," Mr. Lawrence had soon after the gratification of knowing that the application had been successful, and that the necessary sum had been contributed by his correspondent.

About the same date, he writes to his friend, Professor Packard, of Bowdoin College, as follows:

"Your visit to us the last week has opened new views and visions, that are better described in the last chapter of Revelations than in any account I can give. Bowdoin College is connected with all that is near and dear to President Appleton,— not only those on the stage of action with him, but all who came after, embracing in this latter class your own loved ones, who may continue to exercise an important agency in making the college what the good man, in his lifetime, strove to make it. The love, veneration, and respect, my dear wife had for him, makes her feel a peculiar pleasure in doing what would have cheered and comforted him so much had he lived till this time. The thousand dollars handed to you is a first payment of six thousand that she will give to the college in aid of the fund now in progress of collection; and she directs that the Lawrence Academy, at Groton, may be allowed to send one scholar each year to Bowdoin College, to be carried through the four years without charge for instruction; and that, whenever the trustees of the academy do not supply a pupil, the college may fill the place. I will hold myself responsible to make good Mrs. L.'s intentions, should she be deprived in any way of this privilege before the work is done."

Early in the summer of this year, the Hon. Abbott Lawrence made his munificent donation of fifty thousand dollars to Harvard College, for the purpose of founding what was afterwards called, in honor of the donor, the Lawrence Scientific School. After reading the letter accompanying this donation, Mr. Lawrence addressed to his brother the following :

"Wednesday morning, June 9, 1847.

"DEAR BROTHER ABBOTT: I hardly dare trust myself to speak what I feel, and therefore write a word to say that I thank God I am spared to this day to see accomplished by one so near and dear to me this last best work ever done by one of our name, which will prove a better title to true nobility than any from the potentates of the world. It is more honorable, and more to be coveted, than the highest political station in our country, purchased as these stations often are by time-serving. It is to impress on unborn millions the great truth that our talents are trusts committed to us for use, and to be accounted for when the

Master calls. This magnificent plan is the great thing that you will see carried out, if your life is spared; and you may well cherish it as the thing nearest your heart. It enriches your descendants in a way that mere money never can do, and is a better investment than any one you have ever made.

"Your affectionate brother, AMOS.
"To ABBOTT LAWRENCE."

To a friend he writes, soon after:

"This noble plan is worthy of him; and I can say truly to you, that I feel enlarged by his doing it. Instead of our sons going to France and other foreign lands for instruction, here will be a place, second to no other on earth, for such teaching as our country stands now in absolute need of. Here, at this moment, it is not in the power of the great railroad companies to secure a competent engineer to carry forward their work, so much are the services of such men in demand."

"BOSTON, June 18, 1847.

"DEAR PARTNERS: Please pass to the credit of my friend, the Rev. Mark Hopkins, two thousand dollars, to pay for four scholarships at Williams College, to be used through all time by the Trustees of Lawrence Academy, in Groton. The said trustees, or their représentatives, may send and keep in college four pupils from the academy, without any charge for tuition; and, whenever they omit or decline keeping up their full number, the government or the proper authorities of the college are authorized to fill the vacancy or vacancies from their own college pupils. Charge the same to my account. A. L.
"To A. & A. L. & Co."

During the last twenty years of his life, Mr. Lawrence was unable to attend more than the morning services of the church on Sunday, on account of the state of his health.

He was a most devout and constant worshipper, and many of those who have conducted the religious services of the church which he attended will well remember the upturned countenance, the earnest attention, and the significant motions of his head, as he listened with an expression of approval to the faithful declarations of the speaker. He loved to listen to those who "did not shun to declare all the counsel of God," and would sometimes express disappointment when the preacher failed to declare what he considered the important truths of the Gospel.

In writing to a friend, after listening to a discourse of the latter description from a stranger, he compares it, in its adaptation to the spiritual wants of the hearers, to the nourishment which a wood-chopper would receive by placing him in the top of a flowering tree, and allowing him to feed only on the odor of its blossoms. His feelings on this subject are expressed in a letter to an esteemed clergyman, who had solicited his aid in behalf of a church in a distant city.

"BOSTON, June 11, 1847.

"MY FRIEND: I have your letter of yesterday; and, in reply, I offer it as my opinion that the Unitarianism growing up among us the few years past has so much philosophy as to endanger the Christian character of our denomination, and to make us mere rationalists of the German school, which I dread more than anything in the way of religious progress. The church at —— may be of use in spreading Christianity; but it may also be a reproval to it. I do not feel sufficient confidence in it to give money to keep life in it until I see evidence of some of the conservative influences that my own beloved and honored pastor is calling back among us. Your well-wisher and friend,

"A. L.

"P. S. — I fully agree in the opinion that —— is an important point for the dissemination of truth; and, before giving aid, I must know the man before I help support the minister, having small confidence in the teachings of many who enjoy considerable reputation as teachers of righteousness. I may have expressed doubts and fears that may not seem well founded; but I feel them."

The following entry in his diary will give some idea of Mr. Lawrence's exactness in his daily business:

"*Saturday, July* 24, 1847. — Enclosed in a note to the Rev. —— ——, of ——, a fifty-dollar bank-note, of the Atlantic Bank, No. 93, dated Jan. 1, 1846, payable to George William Dodd; letter A at each end of the bill, and A. P. P. in blue ink, in my writing, at the top. Sent the letter to the post-office by coachman, and paid the postage; he keeping a memorandum of his having delivered it, and paid for it. A. L."

"*Sept.* 14. — Professor ——, of the Baptist College in —— has called, to whom I shall give a parcel of books for the use of the college, and also a good word, which I hope will make him remember in whose service he is engaged."

"*Sept.* 15. — Delivered him about two hundred and fifty volumes, various; all of value to him and his college, he said. He is a young man (under thirty years) and a minister."

"*September* 16, 1847, *Sabbath-day.** —' O most blessed Lord and Saviour; thou who didst, by thy precious death and burial, take away the sting of death and the darkness of the grave! grant unto me the precious fruit of this holy triumph of thine, and be my guide both in life and in death. In thy name will I lay me down in peace and rest; for thou, O Lord, makest me to dwell in safety! Enlighten, O Lord, the eyes of my understanding, that I may not sleep the sleep of death! Into thy hands I commend my spirit; for thou hast redeemed me, O thou covenant-keeping God! Bless and preserve me, therefore, both now and forever! Amen!'

"These are suitable thoughts and aspirations, such as every Christian may profitably indulge on retiring each night. His bed should remind him of his grave; and, as the day past brings him so much nearer to it, the appearance, when summoned hence, should be the point most distinctly before him. If he pass on with the 'Well done,' no time can be amiss when called up. O God! grant me to be ever ready; and, by thy blessing and thy mercy, grant me to be allowed to join company with those loved and precious ones whom I feel entirely assured are at thy right hand, then to be no more separated! AMOS LAWRENCE."

The following note and memorandum by Mr. Lawrence will show how he dealt with an old debtor:

* The opposite page is a fac-simile of the original manuscript found in Mr. Lawrence's pocket-book after his death. It may serve as a fair specimen of his chirography during his latter years.

Fac-Simile of Mr. Lawrence's Hand-writing in 1847.

"O most blessed Lord & Saviour! Thou who
didst by Thy precious death & burial take
away the sting of death & the darkness of
the grave grant unto me the precious
fruit of this Holy Triumph of thine, & be my
guide both in life & death. — In thy name
I will lay me down in peace & rest, for thou O
Lord makest me to dwell in safety. —
Enlighten O Lord, the eyes of mine understand
-ing that I may not sleep the sleep of death.
Into thy hands, I commend my spirit for
thou hast redeemed me O thou covenant
keeping-God! Bless & preserve me
therefore both now & forever. — Amen!"

These are suitable thoughts & aspirations
such as every christian may profitably
indulge, on retiring each night.
His bed should remind him of his grave &
as the day past brings him so much nearer
to it, the appearance, when summoned
hence should be the point, most distinct
-ly before him — If he pass on with the
"Well done" no time can be amiss
when called up — O God! grant me
to be ever ready; & by thy blessing & thy mercy
grant me to be allowed to join company
with those loved and precious ones,
whom I feel entirely assured are at
Thy right hand" then to be no more separated

Amos Lawrence

Sept 16. 1847 Sabbath day.

(TO MR. G.)

"MY DEAR SIR: If you have any mode by which I can have the pleasure of receiving your note and interest, amounting to twenty-three hundred dollars, to be vested by me for the benefit of your wife, I shall be pleased to do it, having long since determined to appropriate this money, whenever received, in this way.

"Yours, truly,   A. L.
"For himself and brother A."

"MEM. — Mr. —— was an invalid, and confined to his house at that period, and sent for me to call and see him. I did so, and he seemed much affected at my offer; but told me he was in better circumstances than I had supposed him, and declined the proffered aid. The information thus given me in this last interview was most welcome: from that time, I never mentioned his debt. After his decease, it was paid by his sons; and the family has been prosperous since. I spent the money for others in need, and am rejoiced that all his are so comfortable."

Many of our readers who can look back a few years will recall to memory the manly form, and fine, open countenance, of William L. Green, who was so suddenly cut off at the very threshold of what promised to be an honorable and useful career. He had come to Boston from his native town of Groton; and, after serving an apprenticeship, had entered upon a successful business. He had endeared himself to a large circle of friends, and possessed such qualities of mind and heart as had made him the stay and hope of his parents in their declining years.

Upon hearing of the death of this nephew, Mr. Lawrence addressed to his parents the following letter of sympathy:

"Boston, October 22, 1847

"Dear Brother and Sister: God speaks to us through the rustling of the leaves no less distinctly than in the voice of the whirlwind and the storm; and it is now our business and our privilege to look at him and to him for the lesson of yesterday. Dear W., as he parted from me the Sabbath noon before the last, looked the embodiment of health, long life, and happiness. Now, that noble figure, face, expression, and loved spirit, which lightened his path, is no longer among us, to be in danger of injury from our yielding him that which belongs to God only. Were we not liable, dear brother and sister, to interrupt those communings which God calls us to with himself? He is our merciful Father, and does for us what he sees is best; and, if we receive his teachings, however dark they may appear to us at present, all will be made clear at the right time. Your precious treasure is secured, I trust, and will prove an increased attraction to you to follow; and it seems to me that our children are uniting in their joyful meeting in heaven. May we see in this event, more clearly than ever, where we are to look for direction, instruction, and support! May we be ready when called! So prays your affectionate and afflicted brother, A. L."

To a friend he writes, Dec. 27:

"In our domestic relations, we are all as we could desire, save the individual case of my brother William, who is barely remaining this side Jordan, and in a happy state, I trust, to pass over.

For a number of days, we have supposed each might be the last · but he may continue for some days, or possibly weeks. Death strikes right and left, and takes from our midst the long-honored and beloved, in their maturity. Dr. Codman and Judge Hubbard are both to be buried to-day; two men whose places will not soon be filled, I fear. Only last Tuesday, in my ride with good Dr. Sharp, we agreed to call and pay our respects to Dr. C. on Thursday; but, on that morning, learned that he was dead. On Thursday, Judge Hubbard rode out, and transacted legal business as a magistrate; in the evening went to bed as usual; in the night-time was turned over in bed, as he requested to be, and ceased to breathe. How could a good man pass over Jordan more triumphantly and gloriously?"

The reader will not fail to note the coïncidence, that, almost exactly five years later, Mr. Lawrence was summoned to "pass over" in the same manner, which, from the expression used, seems to have been to him so desirable; though his own departure was still more sudden and striking.

(TO A PHYSICIAN.)

"Sabbath evening, seven o'clock.

"DEAR W.: I have been reading to —— the last hour, beginning at the second chapter of Matthew, and so on in course. Please look at the fourth chapter, and the latter part of the twenty-third verse, and I think you will need no apology for doing what you do, with such instruction. Christ's example, no less than his precepts, is designed to be practically useful to the whole family of man; and I feel humbled and grieved that I have not followed him better, and preached better by all the motives he has thus spread out. I say, then, to you and yours, God bless you in your good work, and make you a worthy follower of the Beloved! A. L."

CHAPTER XXVIII.

REFLECTIONS. — VIEWS ON HOLDING OFFICE. — LETTERS. — CAPTAIN A. SLIDELL McKENZIE. — DEATH OF BROTHER, AND OF HON J. MASON.

"*Jan.* 1, 1848. — In reviewing the scenes and the business of the past year, I have continued evidence of that mercy which a Father bestows on his children, and a louder call to yield more fully than I ever yet have done to the teachings he designs. Many things that seem dark, of which the reasons are not understood, will be made clear at the right time. It is manifest that my stewardship is not so far well done as to permit me to fold my arms and feel easy. No: my life is spared for more work. May its every day be marked by some token that shall meet Thine approval, when the final call shall come!"

(TO PRESIDENT HOPKINS.)

"Boston, March 9.

"This religious awakening among your college students is among the blessings that our Father vouchsafes to his servants who labor faithfully in their work; and I can see his hand as plainly in it as though it were thrust before my face as I write this sentence. Let us, then, bless his holy name, and thank him, as disciples and followers of Christ the Beloved; and urge upon these young men to come forward, as doves to their windows. If my life and my trusteeship have been in any manner instrumental in this good work in your college, it will be matter of grateful thanksgiving while I live. Mrs. L. and myself both felt our hearts drawn out to you as we read your letter; and we commend you, and the good work of guiding these interesting young Christians in the ways and the works that lead to that blessed home to which our loved ones have been called, and to which we hope to be welcomed. To his grace and guidance we commend all things touching this onward and upward movement. I have been under the smarting-rod a few days within the past fortnight. Severe pain took all my courage and light-heartedness out of me, and made me a sorry companion; and my friends, seeing me in my every-day dress, would hardly know me in this sombre garb. Again, dear friend, I bid you God-speed in the good work; and, at last, may you receive the 'Well done' promised to the faithful!"

In the presidential campaign of 1848, the Hon. Abbott Lawrence was made a prominent candidate of the Whig party for the Vice-Presidency; and, in the convention which assembled at Philadelphia in June, was voted for, and received but one vote short of that which would have secured the nomination. Mr. Fillmore, it will be recollected, was the successful candidate. During the canvass, a gentleman, editing a newspaper which strongly advocated the nomination of Taylor and Lawrence, addressed a very courteous letter to Mr. Amos Lawrence, asking for aid in supporting this movement, which he supposed he would of course be deeply interested in. The reply is given here, as an illustration of his views in regard to holding high political office:

"DEAR SIR: In reply to yours, this moment handed me, I state that my income is so reduced, thus far, this year, that I am compelled to use prudence in the expenditure of money, and must therefore decline making the loan. If my vote would make my brother Vice-President, I would not give it, as I think it lowering his good name to accept office of any sort, by employing such means as are now needful to get votes. I hope 'Old Zack' will be President.

"Respectfully yours, A. L."

To President Hopkins he writes, April 15:

"What should we do, if the Bible* were not the foundation of our system of self-government? and what will become of us, when we wilfully and wickedly cast it behind us? We have all more than common reason to pray, in the depths of our sins, God be merciful to us sinners. The efforts made to lessen respect for it, and confidence in it, will bring to its rescue multitudes who otherwise would not have learned how much they owe it. The 'Age of Reason,' fifty years ago, told, on the whole, in advancing truth, by bringing to its support the best minds of Christendom. I hope it may be so now. This is a theme for your head and heart and pen. No man in New England can make a deeper mark. What say ye? The Bible is our great charter, and does more than all others, written or unwritten."

"W. C. writes from N., asking me to loan him three thousand

---

* In looking over the list of Life Directors of the American Bible Society, made such by the payment of one hundred and fifty dollars each, there are found at least ten who are known to have been constituted by Mr. Lawrence.

dollars to buy a farm, and to improve his health and mind; stating that he is a cripple, but wants to do something for the world."

> "That man may last, but never lives,
> Who much receives, but nothing gives,
> Whom none can love, whom none can thank,
> Creation's blot, creation's blank."

(TO PRESIDENT HOPKINS.)

"BOSTON, June 12, 1848

"MY DEAR FRIEND: Only think what changes a few weeks have produced in Europe, and the probable effects upon this country. It seems now certain that vast numbers will emigrate here, rich and poor, from the continent and from England. The question for us is, How shall we treat them? It is certain that foreigners will come here. We have land enough for them, but have not the needful discipline to make them safe associates in maintaining our system of government. Virtue and intelligence are our platform; but the base passions of our country have been ministered to so abundantly by unscrupulous politicians, that our moral sense has been blunted; and these poor, ignorant foreigners are brought into use for selfish purposes, and the prospects for the future are appalling. Yet a ray of light has just broken in upon us by the nomination of General Taylor for President; and my belief is, he is the best man for the place who can be named, with any prospect of success. He is not a politician, but a plain, straight-forward, honest man, anxious to do his duty in all his relations. As to my brother's nomination for Vice-President, I am thankful they did not make it in convention: he is in a higher position before the country than he would be if chosen Vice-President. His course has been elevated and magnanimous in this matter; for he might, by his personal influence and efforts, have received the nomination.

"ADDITIONAL. — It is now almost two, P. M., and I have but just returned from Mount Auburn. The visit has been deeply interesting, on many accounts, and has almost unfitted me to finish this letter. However, there is nothing in the visit but what ought to make me thankful that my treasures, though removed, are secured; and, if my poor efforts can bring me again into their society through the blessed Saviour, I ought not allow this gush of feeling to unman me."

A few days later, he writes to the same friend:

"I have not as yet heard of the examination of yesterday at the Lawrence Academy, which son A. A. attended, but hope for a good report. In truth, I feel as if that school and your college are to go hand in hand in making whole men for generations to come. There is a pleasant vision which opens to me when I look forward to the characters that the academy and the college are to send forth for the next hundred years. I bless God for my old home, and the great elm in front, which has a teaching and a significance that I shall endeavor to make use of in training my grandchildren and dear ones of my family connection. How important, then, that our places of education be sustained, as supplying the pure and living streams that shall irrigate every hill and valley of this vast empire, and train men to know and do their duty! I will not quarrel with a man's Presbyterian, Episcopal, or Baptist creed, so be he will act the part of a good soldier of Christ; for I verily believe great multitudes, of all creeds, desire to serve him faithfully."

"*Aug.* 23. — T. G. sent me a paper this morning, having

many names on it, with a polite note. The paper I returned without reading; telling him I did not read such, or hear stories, and must be excused. He took the answer in high dudgeon, and sent another note, saying he had mistaken me, and desired that his first note should be returned. I wrote upon it that I lived by the day and hour, an invalid, and, for two years, had adopted this course, and had treated bishops, clergymen, and laymen, with the fewest words; that I intended no disrespect, and begged his pardon if I had done anything wrong. I also told him this course was urged upon me by my medical adviser; but, with all my care, there is now an average of six applications a day through the year."

Mr. Lawrence had, many years previous to this date, formed an acquaintance with Captain Slidell McKenzie, of the United States Navy, which had been continued, and was a source of mutual pleasure. Among other relics in the possession of the writer, is a cane of palm-wood, presented by Capt. McKenzie, on his return from Mexico as commander of the United States Steamship "Mississippi," to Mr. Lawrence, who had caused to be engraven upon it, on a silver plate, the following inscription:

ALEXANDER SLIDELL McKENZIE TO AMOS LAWRENCE.
1845.
PALM-WOOD FROM THE BANKS OF THE TOBASCO RIVER.
FROM THE UNITED STATES NAVAL COMMANDER WHO WAS NOT AFRAID TO DO HIS DUTY WHEN LIFE WAS REQUIRED AT THE YARD-ARM.

The latter part of the inscription is in allusion to

the course which Capt. McKenzie felt obliged to adopt in the mutiny on board the United States Brig "Somers," in 184–.

On Sept. 15, he thus notices the death of that officer in his diary:

"This morning's newspapers give the intelligence that the excellent and accomplished Capt. McKenzie died at Sing Sing, N. Y., two days ago. He fell from his horse by an affection of the heart, and died almost instantly. Thus has departed a man whom I esteemed as among the best and purest I am acquainted with, and whose character should be a treasure for his family and the nation. I think him a model officer and a good Christian."

"*Oct.* 11.—

CANADIAN BOAT-SONG.

'Faintly as tolls the evening chime,
Our voices keep tune, and our oars keep time;
Soon as the woods on shore look dim,
We'll sing at St. Ann's our parting hymn.
Row, brothers, row: the stream runs fast,
The rapids are near, and daylight's past.'

I first heard this song sung and played on the piano by ——, afterwards Mrs. ——, at her house in —— street, in 1809. The song rang in my ears sweetly for weeks, as I was taken down with fever the next morning. I never think of it but with delight."

"*Oct.* 15.— My brother William died on Saturday, Oct. 14, at three, P. M., in the sixty-sixth year of his age; and my brother Mason died only five hours afterwards, in his eighty-first year,—

within three doors of each other. Both were very dear to me in life, and both are very dear to me in death; and, in God's good time, I trust that I shall meet them again, not subject to the ills and changes of my present abode."

In a letter of the same date to a friend, he says:

"My letter of last Tuesday will have prepared you for the sad intelligence in this. Brother William continued without much suffering or consciousness till two o'clock yesterday, and then ceased breathing, without a groan. Yesterday morning, the hand of death was manifestly upon Brother Mason, who was conscious to objects around, and requested C. to pray with him; and, when asked if he understood what was said, answered, 'Yes,' and expressed by words and signs his wants and feelings. He continued in a quiet, humble, and hopeful frame, we judge, until just eight o'clock, when, with a single gasp and a slight noise, his mighty spirit passed out of its immense citadel of clay, to join the throng of the loved ones gone before. Brother W. was in his sixty-sixth year, Brother M. in his eighty-first; and both were such men as we need, true as steel in all good works and words. Mr. M. was never sick a day to disable him from attending to his professional and public duties in fifty years, and, until within a short time, never confined a day to his house by illness. On the last Sunday evening, I passed a most refreshing half-hour with him. He appeared as well as he had done for a year; inquired very particularly into Brother W.'s state; expressed the opinion that his own time was near at hand, and a hope that he might be taken without losing his mental and bodily powers. He remarked that protracted old age, after the loss of power to give and receive comfort, was not to be desired.

He has often expressed to me the hope that he should be taken just as he has been. Have we not reason to praise and bless God in taking, no less than in sparing, these honored and loved ones?"

CHAPTER XXIX.

SYSTEM IN ACCOUNTS. — LETTER FROM PROF. STUART. — LETTERS. — DIARY. — DR. HAMILTON. — FATHER MATTHEW.

"*January* 1, 1849. — THE habit of keeping an account of my expenditures for objects other than for my family, and for strictly legal calls, I have found exceedingly convenient and satisfactory; as I have been sometimes encouraged, by looking back to some entry of aid to a needy institution or individual, to do twice as much for some other needy institution or individual. I can truly say, that I deem these outlays my best, and would not, if I could by a wish, have any of them back again. I adopted the practice, ten years ago, of spending my income. The more I give, the more I have; and do most devoutly and heartily pray God that I may be faithful in the use of the good things intrusted to me."

"*January* 2. — Yesterday, Peter C. Brooks died, aged eighty-two; a man who has minded his own business through life, and from a poor boy became the richest man in the city. I honor him as an honest man."

(FROM PROF. STUART, OF ANDOVER.)

"ANDOVER, January 23, 1849.

"MY DEAR SIR: Soon after my daughter's return from Boston, I received a garment exceedingly appropriate to the severe cold to which I am daily exposed in my rides. Many, many hearty thanks for your kindness! To me the article in question is of peculiar value. The cold can hardly penetrate beneath such a garment. God has blessed you with wealth; but he has given you a richer blessing still; that is, a heart overflowing with kindness to your fellow-beings, and a willingness to do good to all as you have opportunity. I accept, with warm emotions of gratitude and thankfulness, the kindness you have done to me. I would not exchange your gift for a large lump of the California gold. Be assured you have my fervent prayer and wishes, that you may at last receive a thousand-fold for all the kindness that you have shown to your fellow-men. You and I are near our final account. May I not hope that this will also be entering on our final reward? I do hope this; I must hope it. What else is there in life that can make us patiently and submissively and calmly endure its ills? God Almighty bless and sustain and guide and comfort you until death; and then may you pass through the dark valley without a fear, cheerfully looking to what lies beyond it!

"I am, my dear sir, with sincere gratitude, your friend and obedient servant, MOSES STUART."

To President Hopkins he writes, Jan. 3:

"Your letters always bring light to our path, and joy to our hearts, in one way or another. The two last seemed to come at the very time to do both, in a way to impress our senses and feelings, as the clear heavens, and brilliant sky, and exhilarating atmosphere, of this charming cold day, do mine, in contrast with a beautiful bouquet of flowers on my table as a love-token from some of my young sleigh-riding friends, and which makes me feel a boy with these boys, and an old man with such wise ones as you.

"In the scenes of the past year, much that will mark its character stands out in bold relief; and, if we of this country are true to our principles, the great brotherhood of man will be elevated; for there have been overturns and overturns which will act until He whose right it is shall reign. If we live up to our political professions, our Protestant religion will elevate the millions who will be brought under our levelling process. 'Level up,' but not down, was Judge Story's maxim of democratic levelling, as he began his political career. In the business of levelling up, the Lawrence Academy, I trust, may do something. The late notices of it have been somewhat various by the newspaper editors to whom the preceptor sent catalogues."

"*February* 25. — Attended Brattle-street Church this morning, and heard a consolatory sermon; and, at the closing prayer, the giving of thanks to our Father in heaven, through Jesus Christ, who lived to serve us, and died to save us."

On the 28th, he writes to his brother Abbott, who had had tendered to him, by General Taylor, the office of Secretary of the Navy:

"DEAR BROTHER: I have heard since noon that you have the invitation of General Taylor to take a seat in his cabinet, and that you will proceed to Washington forthwith to answer for yourself. I am not less gratified by the offer than you can be; but I should feel deep anguish, if I thought you could be induced to accept it, even for a brief period. Your name and fame as a private citizen is a better inheritance for your children than any distinction you may attain from official station; and the influence you can exercise for your country and friends, as you are, is higher and better than any you can exercise as an official of the government."

On March 3, he writes to his brother at Washington:

"I awoke this morning very early, and, after a while, fixed my mind in prayer to God, that your duty may be clearly seen, and that you may perform it in the spirit of a true disciple."

And again on March 5, after hearing that his brother had declined the proffered seat in the cabinet, he writes to him:

"The morning papers confirm my convictions of what you would do; and I do most heartily rejoice, and say that I never felt as proud before."

"*April* 11. — A subscription paper, with an introductory letter from ———, was handed me, on which were seven or eight names for a hundred dollars each, to aid the family of ———, lately deceased. Not having any acquaintance with him or family, I did not subscribe. Applications come in from all quarters, for all objects. The reputation of giving freely is a very bad reputation, so far as my personal comfort is concerned."

April 21, he writes to a friend:

"The matters of deepest interest in my last were ———, the religious movement, ———'s ill-health, and ———'s accident. All these matters are presenting a sunny show now. Our dead Unitarianism of ten or fifteen years ago is stirred up, and the deep feelings of sin, and salvation through the Beloved, are awakened, where there seemed to be nothing but indifference and coldness; my hope and belief are that great good will follow. In the matter of the enjoyment of life, you judge me rightly; few men have so many and rich blessings to be thankful for; and, while I am spared with sufficient understanding to comprehend these, I pray that I may have the honesty to use them in the way that the Master will approve. Of what use will it be to have my thoughts directed to the increase of my property, at the cost of my hopes of heaven? There, a Lazarus is better off than a score of Dives. Pray without ceasing, that I may be faithful."

The following extract of a letter is taken from a work entitled "A Romance of the Sea-Serpent, or the Ichthyosaurus," and will show Mr. Lawrence's views respecting the much contested subject of which it treats:

"Boston, April 26, 1849.

"I have never had any doubt of the existence of the *Sea-Serpent* since the morning he was seen off Nahant by Martial Prince, through his famous mast-head spy-glass. For, within the next two hours, I conversed with Mr. Samuel Cabot, and Mr. Daniel P. Parker, I think, and one or more persons beside, who had spent a part of that morning in witnessing his movements. In addition, Colonel Harris, the commander at Fort Independence, told me that the creature had been seen by a number of his soldiers while standing sentry in the early dawn, some time before this show at Nahant; and Colonel Harris believed it as firmly as though the creature were drawn up before us in State-street, where we then were.

"I again say, I have never, from that day to this, had a doubt of the *Sea-Serpent's existence*. The revival of the stories will bring out many facts that will place the matter before our people in such a light as will make them *as much ashamed* to doubt, as *they formerly were* to believe in its existence.

" Yours truly,   AMOS LAWRENCE."

To a friend he writes, July 18:

"Brother A. has received the place of Minister to the Court of St. James; the most flattering testimony of his worth and character that is within the gift of the present administration, and the only office that I would not advise against his accepting."

About this time, Mr. Lawrence read a small work, entitled "Life in Earnest," by the Rev. James Hamilton, D.D., Minister of the Scotch Church, Regent's Square, London. The sentiments of this little volume were so much akin to his own, and were withal so forcibly exemplified, that he commenced a correspondence with the author, which became a most interesting one, and continued until the close of his life.

" BOSTON, July 18, 1849.

" To REV. J. HAMILTON, D.D.

" SIR: The few lines on the other side of this sheet are addressed to me by our excellent governor, whose good word may be grateful to you, coming as it does from a Christian brother across the Atlantic. If it should ever happen to you to visit this country, I need not say how great would be my pleasure to see you. I am a minute-man, living by the day and by the ounce; but am compensated for all privations, by reading such tracts as 'Life in Earnest,' in such a way that few are allowed. I have cleared out the Sunday-school depository three times in the last four weeks, and have scattered the work broadcast, and intend to continue to do so if my health allows. Among those to whom I have given one is my younger brother, who is soon to be with you in England, as Minister to your Court. I recommend him to your prayers and your confidence.

"With great respect for your character, I am yours,
"AMOS LAWRENCE."

"*July* 23. — We are to have Father Matthew here to-morrow: he is a lion, but I probably shall only see him at a distance. The influence he is said to have upon his Irish people may result in making many of them industrious citizens, who would, without him, be criminals, and a pest to honest people. The evil of such masses being thrown upon us we must bear, and study how to relieve ourselves in any practicable way. I see none but to educate the children, and circulate the Bible and good books among them, which shall encourage them to do the best they can for themselves.

"The Christian banner may have many local influences and teachings; but its broad folds, I trust, will cover many true followers, however exact its worldly interpreters may be of what constitutes a true follower. I saw, in the *New York Observer* (I think it was), a statement of a district in the South-west, where were forty-one Christian denominations, and no two of whose ministers could exchange pulpit labors. Do not these people need a Christian teacher?"

"*August* 3. — Father Matthew is doing a good work here; and the result of his power is in his benevolent and sincere expression, and charming head and face. He has called to see me twice, and I intend to call and see him to-morrow. His ease and eloquence could not do for him what his heavenly expression does."

CHAPTER XXX.

CODICIL TO WILL. — ILLNESS. — GEN. WHITING. — LETTERS. — DIARY.

In August, 1849, Mr. Lawrence reviewed his will and added to it the following codicil:

"Through the mercy of God, my life has been prolonged to this time, and my mental and bodily powers continued to me to an extent that has enabled me to see to the application of those trusts that have been confided to me; and, should my stewardship end now or next year, and the 'Well done' of the Master be pronounced upon my labors, all things here will seem nothing, and less than nothing, in comparison.

"In short, my life, cheerful and happy as it is made by the three blessings conferred upon man after his fall (wife, children, and friends), is in the keeping of a merciful Father, who, by thus continuing it, allows me a foretaste of that future home I hope for whenever he calls.

"In reviewing my will, above written, executed on the 21st day of February, A. D. 1846, I see nothing to alter, and everything to confirm. And I do hereby declare it still my will, and this codicil is to be taken as a confirmation of it; and I do earnestly hope all in interest will see clearly the meaning of every clause, and carry out my meaning without any quibbling, question, or controversy. I have been my own executor, for many years. of the surplus property I have received, and intend to be while my powers of mind will allow it. Many near and dear friends to whom I looked for counsel and direction, at the time my will was executed, have been taken hence, which makes me more desirous of giving a renewed expression at this time."

In this connection was the following note to his sons, found in his pocket-book after his decease:

"DEAR W. AND A.: In my will, I have made no bequests as tokens of remembrance, and have endeavored to do for all (whom I am interested in out of my own family connections) what is needful and proper and best; yet I wish some expression of kindness to M. and F., if in the family when I am taken."   *   *   *   *

Here follow donations to domestics who had been for many years in his family.

About the 20th of September, Mr. Lawrence experienced a severe attack of cholera morbus, which was then a sort of epidemic in the community. Of this attack, he writes to President Hopkins as follows:

"I hardly know how to address you, since I find myself once more spared to lay open my heart to you; for I do indeed feel all the force of the words, What shall I render unto God for all his unspeakable goodness? I have been upon the brink of Jordan, and, with my outstretched hand, seized hold of our merciful Father's hand, that was held out towards me, and was supported by his grasp as plainly as I could have been by your own hand. I was waiting, and praying to him to conduct me to the other side and permit me to join the company of loved ones *passed on*, and felt almost sure I should never see the sunlight of this world again, when, to my amazement, I found my pains subsiding, and that I had not finished the work he had assigned. When you were here, I gave you some little outline of my plan of work for ——. On the 18th of September, I completed that work, and felt stronger on that day than on any day for a month. Under the excitement of the scene and a sudden change of weather, I took cold, and had a terrible attack of cholera, which, by the immediate administration of remedies, was in a degree quieted. Thus my poor old worn-out machine was still kept from parting, as the sole of the shoe is sometimes kept on by freezing snow and water upon it."

In the beginning of this volume, mention is made of the first clerk whom Mr. Lawrence employed after entering business in the year 1807. To that gentleman, now Brigadier-General Whiting, was addressed the following letter, which was the recommencement of a correspondence which had ceased for many years:

"BOSTON, November, 1849.

"MY DEAR GENERAL: I have been deeply interested in overlooking your volume of revolutionary orders of Washington, selected from your father's manuscripts, as it brought back scenes and memories of forty years and more ago, when I used to visit at your house in Lancaster, and to read those papers with a relish that might well be coveted by the youth of the present day. I thank you for this token of auld lang syne, and shall feel the more thankful if you will come and see me. I would certainly go to you, if I had the strength, and could do it safely; but shall never go so far from home, being at any moment liable to be called off. My earnest desire is to be 'in line,' and to be able to answer, promptly, 'here.' I hope to hear from you and your wife and wee things: all have a hold upon me, and you will give them an old man's love. I have taken the opportunity to send you some little reminiscences of old times. Butler's 'History of Groton' (which connects Lancaster in early days) is a model for its exact truthfulness: he was the preceptor of the academy until long after you entered the army. Then I have sent a catalogue of the school, from its beginning for fifty years or more; 'History of Lowell as it Was, and Lowell as it Is,' well written and true; 'Boston Notions,' put together by old Mr. Dearborn, the printer, whom you knew; and some other little matters, which will serve to freshen old things, as your 'Revolutionary Orders of Washington' have done with me. I have just looked into my first sales-book, and there see the entries made by you more than forty years ago. Ever since, you have been going up, from the cornet of dragoons to the present station.

"Farewell. Your old friend, AMOS LAWRENCE.
"GEN. HENRY WHITING, Fort Hamilton, N. Y."

(TO ROBERT BARNWELL RHETT, ESQ., OF SOUTH CAROLINA.)

"BOSTON, Dec. 12, 1849.

"MY DEAR SIR: Your letter of November 30 reached me in due course, and gave me unfeigned pleasure in seeing my hopes confirmed, that the practical common sense of South Carolina was returning, and that the use of their head and hands was getting to be felt among the citizens, as necessary to their salvation as common brethren in the great family of States. Without the use of those trusts placed in their hands by our common Father, the State will not be worth the parchment on which to draw the deeds fifty years hence; and I most earnestly pray God to guide, guard, and save the State from their childishness in their fears that our northern agitators can harm them. I spent the winter of 1819 in Washington, and heard the whole of the debate upon admitting Alabama and Missouri into the Union. Alabama was admitted, Missouri rejected; and I made up my mind then that I would never interfere until requested by my brethren of the Slaveholding States; which resolution I have carried out from that day to this; and I still hold to it. But I would not have admitted Alabama then or Missouri on the terms they were admitted. We of the North have windy, frothy politicians, who hope to make capital out of their ultraism; but, in the aggregate, they soon find their level. Now, of the point to which I desire to come, I do earnestly desire your State to carry out your prophecy, that, in ten years, you will spin all your own crop of cotton; for we of Massachusetts will gladly surrender to you the manufacture of coarse fabrics, and turn our industry to making fine articles. In short, we could now, if you are ready, give up to you the coarse fabrics, and turn one half of our machinery into spinning and weaving cotton hose; and nothing will help us all so much as specific duties. The whole kingdom of Saxony is employed at this moment in making cotton hose for the United States from yarns purchased in England, and made of your cotton. How much better would it be for you and for us to save these treble profits and transport, by making up the cotton at home! Think of these matters, and look at them without the prejudice that prevails so extensively in your State. A few years ago, I asked our kinsman, Gen. ——, of your State, how the forty-bale theory was esteemed at that time. His answer was, 'We all thought it true when it was started, and it had its effect; but nobody is of that mind now.' Still, I believe, when an error gets strong hold of the popular mind, it is much more difficult to eradicate it than it is to supply the truth in its place. If I know myself, I would not mete to you any different measure from what I would ask of you; and I must say to you, that your State and people have placed themselves in a false position, which will be as apparent to them in a few years as the sun is at noonday. My own family and friends are in usual health; and no man this side heaven enjoys earth better than I do. I do pray you to come and see us. I hope to see your son at Cambridge this week. Most respectfully yours,

"AMOS LAWRENCE."

"BOSTON, December 11, 1849.
"To Gen. HENRY WHITING, U. S. A., Fort Hamilton, N. Y.

"MY EARLY FRIEND: Forty years and more ago, we used to talk over together the dismemberment of Poland and the scenes that followed, and to pour out together our feelings for those martyrs of liberty. At the present moment, my feelings are deeply moved by taking by the hand Colonel P. and Major F., just landed here, and driven from their country, martyrs to the same cause. I need only say to you that they are strangers among us, and any attentions from you will be grateful to them, and duly felt by your old friend, A. L."

"*December* 24, 1849.— I have been daily employed, of late, in accompanying visitors to our public institutions; among these, Mr. Charles Carroll, of Maryland, to the Mather School and the Perkins Asylum for the Blind. The effect of kindness upon the character of children is more strikingly illustrated in the Mather School than in any other I know of. Three fifths of the pupils are children of foreigners,— English, Irish, Scotch, German, Swiss, and the like,— mostly very poor. Two fifths are American; and these foreign children, after a few months, are ambitious to look as well and do as well as the best. The little Irish creatures are as anxious to have their faces clean, their hair smooth, their clothes mended, and to learn to read, write, and explain their lessons, as the upper children. These upper children, to the number of about one hundred, belong to the Lawrence Association."

"*December* 25, *Christmas afternoon.* — The following beautiful little note, accompanied by a silver cup, almost unmanned me. Forty-three girls signed the note; two others engaged in it are sick; and one died, and was buried at Mount Auburn by her particular request,— making forty-six of these children, who, of their own motion, got up this token. Their note is dated to-day, and runs thus:

" 'RESPECTED SIR : The misses of the Lawrence Association, anxious to testify their gratitude for the kind interest which you have ever manifested towards them, would most respectfully request your acceptance of this small token of their gratitude.' " (Signed by forty-three girls.)

" 26. — We had great times with the children last evening at Sister M.'s. It really seemed to me that the entertainment gave me as much pleasure as any child among them; beside which, I went to the house of my old friend Dr. Bowditch (where I used to visit twenty-five years ago on like occasions), for a few minutes, and there found seventeen of his grandchildren enjoying the fruits of the Christmas-tree in the best manner possible."

CHAPTER XXXI.

DIARY. — REFLECTIONS. — SICKNESS. — LETTER FROM REV. DR. SHARP. — CORRESPONDENCE.

ON the first of January, 1850, Mr. Lawrence, as usual, reviews, in his property-book, the state of his affairs during the preceding year, with an estimate of his expenditures. The entry for the present year is as follows:

"The amount of my expenditures for all objects (taxes included) is about one hundred and twenty thousand dollars. I consider the money well spent, and pray God constantly that I may be watchful in the use of the blessings he bestows, so that at last he may admit me among the faithful that surround his throne."

The above entry will give some idea of the fidelity with which his trusts had been fulfilled, so far as regarded his worldly possessions. Each year, as it rolled by, as well as each successive attack of illness, seemed only to stimulate him in his efforts to accomplish what he could while the day lasted. No anxious fears disturbed him as he looked forward to the near approach of "that night when no man can work."

That night to him was but a prelude of rest from bodily weakness and suffering, and the forerunner of a brighter day, of which, even in this world, he was sometimes permitted to obtain a glimpse. He says:

"My own health and strength seem renewed. That cholera attack has changed the whole man; and it is only now and then I am brought to a pause that quickens me in my work when again started. A week since, I ventured on two ounces of solid food for my dinner, differing from what I have taken for many years. Nine hours after, in my sleep, I fainted, and was brought to life by dear N. standing over me, giving ammonia, rubbing, and the like. Fasting the day following brought me back to the usual vigor and enjoyments. Do you not see in this the sentence, 'Do with thy might what thy hand findeth to do,' stereotyped in large letters before me. This it is that brings me to the work at this hour in the morning."

"*March* 24. — Received a letter from Rev. Mr. Hallock, Secretary of the American Tract Society, saying that the Society will publish Dr. Hamilton's lecture on the literary attractions of the Bible, which I had sent them a few weeks since; and will supply me with two thousand copies, as I requested.

"Received also, this morning, another tract of Dr. H. from sister K., in London, called the 'Happy Home,' which finished that series to the working people. After reading this number, I feel a strong desire to see the preceding nine numbers."

(TO THE REV. JAMES HAMILTON, D.D.)

"BOSTON, March 24, 1850.

"REV. AND DEAR SIR: I need not repeat to you how deeply interesting all your writings which I have seen have been to me:

but you may not feel indifferent to the fact that the lecture you delivered four months ago, on the literary attractions of the Bible (which I received from my sister, Mrs. Abbott Lawrence, a few weeks since), is now in process of republication by the American Tract Society, agreeably to my request. I hope to assist in scattering it broadcast over our broad land; and thus you will be speaking from your own desk, with the speed of light, to an audience from Passamaquoddy to Oregon. Will you do me the favor to give me a copy of 'Happy Home,' from which I may teach my children and grandchildren.

"Respectfully your friend, and brother in Christ,
"AMOS LAWRENCE."

(TO A COUNTRY CLERGYMAN (ORTHODOX CONGREGATIONAL).)

"BOSTON, May 16, 1850.

"REV. AND DEAR SIR: I make no apology in asking your acceptance of the above, as I am quite sure it cannot come amiss to a poor clergyman, situated as you are. I pray that you will feel, in using it, you cheer my labors, and make me more happy while I am able to enjoy life, in thus sending an occasional remembrancer to one for whom I have always felt the highest respect and esteem. Your friend, "AMOS LAWRENCE."

The above letter contained a draft for one hundred dollars, of which Mr. Lawrence makes the following memorandum, dated on the 18th:

"Mr. —— acknowledges the above letter in very grateful terms, being what his pressing wants require."

In a letter to President Hopkins, dated June 22, Mr. Lawrence says:

"If I cannot visit you bodily, as I had vainly hoped to do, I can convince you that the life and hope of younger days are still in me. Your parting word touched me to the quick, and I cannot repeat or read it without a sympathetic tear filling my own eye. I am not able to stand up; but am cheered by the hope that, before many weeks, I may be able to stand alone. Our good friend Governor Briggs called to see me this week, and was quite horrified to see me trundled about on a hospital chair; however, after a good talk, he concluded that what was cut off from the lower works was added to the upper, and the account in my favor. It has always been so with me; the dark places have been made clear at the right time; so I am no object of pity."

The lameness here mentioned was caused by a slight sprain of the ankle, but was followed by great prostration of the bodily strength, and a feeble state of all the functions, resulting in that vitiated state of the blood called by physicians "purpura." Violent hemorrhages from the nose succeeded; and these, with the intense heat of the weather, so reduced his strength, that the only hope of recovery seemed to be in removing him from the city to the bracing air of the sea-shore. Towards the end of July, he was accordingly removed upon a mattress to the house of his son, at Nahant; and, from the moment he came within the influence of the fresh sea-breeze, he began to recover his spirits and his strength. A day or two after reaching Nahant, he received from his friend, the Rev. Dr. Sharp, the following letter, which is so characteristic, and reminds one so forcibly of the calm and staid manner of that venerable man, that it is given entire:

"BOSTON, July 30, 1850.

"MY VERY DEAR FRIEND: It was with deep regret I learned, on Friday last, that you were quite unwell, and at Nahant. It was in my mind yesterday morning to visit you; nothing prevented me but an apprehension that it might be deemed inexpedient to admit any one to your sick room, except your own family. But, although I have not seen you in person since your last sickness, yet I have been with you in spirit. I have felt exceedingly sad at the probability of your earthly departure. Seldom as we have seen each other, your friendship has been precious to me; and, to say nothing of your dear family, your continuance in life is of great importance to that large family of humanity, the poor, who have so often participated in your bounty. Indeed, as we cannot well spare you, I rather cherish the hope that, in his good providence, God will continue you to us a little longer. But, whatever may be the issue of your present illness, I trust that you, with all your friends, will be enabled to say, 'The will of the Lord be done.' If he 'lives the longest who answers life's great end,' your life, compared with most, has not been short. Not that any of us have done more than our duty. Nay, we have all come short, and may say, with all modesty and truthfulness, we are unprofitable servants; although, in some respects, and to our fellow-beings, we may have been profitable. I trust, my dear friend, you are looking for the mercy of God, through our Lord Jesus Christ, unto eternal life. Death is not an eternal sleep; no, it is the gate to life. It opens up a blessed immortality to all who, in this world, have feared God and wrought righteousness. This world is a probationary state; if we have been faithful, in some humble degree, to our convictions of duty; if we have regretted our follies and sins; if we have sought to do the will of our heavenly Father, and sought forgiveness through the mediation of his Son, — God will receive us to his heavenly glory. I believe, in his own good time, he will receive you, my very dear friend; although my prayer is, with submission, that he will restore you to comfortable health, and allow you to remain with us a little longer. May God be with you, and bless you, in life, in death, and forevermore! With most respectful regard to Mrs. L., and sympathy with you in your afflictions, in which my dear wife joins, I am truly yours, DANIEL SHARP."

From Little Nahant, Mr. Lawrence writes to a friend, under date of Aug. 16:

"I have just arisen from bed, and am full of the matter to tell you how much good your letter has done. I came here as the last remedy for a sinking man; and, blessed be God, it promises me renewed life and enjoyment. What is it for, that I am thus saved in life, as by a miracle? Surely it must be in mercy, to finish out my work begun (in your college and other places), yet unfinished. Pray, give us what time you can when you visit Andover. If I continue to improve as I have done for ten days, I hope to return home next week; but may have some drawback that will alter the whole aspect of affairs. This beautiful Little Nahant seems to have been purchased, built up, and provided, by the good influence of our merciful Father in heaven upon the heart of ——, that he might save me from death, when it was made certain I could not hold out many days longer. Surely I am called on by angel voices to render praise to God."

The five weeks' residence upon the sea-shore was greatly enjoyed by Mr. Lawrence. As the weather was generally fine, much of his time was passed in the open air, in watching the ever-varying sea-views, in reading, or in receiving the visits of his friends. Near the end of August, his health and strength had become so far restored as to warrant his return to the city, and, as his memoranda show, to increased efforts in the field of charity.

CHAPTER XXXII.

AMIN BEY. — AMOUNT OF DONATIONS TO WILLIAMS COLLEGE.

In November, 1850, Amin Bey, Envoy from the Sultan of Turkey to the United States, visited Boston. Among other attentions, Mr. Lawrence accompanied him on a visit to the Female Orphan Asylum, then containing about one hundred inmates; and the pleasant intercourse was continued by a visit of the minister at Mr. Lawrence's house.

The following note accompanied a number of volumes relating to Boston and its vicinity:

(TO HIS EXCELLENCY AMIN BEY.)

"My Brother: The manifest pleasure you felt in visiting our Female Orphan Asylum yesterday has left a sunbeam on my path, that will illumine my journey to our Father's house. When we meet there, may the joy of that reünion you hope for with the loved ones in your own country be yours and mine, and all the good of all the world be our companions for all time! With the highest respect, believe me your friend, A. L."

(TO PRESIDENT HOPKINS.

"Boston, November 11, 1850.

"My dear Friend: My brief letter of introduction by my young friend S., and your answer to it, which I mislaid or lost soon after it came, has made me feel a wish to write every day since the first week after I received yours. S. made me out better than I was when he saw me. I could walk across the rooms, get down and up stairs without much aid, and bear my weight on each foot; having strength in my ankle-bones that enabled me to enter the temple walking, not leaping, but praising God. If ever I am able to walk so far as around the Common, what gratitude to God should I feel to take your arm as my support! I am frequently admonished by faint turns that I am merely a 'minute-man,' liable to be called for at any moment. Only a few days since, I had a charming call from Amin Bey and suite, whom I received in my parlors below, where were some friends to meet him. All seemed interested, and Amin as much so as a Turk ever does. When he left us, I went with him to the door, saw him out and in his carriage, turned to open the inner entry-door, became faint just as M. was leaving the party, and leaned on her to get into the parlor. I was laid on the sofa, insensible for a short time, but, by labor, abstinence, and great care, for two or three days, have got upon my high horse again, and rode with N. to make calls upon the good people of Cambridge. After dinner, when I awoke, I tried to go about my work, but was called off again, and, from that time to this, have been up a little, and then down a little; thus asking me, with angels' voices, Why are you left here? The answer is plain: You have more work to do. Pray, my dear friend, for me to be faithful while my powers are left with me. The reports of and from your college make me feel that my labors in helping it to get on its legs have been repaid four-fold. I am its debtor, and will allow the money out of the next year's income to be used for a telescope, if you deem it best. I have made no further inquiry for the one in progress here, but will ask W. to look and see what progress is making.

When I leave off writing, I shall ride to the office in Court-square, and deposit my Whig vote for Governor Briggs and the others. We are so mixed up here as hardly to know who are supporters of the regular ticket, and who not. This fugitive-slave business will keep our people excited till the law is blotted out. In some of our best circles the law is pronounced unconstitutional; and my belief is that Franklin Dexter's argument on that point will settle the question by starting it, our great men to the contrary notwithstanding."

In the above letter Mr. Lawrence speaks of the gratification which he had derived from the results of his efforts in behalf of Williams College; and, as there may be no more fitting place to give an account of these efforts, the following record is here introduced, from the pen of President Hopkins. It is found in his sermon commemorative of the donor, delivered at the request of the students, on February 21, 1853.

"In October, 1841, the building known as the East College was burned. Needy as the institution was before, this rendered necessary an application to the Legislature for funds; and, when this failed, to the public at large. Owing to a panic in the money market, this application was but slightly responded to, except in this town. In Boston the sum raised was less than two thousand dollars; and the largest sum given by any individual was one hundred dollars. This sum was given by Mr. Lawrence, who was applied to by a friend of the college; and this, it is believed, was the only application ever made to him on our behalf. This directed his attention to the wants of the college; but nothing more was heard from him till January, 1844. At that time, I was delivering a course of the Lowell Lectures, in Boston, when his son, Mr. Amos A. Lawrence, called and informed me that his father had five thousand dollars which he wished to place at the disposal of the college. As I was previously but slightly acquainted with Mr. Lawrence, and had had no conversation with him on the subject, this was to me an entire surprise; and, embarrassed as the institution then was by its debt for the new buildings, the relief and encouragement which it brought to my own mind, and to the minds of others, friends of the college, can hardly be expressed. Still, this did not wholly remove the debt. On hearing this casually mentioned, he said, if he had known how we were situated, he thought he should have given us more; and the following July, without another word on the subject, he sent me a check for five thousand dollars. This put the college out of debt, and added two or three thousand dollars to its available funds. In January, 1846, he wrote, saying he wished to see me; and, on meeting him, he said his object was to consult me about the disposition of ten thousand dollars, which he proposed to give the college. He wished to know how I thought it would do the most good. I replied, at once, By being placed at the disposal of the trustees, to be used at their discretion. He said. 'Very well;' and that was all that passed on that point. So I thought; and, knowing his simplicity of character, and singleness of purpose, I felt no embarrassment in making that reply. Here was a beautiful exemplification of the precept of the apostle, 'He that giveth, let him do it with simplicity.' Such a man had a right to have, for one of his mottoes, 'Deeds, not words.' This was just what was needed; but it gave us some breadth and enlargement, and was a beginning in what it had long been felt must, sooner or later, be undertaken,— the securing of an available fund suitable as a basis for such an institution. His next large gift was the library. This came from his asking me, as I was riding with him the following winter, if we wanted anything. Nothing occurred to me at the time, and I replied in the negative; but, the next day, I remembered that the trustees had voted to build a library, provided the treasurer should find it could be done for twenty-five hundred dollars. This I mentioned to him. He inquired what I supposed it would cost. I replied, 'Five thousand dollars.' He said, at once, 'I will give it.' With his approbation, the plan of a building was subsequently adopted that would cost seven thousand dollars; and he paid that sum. A year or two subsequently, he inquired of me the price of tuition here, saying he should like to connect Groton Academy with Williams College; and he paid two thousand dollars to establish four scholarships for any one who might come from that institution. His next gift was the telescope, which cost about fifteen hundred dollars. The history of this would involve some details which I have not now time to give. In 1851, accompanied by Mrs. Lawrence, he made a visit here. This was the first time either of them had seen the place. In walking over the grounds, he said they had great capabilities, but that we needed more land; and authorized the purchase of an adjoining piece of four acres. This purchase was made for one thousand dollars; and, if the college can have the means of laying it out, and adorning it suitably, it will, besides furnishing scope for exercise, be a fit addition of the charms of culture to great beauty of natural scenery. In addition to these gifts, he has, at different times, enriched the library with costly books, of the expense of which I know nothing. Almost everything we have in the form of art was given by him. In December, 1845, I received a letter from him, dated the 22d, or 'Forefathers' Day,' which enclosed one hundred dollars, to be used for the aid of needy students in those emergencies which often arise. This was entirely at his own suggestion; and nothing could have been more timely or appropriate in an institution like this, where so many young men are struggling to make their own way. Since that time, he has furnished me with at least one hundred dollars annually for that purpose; and he regarded the expenditure with much interest. Thus, in different ways, Mr. Lawrence had given to the college between thirty and forty thousand dollars; and he had expressed the purpose, if he should live, of aiding it still further. Understanding as he did the position and wants of this college, he sympathized fully with the trustees in their purpose to raise the sum of fifty thousand dollars, and, at the time of his death, was exerting a most warm-hearted and powerful influence for its accomplishment. In reference to this great effort, we feel that a strong helper is taken away. The aid which Mr. Lawrence thus gave to the college was great and indispensable; and probably no memorial of him will be more enduring than what he has done here. By this, being dead, he yet speaks, and will continue to speak in all coming time. From him will flow down enjoyment and instruction to those who shall walk these grounds, and look at the heavens through this telescope, and read the books gathered in this library, and hear instruction from teachers sustained, wholly or in part, by his bounty. Probably he could not have spent this money more usefully; and there is reason to believe that he could have spent it in no way to bring to himself more enjoyment. The prosperity of the college was a source of great gratification to him; and he said, more than once, that he had been many times repaid for what he had done here. That he should have thus done what he did unsolicited, and that he — and, I may add, his family — should have continued to find in it so much of satisfaction, is most grateful to my own feelings, and must be so to every friend of the college. In doing it, he seemed to place himself in the relation, not so much of a patron of the college, as of a sympathizer and helper in a great and good work."

CHAPTER XXXIII.

LETTERS. — DIARY.

At the beginning of the year 1851, Mr. Lawrence writes to President Hopkins:

"The closing of the old year was like our western horizon after sunset, bright and beautiful; the opening of the new, radiant with life, light, and hope, and crowned with such a costume of love as few old fathers, grandfathers, and uncles, can muster; in short, my old sleigh is the pet of the season, and rarely appears without being well filled, outside and inside. It is a teacher to the school-children, no less than to my grandchildren; for they all understand that, if they are well-behaved, they can ride with me when I make the signal; and I have a strong persuasion that this attention to them, with a present of a book and a kind word now and then, makes the little fellows think more of their conduct and behavior. At any rate, it does me good to hear them call out, 'How do you do, Mr. Lawrence?' as I am driving along the streets and by-ways of the city."   *   *   *

To an aged clergyman in the country, who was blind and in indigent circumstances, he writes:

"Jan. 14.

"Your letter of last week reached me on Saturday, and was indeed a sunbeam, which quickened me to do what I had intended for a 'happy new-year,' before receiving yours. I trust you will have received a parcel sent by railroad, on Monday, directed to you, and containing such things as I deemed to be useful in your family; and I shall be more than paid, if they add one tint to the 'purple light' you speak of, that opens upon your further hopes of visiting us the coming season. For many months I was unable to walk; but my feet and ankle-bones have now received strength. I feel that the prayers of friends have been answered by my renewed power to do more work. How, then, can I enjoy life better than by distributing the good things intrusted to me among those who are comforted by receiving them? So you need not feel, my friend, that you are any more obliged than I am. The enclosed bank-bills may serve to fit up the materials for use; at any rate, will not be out of place in your pocket. I trust to see you again in this world, which has to me so many interesting connecting links between the first and only time I have ever seen you (thirty-five or more years ago, in Dr. Huntington's pulpit, Old South Church) and the present."

(FROM REV. JAMES HAMILTON, D.D.)

"42 GOWER-STREET, LONDON, Feb. 15, 1851.

"MY DEAR SIR: No letter which authorship has brought to me ever gave me such pleasure as I received from yours of July, 1849, enclosing one which Governor Briggs had written to you. That strangers so distinguished should take such interest in my writings, and should express yourselves so kindly towards myself, overwhelmed me with a pleasing surprise, and with thankfulness to God who had given me such favor. I confess, too, it helped to make me love more the country which has always been to me the dearest next to my own. In conjunction with some much-prized friendships which I have formed among your ministers, it would almost tempt me to cross the Atlantic. But I am so bad a sailor that I fear I must postpone personal intercourse with those American friends who do not come to England, until we reach the land where there is no more sea. However feebly expressed, please accept my heartfelt thanks for all the cost and trouble you have incurred in circulating my publications. It is pleasant to me to think that your motive in distributing them, in the first instance, could not be friendship for the author; and to both of us it will be the most welcome result, if they promote the cause of practical Christianity. Owing to weakness in the throat and chest, I cannot preach so much as many of my neighbors, and therefore I feel the more anxious that my tracts should do something for the honor of the Saviour and the welfare of mankind. You were kind enough to reprint my last lecture to young men. I could scarcely wish the same distinction bestowed on its successor, because it is a fragment. I have some thoughts of extending it into a short exposition of Ecclesiastes, which is a book well suited to the times, and but little understood. * * *

"Yours, most truly, JAMES HAMILTON."

In reply to the above letter, Mr. Lawrence writes, April 8:

"I will not attempt to express to you in words my pleasure in receiving your letter of Feb. 15, with its accompaniments. The lecture delivered to the young men on the 4th of February, although designated by you as a fragment, I sent to my friend, with a copy of your letter, asking him whether he would advise its publication, and whether he would scatter it with its predecessor; and, if so, I would pay the expense. His answer you have here, and I have the pleasure of saying that the 'Fragment' will be ready to circulate by thousands the present week;

and, when you shall have added your further comments upon Solomon and his works, our American Tract Society will be ready to publish the whole by hundreds of thousands, I trust, thus enabling you to preach through our whole country. The Memoir of Lady Colquhon is a precious jewel, which I shall keep among my treasures to leave my descendants. I had previously purchased a number of copies of the American edition, and scattered them among my friends, so that there is great interest to see your copy sent me. The part of your letter which touched my heart most was that in which you speak of my brother Abbott, and say of him that 'no foreign minister is such a favorite with the British public.' It brought him before me like a daguerreotype likeness, through every period of his life for fifty years. First, as the guiding spirit of the boys of our neighborhood, in breaking through the deep snow-drifts which often blocked up the roads in winter; then as my apprentice in the city; and, in a few years, as the young military champion, to watch night and day, under arms, on the point of Bunker Hill nearest the ocean, the movements of a British fleet lying within four or five miles of him, and threatening the storming of Boston; then, soon after, as embarking in the very first ship for England, after the close of the war, to purchase goods, which were received here in eighty-three days after he sailed. Since that time, our firm has never been changed, except by adding '& Co.,' when other partners were admitted. He has been making his way to the people's respect and affection from that time to this, and now fills the only public station I would not have protested against his accepting, feeling that *place* cannot impart *grace*. My prayers ascend continually for him, that he may do his work under the full impression that he must give an account to Him whose eye is constantly upon him, and whose 'Well done' will be infinitely better than all things else. I believe he is awakening an interest to learn more about this country; and the people will be amazed to see what opportunities are here enjoyed for happiness for the great mass. What we most fear is *that* ignorance which will bring everything down to its own level, instead of that true knowledge, which shall level up the lowest places, now inundated with foreign emigrants. Our duty is plain; and, if we do not educate and elevate this class of our people, they will change our system of government within fifty years. Virtue and intelligence are the basis of this government; and the duty of all good men is to keep it pure. * * *

" And now, my friend, what can I say that will influence you to come here, and enjoy with me the beautiful scenes upon and around our Mount Zion?

" With the highest respect and affection, I am most truly yours,

"AMOS LAWRENCE.

" P. S. — Mrs. L. desires me to present to you and your lady her most respectful regard, with the assurance that your writings are very precious to her. She is a granddaughter to a clergyman of your ' Kirk,' and enjoys much its best writings."

To the same gentleman he writes soon after :

" And now let me speak about the ' Royal Preacher.' * I expected much, but not so much as I found in it. We, on this side the Atlantic, thank you ; and the pictures of some of our own great men are drawn to the life, although their history and character could not have been in your eye. Truth is the same now as in Solomon's time ; and it is surprising that the mass of men do not see and acknowledge that ' the saint is greater than

---

* A tract by Dr. Hamilton.

the sage, and discipleship to Jesus the pinnacle of human dignity. I have had, this morning, two calls, from different sections of our Union, for your 'Life in Earnest,' 'Literary Attractions of the Bible,' 'Solomon,' 'Redeemed in Glory,' &c., which I responded to with hearty good-will. Some of the books will go out of the country many thousand miles, and will do good. I must shake hands with you across the Atlantic, if you can't 'screw up' your courage to come here, and bid you God-speed in all your broad plans for the good of your fellow-men.

"I have a great respect for deep religious feelings, even when I cannot see as my friends do; and therefore pray God to clear away, in his good time, all that is now dark and veiled.

"It is time for me to say farewell."

CHAPTER XXXIV.

SIR T. F. BUXTON. — LETTER FROM LADY BUXTON. — ELLIOTT CRESSON. — LETTERS.

AFTER the death of Sir Thomas Fowell Buxton, Mr. Lawrence had read what had been published respecting his life and character, and had formed an exalted opinion of his labors in behalf of the African race. A small volume had been issued, entitled "A Study for Young Men, or a Sketch of Sir T. F. Buxton," by Rev. T. Binney, of London Mr. Lawrence had purchased and circulated large numbers of this work, which recorded the deeds of one upon whom he considered the mantle of Wilberforce to have fallen; and, through a mutual friend, he had been made known to Lady Buxton, who writes to him as follows .

"Very, very grateful am I for your love for him, and, through him, to me and my children. I desire that you may be enriched by all spiritual blessings; and that, through languor and illness and infirmity, the Lord may bless and prosper you and the work of your hands. I beg your acceptance of the third edition, in the large octavo, of the memoir of Sir Fowell."

Those who have read the memoir referred to will

remember the writer, before her marriage, as Miss Hannah Gurney, a member of that distinguished family of Friends of which Mrs. Fry was the elder sister. During the remaining short period of Mr. Lawrence's life, a pleasant correspondence was kept up, from which a few extracts will hereafter be given.

To Elliott Cresson, of Philadelphia, the enthusiastic and veteran champion of the colonization cause, Mr. Lawrence writes, June 12, 1851·

"MY DEAR OLD FRIEND CRESSON: I have just re-read your kind letter of June 2, and have been feasting upon the treasure you sent me in the interesting volume entitled 'Africa Redeemed.' I will set your heart at rest at once by assuring you that I feel just as you do towards that land. Do you remember visiting me, a dozen or more years ago, to get me to lead off with a thousand-dollar subscription for colonization, and my refusing by assuring you that I would not interfere with the burden of slavery, then pressing on our own Slave States, until requested by them? * * * * Liberia, in the mean time, has gone on, and now promises to be to the black man what New England has been to the Pilgrims, and Pennsylvania to the Friends. I say, with all my heart, to Gov. Roberts and his associates, God speed you, and carry onward and upward the glorious work of redeeming Africa! I had a charming message from a young missionary in Africa a few days since,— the Rev. Mr. Hoffman, of the Episcopal Mission; and you will be glad to hear that the good work of education for Liberia progresses surely and steadily here. My son A. is one of the trustees and directors (Prof. Greenleaf is president), and has given a thousand dollars from 'a young merchant;' and I bid him give another thousand from 'an old merchant,' which he will do as soon as he returns from our old home with his family. Now I say to you, my friend, I can sympathize and work with you while I am spared. God be praised! we are greatly favored in many things. No period of my life has been more joyous.

"With constant affection, I am yours,

"AMOS LAWRENCE."

Among other memoranda of the present month is found a cancelled note of five hundred dollars, which had been given by a clergyman in another State to a corporation, which, by reason of various misfortunes, he had not been able to pay. Mr. Lawrence had heard of the circumstance, and, without the knowledge of the clergyman, had sent the required sum to the treasurer of the corporation, with directions to cancel the obligation.

(TO LADY BUXTON.)

"BOSTON, July 8, 1851.

"DEAR LADY BUXTON: Your letter, and the beautiful copy of the memoir of your revered and world-wide honored husband, reached me on the 26th of June. I have read and re-read your heart-touching note with an interest you can understand better than I can describe. I can say that I thank you, and leave you to imagine the rest. Sir Fowell was born the same year, and in the same month, that I was; and his character and his labors I have been well acquainted with since he came into public life; and no man of his time stood higher in my confidence and respect Although I have never been in public life, I have been much interested in public men; and have sometimes had my confidence abused, but have generally given it to men who said what they meant, and did what they said. I feel no respect for the demagogue, however successful he may be; but am able to say, with the dear and honored friend whose mantle fell upon Sir Fowell, 'What shadows we are, and what shadows we pursue!' I feel pity for the man who sacrifices his hopes of heaven for such vain objects as end in the mere gaze of this world. The 'Study for Young Men,' republished here a short time since, is doing such work among us as must cheer the spirit of your husband in his heavenly home.

"I enclose you a note from Laura Bridgman, a deaf, dumb, and blind girl, who has been educated at our asylum for the last twelve years or more (now about twenty-two years old), which may interest you from the fact of her extraordinary situation.

"With great respect, I remain most truly yours,
"AMOS LAWRENCE."

(TO A LADY IN PHILADELPHIA.)

"DEAR L.: Your call on me to 'pay up' makes me feel that I had forgotten, and therefore neglected, my promise. I begin without preface. When a child, and all the way up to fifty years of age, the incidents of revolutionary history were so often talked over by the old soldiers who made our house their rendezvous whenever they came near it, that I feel as if I had been an actor in the scenes described. Among these, the Battle of Bunker Hill was more strongly impressed upon my mind than any other event. My father, then twenty-one years old, was in Captain Farwell's company, a subaltern, full of the right spirit, as you may know, having some sparks left when you used to ride on his sled and in his wagon, and eat his 'rattle apples,' which were coveted by all the children. He was in the breastwork; and his captain was shot through the body just before or just after Pitcairn was shot. My father did not know Major Pitcairn personally, but understood it was he who mounted the breastwork, calling to his soldiers to follow, when he pitched into the slight trench outside, riddled and dead, as my father always thought as long as he lived. But it turned out otherwise. He was brought from the field, and lodged in a house in Prince-street, now standing (the third from Charlestown Bridge); and the intelligence was immediately communicated to the Governor, then in the Royal House, now called the Province House. He sent Dr. Kast and an officer, accompanied by young Bowdoin as an amateur, to see to the major, and report. On entering the chamber, the doctor wished to examine the wound; but Pitcairn declined allowing him, saying it was of no use, as he should soon die. When pressed by the argument that his excellency desired it, he allowed Dr. Kast to open his vest, and the blood, which had been stanched, spirted out upon the floor; so that the room carried the mark, and was called 'Pitcairn's Chamber' until long after the peace. The doctor returned immediately to the Governor to report; and, before he could get back, life had fled. He was laid out in his regimentals, and was deposited in the vault of St. George's Church, now the Stone Chapel, and there remained until 1788, when Dr. Winship, of Roxbury, then on a visit to London, had occasion to call on Dr. C. Letsom, and informed him that he had in his possession the key of the vault; that he had examined the body, which was in so good a state of preservation, that he recognized the features; and that he had counted at least thirty marks of musket-balls in various parts of the body. An arrangement was made, through Dr. Winship, for the removal of the body to England. Dr. William Pitcairn built a vault in the Burying-ground of St. Bartholomew, near the hospital, for its reception. Capt. James Scott, the commander of a trading vessel between Boston and London at that period, undertook the service of removal, although he foresaw difficulty in undertaking the business, on account of the strong prejudice of sailors to having a corpse on board. With a view to concealment, the coffin was enclosed in a square deal case, containing the church-organ, which was to be sent to England for repairs. This case, with 'Organ' inscribed upon it, was placed, as it was said, for better security, in a part of the ship near the sailors' berths, and in that situation was used occasionally during the passage for their seat or table. On arrival of the ship in the river, an order was obtained for the landing of the case; and, as it was necessary to describe its contents, the order expressed permission to land a corpse. This revealed the stratagem of Capt. Scott, and raised such a feeling among the sailors as to show that they would not have been quiet had they known the truth respecting their fellow-lodger. Major Pitcairn was the only British officer particularly regarded by our citizens, as ready to listen to their complaints, and, as far as in his power, to relieve them, when not impeded by his military duties. Our excellent old friend B. will be interested in the 'Stone Chapel' part of this story, and probably can add particulars that I may have omitted.

"Your affectionate   Amos Lawrence."

CHAPTER XXXV.

LETTERS — REV. DR. SCORESBY. — WABASH COLLEGE.

AFTER receiving a note from a relative of Lady Colebrooke, announcing her death, at Dunscombe, in the island of Barbadoes, Mr. Lawrence wrote the following note of sympathy to her husband, Sir William Colebrooke, then Governor of that island. She will be remembered as the lady who had formerly visited Boston, and who was alluded to in one of his letters, as a niece of Major André:

"DEAR SIR WILLIAM: I lose no time in expressing to you the feelings of my heart, on reading the brief notice of the last hours of dear Lady Colebrooke. All my recollections and associations of her are of the most interesting character; and for yourself I feel more than a common regard. We may never meet again in this world; but it matters little, if, when we are called off, we are found 'in line,' and ready to receive the cheering 'Well done' when we reach that better world we hope for. I trust that you, and all your dear ones, have been in the hollow of our Father's hand, through the shadings of his face from you; and that, in his own good time, all will be cleared away.

"Faithfully and respectfully yours, AMOS LAWRENCE.
"BOSTON, Aug. 8, 1851."

(TO THE HON. CHARLES B. HADDOCK, MINISTER OF THE UNITED STATES TO PORTUGAL.)

"BOSTON, Aug. 19, 1851.

"DEAR AND KIND-HEARTED FRIEND: Your letters to me before leaving the country, and after reaching England, awakened many tender remembrances of times past, and agreeable hopes of times to come. In that, I felt as though I had you by the hand, with that encouraging 'Go forward' in the fear of God, and confidence in his fatherly care and guidance. I know your views have always put this trust at the head of practical duties, and that you will go forward in your present duties, and do better service to the country than any man who could be sent. Portugal is a sealed book, in a great degree, to us. Who so able to unlock and lay open its history as yourself? Now, then, what leisure you have may be most profitably applied to the spreading out the treasures before us; and, my word for it, your reputation as a writer and a thinker will make whatever you may publish of this sort desirable to be read by the great mass of our reading population.

*   *   *   *   *   *

"I hold that God has given us our highest enjoyments, in every period, from childhood to old age, in the exercise of our talents and our feelings with reference to his presence and oversight; and that, at any moment, he may call us off, and that we may thus be left to be among the children of light or of darkness, according to his word and our preparation. These enjoyments of childhood, of middle age, of mature life, and of old age, are all greatly increased by a constant reference to the source from whence they come; and the danger of great success in life is more to be feared, in our closing account, than anything else. A brief space will find us in the earth, and of no further consequence than as we shall have marked for good the generation of men growing up to take our places. The title of an honest man, who feared God, is worth more than all the honors and distinction of the world. Pray, let me hear from you, and the dear lady, whom I hope to escort once more over the sides of our Mount Zion, and introduce to some of my children and grandchildren settled upon the borders; and, if any stranger coming this way from you will accept such facilities as I can give to our institutions, I shall gladly render them. It is now many years since I have sat at table with my family, and I am now better than I have been at any time during that period; in short, I am light-hearted as a child, and enjoy the children's society with all the zest of early days. I must say, 'God speed you, my friend,' and have you constantly in the hollow of his hand! In all kind remembrances, Mrs. L. joins me, to your lady and yourself.

"Faithfully and respectfully your friend,

"AMOS LAWRENCE."

On the same day that the preceding letter was penned, Mr. Lawrence, in acknowledgment of some work sent to him by the Rev. Dr. Scoresby, of Bradford, England, wrote the following letter. That gentleman had visited this country twice, and had made many friends in Boston. Once an Arctic traveller, and a man of great scientific acquirement, he has now become an eminent and active clergyman in the Church of England, and has devoted all his energies to the task of elevating the lower orders of the population where his field of labor has been cast.

"Boston, Aug. 19, 1851.

"My dear Friend: Your letter from Torquay, of ninth July, reached me on the sixth of this month. It brought to memory our agreeable intercourse of former years, and cheered me with the hope that I might again see you in this world, and again shake your hand in that cordial, social way that goes direct to the heart. I had been much interested in the account brought by ——, and in your kind messages by him. Your memorials of your father interest me exceedingly, and I thank you most sincerely for the volume and the sermon you sent. This sermon I sent to a friend of mine, and also a friend of yours, who became such after hearing you preach in Liverpool. Professor ——, of —— College, is a most talented, efficient, and popular teacher; and his present position he has attained by his industry and his merit. He was a poor youth, in Liverpool, who followed you in your preaching; came here, and went as an apprentice to a mechanical business; was noticed as a bright fellow; was educated by persons assisting him, and graduated at —— College. He became a tutor, and is now a professor, and is an honor to the college and his nation. We are all at work in New England, and now feel a twinge from too fast driving in some branches of business; but, in the aggregate, our country is rapidly advancing in wealth, power, and strength, notwithstanding the discontent of our Southern brethren. We have allowed the 'black spot' to be too far spread over our land; it should have been restrained more than thirty years ago, and then our old Slave States would have had no just cause of complaint. I am called off, and must bid you farewell, with kind regards of Mrs. L., and my own most faithful and affectionate remembrance.   Amos Lawrence.

"Rev. William Scoresby, D.D., Torquay, Devonshire, Eng."

(TO PRESIDENT HOPKINS.)

"BOSTON, Nov. 15, 1851.

"MY DEAR FRIEND: This is a rainy day, which keeps me housed; and, to improve it in 'pursuit,' I have a bundle made up, of the size of a small 'haycock,' and directed to you by railroad, with a few lines enclosed for the amusement of the children. I have told A. and L. that they couldn't jump over it; but H. could, by having a clear course of two rods. Louis Dwight has spent a half-hour with me this morning, exhibiting and explaining his plan for the new Lunatic Asylum of the State, which I think is the best model I have ever seen, and is a decided improvement on all our old ones. The committee, of which Governor Briggs is chairman, will give it a careful consideration and comparison with Dr. Bell's, and perhaps Dr. Butler's and others; and, with such an amount of talent and experience, the new asylum will be the best, I trust, that there is on this side of the Atlantic. Louis Dwight is in fine spirits, and in full employ in his peculiar line. The new institution in New York for vagrant children will very likely be built on his plan. He is really doing his work most successfully, in classing and separating these young sinners, so that they may be reclaimed, and trained to become useful citizens; in that light, he is a public benefactor. * * *

"Faithfully and affectionately yours,

"AMOS LAWRENCE."

In a letter to a friend, written on Sunday, and within a few days of the preceding, Mr. Lawrence says, after describing one of his severe attacks:

"I am not doing wrong, I think, in consecrating a part of the day to you, being kept within doors by one of those kindly admonitions which speaks through the body, and tells me that my home here is no shelter from the storm. I had been unusually well for some weeks past, and it seemed to me that my days passed with a rapidity and joyousness that nothing short of the intercourse with the loved ones around me could have caused. What can be more emphatic, until my final summons? If my work is done, and well done, I should not dread the summons; pray that it may be, and that we may meet again after a brief separation. I am hoping to be safely housed by and by where cold and heat, splendid furniture, luxurious living, and handsome houses, and attendants, will all be thought of as they really merit."

Mr. Lawrence had, for a considerable time, been interested in the Wabash College, at Crawfordsville, Indiana; and, on the 24th of November, announced to the Trustees a donation from Mrs. L. of twelve hundred dollars, to found four free scholarships for the use of the academy at Groton. He adds:

"I would recommend that candidates for the scholarships who abstain from the use of intoxicating drinks and tobacco always have a preference. This is not to be taken as a prohibition, but only as a condition to give a preference."

Mr. Lawrence speaks of his interest in Wabash College, growing out of his affection and respect for its President, the Rev. Charles White, D.D., who went from New England, and with whom he had become acquainted during a visit which that gentleman had made to his native State. Eight days after this donation to Wabash College, Mr. Lawrence enclosed to Rev. Dr. Pond, of the Theological School at Bangor, Maine, the sum of five hundred dollars; which he says, with other sums already subscribed by others for new professorships, would "prove a great blessing to all who resort to the institution through all time."

CHAPTER XXXVI.

DIARY — AMOUNT OF CHARITIES. — LETTERS. — THOMAS TARBELL. — UNCLE TOBY. — REV. DR. LOWELL.

"*January* 1, 1852. — The value of my property is somewhat more than it was a year ago, and I pray God that I may be faithful in its use. My life seems now more likely to be spared for a longer season than for many years past; and I never enjoyed myself more highly. Praise the Lord, O my soul!

"P. S. — The outgoes for all objects since January 1, 1842 (ten years), have been six hundred and four thousand dollars, more than five sixths of which have been applied in making other people happy; and it is no trouble to find objects for all I have to spare."

This sum, in addition to the subscriptions and donations for the year 1852, makes the amount of his expenditures for charitable purposes, during the last eleven years of his life, to be about five hundred and twenty-five thousand dollars. From 1829 to 1842, the sum expended for like appropriations was, according to his memoranda, one hundred and fourteen thousand dollars; making, for the last twenty-three years of his life the sum of six hundred and thirty-nine thousand dollars expended in charity. Taking the amount of his property at various times, as noted by himself, from the year 1807 to 1829, a period of twenty-two years, with his known liberality and habits of systematic charity, it would be safe to assert that during his life he expended seven hundred thousand dollars for the benefit of his fellow-men. Many persons have done more; but few perhaps have done as much in proportion to the means which they had to bestow.

In a letter to President Hopkins, dated March 31, Mr. Lawrence writes:

"I am interested in everything you write about in your last letter; but among the items of deepest interest is the fact of the religious feeling manifested by the young men; and I pray God it may take deep root, and grow, and become the controlling power in forming their character for immortality. I trust they will count the cost, and act consistently. May God speed them in this holy work!"

A few days later, he writes on the same subject:

"And now let us turn to matters of more importance; the awakening of the young men of your college to their highest interest,— the salvation of their souls. I have been moved to tears in reading the simple statement of the case, and I pray God to perfect the good work thus begun. I have much to think of to-day, this being my sixty-sixth birth-day. The question comes home to me, What I am rendering to the Lord for all his benefits; and the answer of conscience is, Imperfect service. If accepted, it will be through mercy; and, with this feeling of hope, I keep about, endeavoring to scatter good seed as I go forth in my daily ministrations."

The following correspondence was not received in time to be placed in the order of its date, but is now given as an illustration of Mr. Lawrence's views on some important points, and also as an instance of his self-control. In the autumn of 1847, he became acquainted with the Rev. Dr. ——, a Scotch Presbyterian clergyman, then on a visit to some friends in Boston. During a drive in the environs, with this gentleman and the Rev. Dr. Blagden, Mr. Lawrence made a remark of a practical nature upon some religious topic, which did not coincide with the views of his Scotch friend; and a debate ensued, which was characterized by somewhat more of warmth than was warranted by the nature of the subject. Mutual explanations and apologies followed, and the correspondence, which was continued after the return of Dr. —— to Scotland, shows that the discussion on the occasion referred to had caused no diminution of their mutual regard or good-will.

The Rev. Dr. Blagden, in a note to the editor, dated Boston, April 18, 1855, writes as follows:

"As the result of our incidental conversation on Monday last, let me say, that the facts of which we spoke occurred during a drive which the Rev. Dr. ——, of Scotland, and I were enjoying with your father, in his carriage, at his kind invitation, in October, 1847.

"Without being able to recall the precise connection in which the remarks were made, I only now remember that Mr. Lawrence was led to speak with some degree of warmth, but with entire kindness, on the great error of relying on any idea of justification before God by faith, without corresponding works; so that, to one not familiar with the religious events in the history of this community, which, by operating on Mr. Lawrence's habits of thought, might well lead him to be jealous of any view of faith which did not directly express the necessity of good works, his remarks might very readily have seemed like a direct attack on that great truth of justification by faith, which Luther affirmed to be, as it was held or rejected, the test of a falling or rising church.

"Immediately, that which the late Edward Irving, in one of his sermons, under the name of 'Orations,' calls the 'ingenium perfervidum Scotorum,' burst from the Rev. Dr. ——, with something of that zeal for the doctrines of Knox and Calvin for which I understand he has been somewhat remarkable in his own country. He vehemently declared his abhorrence of any such denial of the first and fundamental truth of the Gospel, evidently taking it somewhat in the light of an insult to us as the preachers of that truth. He ended by saying, with much force and warmth, that the apostle Paul sometimes condensed the whole of the Gospel into a single phrase; and one of these phrases, as expressed in the Epistle to the Philippians, he commended to the notice of Mr. Lawrence, namely, 'We are the circumcision which worship God in the spirit; and rejoice in Christ Jesus, and have no confidence in the flesh.'

"Mr. Lawrence met this strong, and apparently indignant and truly honest expression of feeling, with entire courtesy and self-command, but with evident and deep emotion; and, repressing all expression of displeasure, he gradually led the conversation to less unwelcome subjects, so that our ride ended pleasantly, though the embarrassment created by this event continued, in a lessening degree, to its close.

"It will probably add to the interest of the whole transaction, in your own mind, if I state, not only what you seemed aware of on Monday, that your father sent me, a day or two after, 'Barr's Help' (I believe is the name of the volume), with a very kind and polite note, alluding to what had passed, and a paper containing some development of his own religious belief; but Rev. Dr. ———, also, soon after, in alluding to the circumstances in a note to me, on another subject, and which is now before me, wrote:

"'I regret the warmth with which I did so. Alas! it is my infirmity; but it was only a momentary flash, for I was enabled, through a silent act of prayer, to get my mind purged of all heat, before I ventured to resume the conversation on the vital topic which our good and kind friend himself was led to introduce.'

"I suspect this will reach you at an hour too late entirely for the use which you thought might possibly be made of it. It may, however, have some little interest, as a further development of the excellent character of your father; and it refers to a scene of which I have never been in the habit of speaking to others, but which I shall always remember with great interest, as one among many pleasing and profitable recollections of him."

The following extracts are taken from the paper referred to in the preceding communication:

"Boston, November 4, 1847.
"To Rev. G. W. Blagden, D.D.

"Rev. and dear Sir: Our interesting ride last Thursday has peculiar claims upon me as a teacher and a preacher for a better world. To one who knows me well, my unceremonious manner to our friend would not seem so strange; but it was none the less unkind in me to treat him thus.

"My first impressions are generally the right ones, and govern the actions of daily and hourly experience here; and these impressions were entirely favorable to our friend; and my treatment, up to the moment that you 'poured your oil upon the waters,' had been such as I am now well pleased with. But the conversation then commenced; and the lecture, illustrations, arguments, and consequences, were all stereotyped in my mind, having been placed there twenty-seven years ago by a learned and pious Scotchman, whose character came back to my memory like a flash of light. It is enough to say that a multitude of matters wholly adverse to my first impressions left me no command of my courtesies; and I stopped the conversation.   *   *   *

"I believe that our Saviour came among men to do them good, and, having performed his mission, has returned to his Father and to our Father, to his God and our God; and if, by any means, he will receive me as a poor and needy sinner with the 'Well done' into the society of those whom he shall have accepted, I care not what sort of *ism* I am ranked under here.

"There is much, I think, that may be safely laid aside among Christians who are honest, earnest, and self-denying. Again I say, I have no hope in *isms*, but have strong hope in the cross of Christ.

"The little book* I send is a fuller exposition of the Kirk's

---

* "Help to Professing Christians. By Rev. John Barr. Published by Perkins and Marvin. Boston, 1831."

doctrine than our friend's. I have reviewed it, and see no reason to alter a prayer or an expression. Return it at your leisure, with the two notes of our friend to me since our drive. Soon after I left you, I came home, sat down at my table to write a note as an apology to him for my rudeness in stopping his discourse, fainted, went to bed; next day, ate three ounces of crusts, rode out, and went to bed sick with a cold in my face. For the following forty-eight hours, I did not take an ounce of food; the slightest amount of liquid sustained me; and yesterday was the first day of my being a man. To-day, I called to see and apologize to you." * * * * *

(TO A FRIEND IN SOUTH CAROLINA.)

"BOSTON, June 12, 1852.

"MY DEAR FRIEND: The announcement of the death of your beloved wife, and the queries and suggestions you made, touched me in a tender place. You and your dear wife are separated, it is true; but she is in the upper room, you in the lower. She is with Jesus, where, with his disciples, he keeps the feast; and, not long hence, he will say to you, 'Come up hither.' Your spirit and hers meet daily at the same throne,— hers to praise, yours to pray; and, when you next join her in person, it will be to part no more. Is not the prospect such as to gild the way with all those charms, which, in our childhood, used to make our hours pass too slowly? * * * * *

"My connection with the people of your State, growing out of my marriage, has brought me into personal intercourse, for more than thirty years past, with a great family connection, embracing in its circle many of your distinguished characters. All the M. family, of whom your present Governor is one, came from the same stock; and the various ramifications of that family at the South include, I suppose, a great many thousand souls. I, therefore take a lively interest in everything interesting to your people. We have hot heads, and so have you; but I think your people misjudge, when they think of setting up an independent government. The peculiar institution which is so dear to them will never be interfered with by sober, honest men; but will never be allowed to be carried where it is not now, under the Federal government. Politicians, like horse-jockeys, strive to cover up wind-broken constitutions, as though in full health; but hard driving reveals the defect, and, within thirty years, the old Slave States will feel compelled to send their chattels away to save themselves from bankruptcy and starvation. I have never countenanced these abolition movements at the North; and have lately lent a hand to the cause of Colonization, which is destined to make a greater change in the condition of the blacks than any event since the Christian era. * * *

" You need no new assurance of my interest in, and respect for, yourself, and the loved ones around you. I enjoy life as few old men do, I believe; for my family seem to live around and for me. My nephew by marriage, Franklin Pierce, seems to be a prominent candidate for the 'White House' for the next four years. He is the soul of honor, and an old-fashioned Democrat, born and bred, and to be depended on as such; but, as I am an old-fashioned George Washington, John Jay Federalist, from my earliest days, and hope to continue to be, I shall prefer one of this stamp to him. * * *

" With a heart overflowing, I hardly know where to stop. We shall meet in the presence of the Saviour, if we hold fast to the hem of his garment; and I hope may be of the number of those whose sins are forgiven.

"Ever yours, AMOS LAWRENCE."

During the summer, a small volume appeared,

entitled "Uncle Toby's Stories on Tobacco." Mr. Lawrence read it; and the views there inculcated so nearly coincided with his own, so often expressed during his whole life, that he caused two editions, of some thousands of copies, to be published and circulated, principally by the boys of the Mather School. On this subject, he writes to President Hopkins, under date of Aug. 5:

"My two last scraps told their own stories to the children, and to-day you will receive a package by express that may require explanation. Uncle Toby has hit the nail on the head in telling his tobacco stories to American lads; and I think your students will do good service in carrying them among their friends wherever they are, to show them how much better it is to prevent an evil than to remedy it; and, taking school-boys as they are, these stories will do more good than any that have been published. I met the author yesterday accidentally at the American Sabbath School Union Depository, where I had just paid for the fifty copies sent to you, and he was very earnest to have me write a few lines for him to publish in his book; but I referred him to the three hundred boys of the Mather School, who are full of the matter to help other school-boys to do as they are doing. However, I may say to him, that, as a school-boy, I was anxious to be *manly*, like the larger boys; and, by the advice of one, I took a quid, and kept it till I was very sick, but did not tell my parents what the matter was; and, from that time to this, have never chewed, smoked, or snuffed. To this abstinence from its use (and from spirit) I owe, under God, my present position in society. Further, I have always given the preference to such persons as I have employed, for more than forty years past, who have avoided rum and tobacco; and my experience has been such as to confirm me that it is true wisdom to have done so. The evil is growing in a fearfully rapid ratio among us; and requires the steady course of respected and honored men to prevent its spread, by influencing the school-children of our land against becoming its slaves. You will please use the fifty copies in the way you think best. If my life is spared, the Mather School boys will be allowed to tell their own experience to the boys of all the other public schools in this city and neighborhood. In short, I look to these boys influencing three millions of boys within the next thirty or forty years. Is not this work worth looking after?"

The following well-merited tribute to the character of a respected citizen, who devoted his life to the promotion of every good object, is extracted from a note written by Mr. Lawrence to the Hon. Benjamin Seaver, then Mayor of the city, and dated Aug. 23:

"MY FRIEND SEAVER: I have desired, for some weeks past, to inquire of you some further particulars of the disposition our friend Tarbell * made of his property. You mentioned that something would be paid over to A. & A. Lawrence, and something to the Old Ladies' Home, which institution he helped forward by his labors and his influence, in an important stage of its existence; and he was called off just as he was beginning to enjoy the fruits of his labor, in making a multitude of old ladies happy in thus supplying them a home for the remainder of their days on earth. Our friend has passed on; but I doubt not that his labors have

---

* The late Thomas Tarbell, originally from Groton, Mass.

prepared him to enter that world where there is no weariness or want, and all sufferings are at an end. I have journeyed side by side, for more than three-score years, with our friend; and can say, with truth, that I never knew him guilty of a dishonest or dishonorable act, and that his life was a practical exponent of his Christian principles. I pray to our Father to make me more faithful in doing the work our friend had so much at heart, while I can do it. My share of the money,* coming from his estate, I shall wish paid over to the Old Ladies' Home, and I doubt not brother A. will wish the same done with his share. This appropriation will increase our friend's happiness, even in his heavenly home; for the voice from Heaven proclaims, 'Blessed are the dead which die in the Lord from henceforth; that they may rest from their labors, and their works do follow them.' "

The editor feels some delicacy in inserting the following, from a gentleman still living, and in our own vicinity; but the tribute to Mr. Lawrence, coming, as it does, from a divine so distinguished in all those qualities which adorn his own profession, as well as for every Christian virtue, is too flattering to be omitted:

"Elmwood, Sept. 3.

"My dear Friend: I take such paper as happens to be near me, in my sick chamber, to thank you for the books and pamphlets, which I have read as much as my dim sight and weak nerves will allow me at present to read. I wish, when you write to your friend Dr. Hamilton, you would thank him for me for his

---

* This was a debt contracted by Mr. T., in 1826, amounting, at that time, to about fifteen hundred dollars, when he failed in business. The amount of the debt was soon after transferred to the "Old Ladies' Home."

eloquent and evangelical appeals for Christian truth and duty Tell him I am a Congregational Minister of Boston, but no sectarian; that I was matriculated at the University of Edinburgh, fifty years ago, and studied divinity there under Drs. Hunter, Micklejohn, Moodie, &c., and moral philosophy, under Dugald Stewart; — that my particular friends were David Dickson, since Minister of St. Cuthbert's, Edinburgh; David Wilkie, since Minister of Old Gray Friar's Church, Edinburgh; Patrick McFarlane, since Minister in Glasgow and Greenock; Thomas Brown, since Professor of Moral Philosophy at Edinburgh; David Brewster, since Sir David, &c.: most of whom he probably knows. Tell him I should be glad of his correspondence, as I have that of his friend, Principal Lee, of the University of Edinburgh; and that we should be glad to see him in Boston. I was happy to see your name appended to a petition on the subject of the liquor law, though I always expect to find it among the advocates of every benevolent enterprise within your reach. Your visit did me much good. I have much valued your friendship, and your manifestations of respect and regard for me. Heaven bless you and yours, and make you more and more a blessing! Come and see me when you can, my dear friend. With much affection and respect,

"Your old friend,   CHARLES LOWELL.

"P. S. — I write with a feeble hand, dim sight, and nervous temperament."

In enclosing the preceding note to the Rev. Dr. Hamilton, Mr. Lawrence writes, Sept. 4:

"The writer of the foregoing is the Rev. Dr. Lowell, of this city, who is broken down in health, but not at all in his confidence and hope and joy in the beloved Jesus. Of all men I have ever known, Dr. Lowell is one of the brightest exemplars of the character and teachings of the Master; for all denominations respect him, and confide in him. For more than forty years I have known him; and, in all the relations of a good pastor to his people, I have never known a better. I have met him in the sick chamber, with the dying, and in the house of prayer. In the character of a teacher, and a leader of the people heavenward, no one among us has been more valued. Although I have not been a member of his church, he has, in times of great urgency, supplied our pulpit, and has always been ready to attend my family and friends when asked. I sent him such of your writings as I had in store for circulation, 'The Royal Preacher' among them; and I must say to you that I think no living man is preaching to greater multitudes than you are at this day. I have circulated tens of thousands of your tracts and volumes, and, if I am spared, hope to continue the good work. Millions of souls will be influenced by your labors."

CHAPTER XXXVII.

CORRESPONDENCE. — DIARY.

(FROM LADY BUXTON.)

"NORTHRUPP'S HILL, Sept. 8, 1852.

"MY DEAR FRIEND: Again I have to thank you for your kind remembrance of me in your note and little book on the abuse of tobacco, and your sympathy with me in my late deep anxiety, ending in the removal of my most tenderly beloved and valued daughter Priscilla. It pleased God to take her to himself on June 18, to the inexpressible loss and grief of myself, and her husband and children. We surely sorrow with hope; for she had loved and followed the Lord Jesus from her childhood, and had known and obeyed the Holy Scriptures, which did make her, under the influence of the blessed Spirit, wise unto salvation. To her, to live was Christ, and therefore to die, gain; and we are thankful, and rejoice for her. Her spirit is with the Lord, beholding and sharing his glory, and reünited to her dearest father, brothers, and sisters, and many beloved on earth, in joy unspeakable. Still, we do and are permitted to mourn. * *

" Priscilla traced the foundation of her illness to the great exertion she used in revising and altering her father's work on the remedy for the slave-trade. The stress upon her feelings and mind was too great for her susceptible nature. I believe it might be traced further back to her very great efforts to assist her father in his public business; so that I may say, I have had to part with the two most beloved, and gifted nearly, I have ever known, for the cause of God. But the comfort is intense that they cannot lose the abundant recompense of reward given through mercy and favor, not for any merits of their own, to those who love and serve the Lord. I must thank you most warmly again for the valuable gift of 'Uncle Tom's Cabin.' When it arrived, it was unknown in this country; now it is universally read, but sold at such a cheap rate, in such poor print, that this very beautiful copy is quite sought after. How wonderfully successful a work it has proved! I hope your little book upon tobacco may be of use here. I shall send it to my grandsons at Rugby. I fear you have been suffering much from bodily illness and infirmity, my dear friend. I trust your interesting circle about you are all well and prospering, and enjoying the blessing and presence of the Saviour. With kindest regards and affection, I am yours very sincerely, H. BUXTON."

"*September* 23, 1852. — By a singular coincidence, at the same time I received Lady Buxton's letter, I received one from 'Mrs. Sunny Side,'* from her sick chamber, asking the loan of some of Miss Edgeworth's works; also a note from Mrs. Stowe, giving me some information respecting the publication of 'Uncle Tom's Cabin' in England and Germany; also a letter from our minister in Portugal; and, three or four hours later, 'Uncle Toby' called, having spent the day in the Mather School, lecturing on tobacco."

From a letter written about this time, an extract is

* Mrs. Phelps, wife of Professor Phelps, of Andover, and daughter of Professor Stuart, the authoress of "Sunny Side," "Peep at Number Five," and other popular works.

made, which is interesting as showing his system of diet ·

"My own wants are next to nothing, as I live on the most simple food,— crusts and coffee for breakfast; crusts and champagne for dinner, with never more than three ounces of chicken, or two ounces of tender beef, without any vegetable, together eight ounces; coarse wheat-meal crusts, and two or three ounces of meat, in the twenty-four hours,— beginning hungry, and leaving off more hungry. I have not sat at table with my family for fifteen years, nor eaten a full meal during that time, and am now more hale and hearty than during that whole period."

(TO A LADY IN FLORIDA.)

"BOSTON, Oct. 14, 1852.

"DEAR MRS. ——— : Your deeply interesting note reached me within the last half-hour; and I feel that no time should be lost in my reply. My life has been protracted beyond all my friends' expectations, and almost beyond my own hopes; yet I enjoy the days with all the zest of early youth, and feel myself a spare hand to do such work as the Master lays out before me. This of aiding you is one of the things for which I am spared; and I therefore forward one hundred dollars, which, if you are not willing to accept, you may use for the benefit of some other person or persons, at your discretion. Your precious brother has passed on; and, in God's good time, I hope to see him face to face, and to receive, through the Beloved, the 'Well done' promised to such as have used their Lord's trusts as he approves. I enclose you Lieut. ———'s letter on his return from sea. * * * *

"I had a charming ride yesterday with my nephew Frank Pierce, and told him I thought he must occupy the White House tne next term, but that I should go for Scott. Pierce is a fine, spirited fellow, and will do his duty wherever placed; but Scott will be my choice for President of the United States. God bless you, my child, and have you in the hollow of his hand, in these days of trial. Your friend, A. L."

(TO THE HON. JONATHAN PHILLIPS.)

"BOSTON, Oct. 25, 1852.

"TO MY RESPECTED AND HONORED FRIEND: The changing scenes of life sometimes recall with peculiar freshness the events and feelings of years long past; and such is the case with me, growing out of the death of our great New England statesman, who has, for a long period of years, been looked up to as preaching and teaching the highest duties of American citizens with a power rarely equalled, never surpassed. He is now suddenly called to the bar of that Judge who sees not as man sees, and where mercy, not merit, will render the cheering 'Well done' to all who have used their trusts as faithful stewards of their Lord, — the richest prize to be thought of. Our great man had great virtues, and, doubtless, some defects; and I pray God that the former may be written in the hearts of his countrymen, the latter in the sea. Here I begin the story that comes over my thoughts.

'About forty years ago, walking past your father's house, with my wife and some of our family friends, on a bright, moonlight night, we were led to discuss the character of the owner (your honored father); some of the party wishing they might possess a small part of the property which would make them happy, others something else, when my own wish was expressed. It was, that I might use whatever Providence might allow me to possess as faithfully as your father used his possessions, and that I should esteem such a reputation as his a better inheritance for my children than the highest political honors the country could bestow. A few years later, I was visiting Stafford Springs with my wife, and there met you and Mrs. P., and first made your acquaintance. Still a few years later, I became personally acquainted with your father by being chosen a Director of the Massachusetts Bank, he being President. Still later, I became more intimate with yourself by being a member of the Legislature with you, when the seceders from Williams College petitioned to be chartered as Amherst College, which you opposed by the best speech that was made; and we voted against the separation, and, I believe, acted together on all the subjects brought up during that session. Since then, which is about thirty years, I have been a successful business man, although, for the last twenty years, I have been a broken machine, that, by all common experience, should have been cast aside. But I am still moving; and no period of my life has had more to charm, or has had more flowers by the wayside, than my every-day life, with all my privations. The great secret of the enjoyment is, that I am able to do some further work, as your father's example taught me, when the question was discussed near forty years ago. Can you wonder, then, my friend, that I wish our names associated in one of the best literary institutions in this country; viz., Williams College? My interest in it seemed to be accidental, but must have been providential; for we cannot tell, till we reach a better world, what influence your speech had in directing my especial attention to the noble head of the college, when I first met him in a private circle in this city; and, since then, my respect for his character, my love for him as a man and a brother, has caused me to feel an interest in his college that I never should have felt without this personal intercourse. The two hundred young men there need more teachers; and the college, in view of its wants has appealed to the public for fifty thousand dollars, to place it upon an independent footing. * * * * *

"There is money enough for all these good objects; and, if our worthy citizens can only be made to see that it will be returned to them four-fold, in the enjoyment of life in the way that never clogs, it will not be thought presumptuous in me to advise to such investments. From long observation, I am satisfied that we do better by being our own executors, than by hoarding large sums for our descendants. Pardon me for thus writing to you; but knowing, as I do, that the college has commenced its appeal for aid, I am sure you will excuse me, whether you contribute to its aid or not. With great respect, I am, as I have always been,

"Your friend, AMOS LAWRENCE.

"P. S.— If you wish to talk with me, I shall be rejoiced to say what I know about the college."

In his diary of the same date, Mr. Lawrence writes:

"6 P. M.— My good old friend has called to see and talk with me, and a most agreeable conversation we have had. He expressed good wishes for the college, and will subscribe a thousand dollars at once, which is a cheering beginning in this city. The interest in the college will grow here, when people know more about it."

"BOSTON, *Saturday morning, Nov.* 13, 1852.— The circumstances which have brought me the following letter from my valued friend, 'Honest John Davis,' are these: Many years ago, I learned, from undoubted sources, that his pecuniary losses, through the agency of others, had so straitened him as to decide him to take his two sons from Williams College, which seemed to me a pity; and I therefore enclosed to him five hundred dollars, with a request that he would keep his boys in college, and, when his affairs became right again, that he might pay the same to the college for some future needy pupils. Two or three years afterwards, he said he was intending to hand over to the college the five hundred dollars, which I advised not to do until it was perfectly convenient for him. The circumstances which now call him out are very interesting; and, to me, the money seems worth ten times the amount received in the common business of life. Within ten minutes after Mr. Davis's letter was read to me, Dr. Peters, the agent of the college to collect funds for its necessities, called in to report progress in his work. I immediately handed over the five hundred dollars from John Davis, with a request that he would acknowledge its reception to my friend at once."

"WORCESTER, Nov. 12, 1852.

"MY DEAR SIR: I have been in Boston but once since my return from Washington, and then failed to see you. Nevertheless, you are seldom absent from our thoughts; you do so much which reminds us of the duties of life, and fixes in our minds sentiments of cherished regard and unalterable affection. No one can desire a more enviable distinction, a more emphatic name, than he whom all tongues proclaim to be the good man; the man who comprehends his mission, and, with unvarying steadiness of purpose, fulfils it. There is such a thing as mental superiority, as elevated station, as commanding influence, as glory, as honor; and these are sometimes all centered in the same individual; but, if that individual has no heart; if humanity is not mixed in his nature; if he has no ear for the infirmities, the weaknesses, and sufferings of his fellow-beings,— he is like the massive, coarse walls of a lofty fortress, having strength, greatness, and power; but, as a man, he is unfinished. He may have much to excite surprise or to overawe, but nothing to awaken the finer sensibilities of our nature, or to win our love. The divine efflatus has never softened the soul of such a man. The heavenly attributes of mercy, brotherly love, and charity, have never touched his heart with sympathy for his race. He forgets that a fellow-being, however humble, is the work of the same God who made him, and that the work of the Almighty has a purpose. He forgets the great command to love our neighbor. He forgets that all who are stricken down with disease, poverty, affliction, or suffering, are our neighbors; and that he who ministers to such, be he Jew or Samaritan, is, in the lofty, scriptural sense, a neighbor. Neither the hereditary descent of the Levite, nor the purple of the priest, makes a neighbor; but it is he who binds up the bleeding wound. This is the act upon which Heaven places its seal of approval, as pleasing in the sight of him that is perfect. Where there is an absence of purity of heart or generous sympathy, the man lacks the most ornate embellishment of character, that lustrous brightness which is the type of heaven. To minister to the necessities of the humble and lowly is the work of God's angels; and the man who follows their example cannot be far from his Maker. You have the means of doing good; but have what is greater, and a more marked distinction, the disposition to do it when and where it is needed. Your heart is always alive, and your hand untiring. * * * * *,

"Some years ago, you did that for me and mine which will command my gratitude while I live. I needed aid to educate my children; and you, in a spirit of marked generosity, came unasked to my relief. I need not say how deeply, how sincerely thankful I was, that one, upon whom I had no claim, should manifest so generous a spirit. After a while, times changed somewhat for the better; and, feeling that I was able to do it, I asked permission to restore the sum advanced, that you, to whom it belonged, might have the disposition of it, since it had performed with me the good that was intended. You kindly gave me leave to hand it over to the college, but advised me to take my own time, and suit my convenience. That time has now come; and, as you are again extending to the college your sustaining arm, and may wish to take this matter into the account, I herewith enclose a check for five hundred dollars, with the renewed thanks of myself and my wife for the great and generous service which you have done us. We shall, in all respects, have profited greatly by it; and have no wish to cancel our obligations by this act, but to recognize them in their fullest extent. I am, most truly and faithfully,

"Your friend and obedient servant,

"JOHN DAVIS."

Some inquiries having been made of Mr. Lawrence respecting the early history of the Bunker Hill Monument, he writes, on the 12th of November, in a short note:

DEAR SON: You may be glad to copy the twelfth section of my will, executed in 1833. This information is not before the world, but may be interesting to your children. I could have finished the monument, sick as I was, at any time before Edmund Dwight's death, by enlisting with him, who made me the offer, to join a small number of friends (three Appletons, Robert G.

Shaw, and us three Lawrences), without saying, 'by your leave,' to the public."

* * * * * *

"Surety-ship is a dangerous craft to embark in. Avoid it as you would a sail-boat with no other fastenings than mere wooden pegs and cobweb sails."

CHAPTER XXXVIII.

MR. LAWRENCE SERVES AS PRESIDENTIAL ELECTOR. — GEN. FRANKLIN PIERCE. — SUDDEN DEATH. — FUNERAL.

IN November, Robert G. Shaw, Esq., and Mr. Lawrence, were chosen Presidential Electors for the district in which they resided. Both, at that time, were in the enjoyment of their usual health, and yet both were removed within a few months by death. The Electoral College was convened in the State House at Boston, in December; and Mr. Lawrence has noticed the event by a memorandum, endorsed upon his commission of Elector, as follows:

"*December* 1.— I have attended to the duty, and have given my vote to Winfield Scott for President, and William A. Graham for Vice-President."

He did not add, that, before leaving the State House, he gave the customary fee paid in such cases towards freeing the family of a negro from slavery.

But little is found in the handwriting of Mr. Lawrence for the month of December, except his usual record of donations to charitable objects. He seems to have written but few letters, which may in part be accounted for by having had his time much occupied by a most agreeable intercourse with Gen. Franklin Pierce, who, with his family, were his guests during a part of the month. That gentleman had for many years been on terms of intimate friendship with Mr. Lawrence, and had kept up a familiar correspondence from Washington and elsewhere, which no political differences had abated. He had always been a favorite; and now, having been elected to the Presidential chair, and engaged in plans for his future administration, it may be imagined what interest this intercourse excited in Mr. Lawrence, deeply concerned as he was in every movement that tended to promote the political and moral welfare of the country. Many excursions were made to the interesting spots and charitable institutions of Boston and its vicinity, during this visit, which has a melancholy interest from the events which immediately followed it. On the twenty-sixth, General and Mrs. Pierce left Boston for their home at Concord, N. H., with the intention of spending a few days with their friends at Andover. They were accompanied by their only child Benjamin, a bright and promising boy, twelve years of age, whose melancholy death, but a few days afterwards, will give an interest to the following note, which he wrote to Mr. Lawrence in acknowledgment of a little token of remembrance:

"Andover, Dec. 27, 1852.

"Dear Uncle Lawrence: I admire the beautiful pencil you sent me, and I think I shall find it very useful. I shall keep it very carefully for your sake, and I hope that I may learn to write all the better with it. It was kind in you to write such a good little note, too; and I see that being industrious while you were young enables you to be kind and benevolent now that you are old. I think that you have given me very good advice, and I hope I shall profit by it. So, dear uncle, with much love to aunt, I am

"Your affectionate nephew,

"B. Pierce."

The brief history of this promising boy, who exhibited a maturity and thoughtfulness far beyond his years, is soon told. Nine days afterwards, in company with his father and mother, he left Andover on his return home. A few minutes after starting, the cars were precipitated down a steep bank, among the rocks, causing the instant death of Benjamin, and bruising the father and many other passengers severely. The accident sent a thrill of sympathy throughout the Union, and cast a withering blight upon the prospects of the bereaved parents, which, amidst all earthly distinctions, can never be forgotten, and which has perhaps rendered more irksome the great and unceasing responsibilities of high official station.

Dec. 28. — I sent a large bundle of clothing materials, books, and other items, with sixty dollars, by steamer for Bangor, to Professor Pond, of Bangor Theological Seminary, for the students. Also gave a parcel, costing twenty-five dollars, to Mrs. ——, who is a Groton girl, and now having twins, making twenty children: is very poor.

"*Dec.* 30. — To Professor ——, by dear S., one hundred dollars. Books and items to-day, five dollars."

These were his last entries

On the afternoon of the above date, the writer, in his usual walk, passed Mr. Lawrence's door with the intention of calling on his return, but, after proceeding a few steps, decided, from some unaccountable motive, to give up the accustomed exercise, and pass the time with his father. Mr. Lawrence appeared in excellent health and spirits; and nearly an hour was agreeably spent in discussing the topics of the day. He seemed more than usually communicative; and, although always kind and affectionate, there was, on this occasion, an unusual softness of manner, and tenderness of expression, which cannot be forgotten. The last topic touched upon was the character of a prominent statesman, just deceased, and the evidence which he had given of preparation for an exchange of worlds. He spoke somewhat fully upon the nature of such preparation, and expressed a strong hope, that, in the present instance, the exchange had been a happy one.

In the latter part of the evening, Mr. Lawrence addressed to his friend, Prof. Packard, of Bowdoin College, the following note, in reply to some questions asked by that gentleman in regard to the Bunker Hill Monument, of which he was preparing a history for publication among the records of the Maine Historical Society:

"BOSTON, December 30, 1852, evening.

"MY DEAR FRIEND: Your letter of Tuesday reached me just before my morning excursion to Longwood to see our loved one there. In reply to your first query, I answer, that Mr. E. Everett presented a design of Bunker Hill Monument, which was very classic, and was supported by Col. Perkins and Gen. Dearborn, I believe, and perhaps one or two more. Young Greenough (Horatio), then a student of Harvard College, sent in a plan with an essay, that manifested extraordinary talents, and was substantially adopted, although the column was amended by the talents, taste, and influence of Loammi Baldwin, one of our directors. The discussion of the model was very interesting; and, among the whole mass of plans, this of Mr. Everett and Mr. Baldwin, or, as I before said, a modification of Greenough's, were the only ones that were thought of. Mr. Everett, and those who favored his classic plan, were very cordial in their support of the plan of the monument as it is, very soon after its adoption. Mr. Ticknor was very active in support of the plan as adopted; and I have a strong impression that young Greenough's arguments were wholly just, and, abating some assertions which seemed a little strong for a mere college-lad, were true and unexceptionable. I write from memory, and not from overlooking the plans carefully since the time they were considered. Young Greenough I felt a deep interest in, and advanced money to his father to allow him to go abroad to study, which has been repaid since his father's death. Here I have an interesting story to tell you of this debt, which I wished to cancel, that the widow might receive the amount. Mr.

Greenough was near his end, and deeply affected, but fully persuaded that, by the provisions of his will, his widow would soon have an ample income, and declined the offer. It has turned out better than he ever anticipated. The books shall go forward, as you requested. All our family, 'kith and kin,' are pretty well. The President elect has, I think, the hardest time, being overworked; and, as we are now without any one, we shall be rejoiced to see you here. Pray, come. I shall write again when I send the 'red book' you request.

"With love to all, N. and I join; and I bid you adieu.

"From your friend,

"AMOS LAWRENCE.

"To Prof. PACKARD, Brunswick, Me."

The above letter was folded, directed, and left upon his table, and doubtless contained the last words he ever wrote.

After the usual family devotions, he retired at about ten o'clock, and, before his attendant left the room, asked a few questions relating to the situation of a poor family which he had relieved a day or two before. Mrs. Lawrence had been in an adjoining room, and, on returning, found him lying quietly, and apparently engaged in silent prayer. She did not, therefore, disturb him, but retired for the night without speaking. In less than two hours, she was awakened by one of his usual attacks. Remedies were applied; but, no rallying symptoms appearing, the physician and family were summoned. All that medical skill could do was in vain; and, at a quarter past twelve, on the last day of the year, he quietly breathed his last, without having awakened to consciousness after his first sleep.

All his temporal affairs seemed to have been arranged in view of this event. The partnership with his brother, which had existed for nearly forty years, was dissolved in that way which he had resolved in former years should alone terminate it. From various prudential reasons, however, he had changed his opinion, and had decided to withdraw from all business relations, and accordingly furnished the advertisement, which was to appear on the next day in the public prints, announcing his withdrawal. Four days previous, he had executed a codicil to his will; and thus seemed to have settled his concerns with the closing year. The summons did not find him unprepared; for it was such as he had long expected, and had alluded to many times in his conversation, as well as in his letters to friends. The plans of each day were made with reference to such a call. Nor can we doubt that he was, in the highest sense, prepared to exchange what he sometimes was permitted to call " the heaven on earth " for that higher heaven where so many of his most cherished objects of earthly affection had preceded him. On the morning of his death, the editor found upon his table the following lines, which had been copied by him a few days previous, and which are the more interesting from being a part of the same hymn containing the lines repeated by his wife upon her death-bed, thirty-three years before :

> "Vital spark of heavenly flame,
> Quit, O, quit this mortal frame!
> Trembling, hoping, lingering, flying, —
> O, the pain, the bliss, of dying!
> Cease, fond nature, — cease the strife,
> And let me languish into life.
> Hark ! ―――――――"

It would almost seem that a vision of the angel-messenger had been afforded, and that the sound of his distant footseps had fallen upon his ear; for, with the unfinished line, the pen thus abruptly stops.

The funeral ceremonies were performed on Tuesday, the 4th of January. A prayer was first offered before the body was taken from the house, in the presence of the family and friends of the deceased, by the Rev. A. H. Vinton, D.D., Rector of St. Paul's Church. Public exercises in Brattle-street Church were then performed, in the presence of a crowded congregation, composed of the numerous friends and former associates of the deceased, clergymen of all denominations, and large numbers representing the various professions and trades of the community.

The religious services were conducted by three of Mr. Lawrence's most intimate and valued friends representing three different denominations. These were the Rev. Dr. Lothrop, pastor of Brattle-street Church; the Rev. Dr. Hopkins, President of Williams

College; and the Rev. Dr. Sharp, pastor of the Baptist Society in Charles-street. A beautiful and appropriate hymn was sung by the members of the Lawrence Association, from the Mather School, who surrounded the coffin, and, at the conclusion of the hymn, covered it with flowers. The body, followed by a large procession of mourning friends, was then conveyed to Mount Auburn, and deposited by the side of the loved ones who had preceded him, and under the shade of the "Old Oak," where may it rest until summoned to the presence of that Saviour whose example and precepts he so much loved on earth, and through whom alone **he** looked for happiness in heaven!

CHAPTER XXXIX.

SKETCH OF CHARACTER BY REV. DRS. LOTHROP AND HOPKINS.

THE correspondence in the preceding pages will, perhaps, give a clearer view of the character of Mr. Lawrence than anything which can be adduced by others. It may not be amiss, however, to quote what has been written by two of his most intimate friends, who had the most ample means of forming a just estimate of the man, and of the motives by which he was actuated. Dr. Lothrop, in his sermon preached on the Sunday after the funeral, says:

"I have intimated that Mr. Lawrence was intellectually great. I think he was so. By this, I do not mean he was a scholar or learned man, with a mind developed and disciplined by severe training, and enlarged and enriched by varied culture in the various departments of human thought and study. This, we know, he was not; although he was a man of considerable reading, who loved and appreciated the best books in English literature. But I mean that he was a man of great native vigor of intellect, whose mind was clear, strong, comprehensive in its grasp, penetrating, far-reaching in its observation, discerning and discriminating in its judgments, sagacious in its conclusions; a mind, which, if enriched by the requisite culture, and directed to such objects, would have made him eminent in any of the walks of literary or professional life, as, without that culture, it did make him eminent in those walks of practical, commercial life to which he did direct it. I mention this, not to dwell upon it, but simply because some who have known him little, and that only since disease had somewhat sapped his strength, may not do him justice in this respect. Those who remember his early manhood; who saw the strong, bold, and vigorous tread with which he walked forward to his rightful place among the merchants of the city; those who remember the sagacity of his enterprises, his quick and accurate discernment of character, and the commanding influence he exercised over others; the ease and rapidity with which he managed the concerns of a large commercial establishment, and decided and despatched the most important commercial negotiation,— these will be ready to admit that he was intellectually a strong man. To the last this vigor of intellect showed itself; if not always in his conversation, yet always in his letters, many of which will be found to have a force of thought, a fulness of wisdom and sound judgment, a terse, epigrammatic comprehensiveness of expression, of which no man, however distinguished by his learning and scholarship, would have need to be ashamed. The merchants of this city have ever been distinguished, I believe, for their integrity and benevolence. Nowhere is wealth acquired by a more honest and healthy activity; nowhere is a larger portion of it devoted to all the objects which a wise philanthropy, an extended patriotism, and a tender Christian sympathy, would foster and promote. Mr. Lawrence was conspicuous for these qualities. His integrity, I may venture to say, stands absolutely unimpeached, without spot or blemish. His history, as a merchant, from first to last, will bear the strictest scrutiny. Its minutest incidents, which have faded from the memory of those concerned; its most secret acts, those of which no human eye could take knowledge, — might all be brought into the light before us; and like those, I trust, of many of his fraternity, they would seem only to illustrate the purity and integrity of his principles, the conscientious regard to truth and right and justice with which he conducted all the negotiations of business, and all the affairs of his life. He seemed ever to me to have a reverence for right, unalloyed, unfaltering, supreme; a moral perception and a moral sensibility, which kept him from deviating a hair's breadth from what he saw and felt to be his duty. It was this that constituted the strength of his character, and was one of the great secrets of his success. It was this that secured him, when a young man, the entire confidence, and an almost unlimited use of capital, of some of the wealthiest and best men of that day. * * * * *

"The prominent feature in Mr. Lawrence's life and character, its inspiration and its guide, was religion; religious faith, affection, and hope. He loved God, and therefore he loved all God's creatures. He believed in Christ, as the promised Messiah and Saviour of the world; and therefore found peace and strength to his soul, amid all the perils, duties, and sorrows of life. * * * * *

"There was nothing narrow or sectarian about Mr. Lawrence's religious opinions or feelings. He had a large, catholic spirit, which embraced within the arms of its love, and of its pecuniary bounty also when needed, all denominations of Christians; and it is to be hoped that the influence of his example and character has done something, and will continue to do more, to rebuke that bigotry which 'makes its own light the measure of another's illumination.' He took no pleasure in religious disputes or discussions. The practical in Christianity was what interested him.

His great aim was to illustrate his faith by his daily walk, and authenticate his creed by a life of practical usefulness, constant benevolence, and cheerful piety. This aim he successfully accomplished, to the conviction of persons of all creeds and of every name. These will all give him a name in the church universal; will all admit that he was a noble specimen of a true Christian,— a loving and believing disciple, who had the very spirit of his Master. That spirit pervaded his daily life, and formed the moral atmosphere in which he lived and breathed. It quickened in him all holy, devout, and pious affections; gave him a profound reverence, a cheerful submission, a bright and glorious hope,— a hope that crowned every hour with gladness, robbed death of all terrors, and, in *his* soul, brought heaven down to earth."

The following extracts are taken from the sermon, by President Hopkins, before the students of Williams College,— a sermon from which extracts have been already made:

"Having thus spoken of the use of his property by Mr. Lawrence, I observe that it was distinguished by the three characteristics which seem to me essential to the most perfect accomplishment of the ends of benevolence, and that in two of these he was preëminent.

"The first of these is, that he gave the money in his life-time. No man, I presume, has lived on this continent, who has approximated him in the amount thus given; and in this course there are principles involved which deserve the careful attention of those who would act conscientiously, and with the highest wisdom. There may doubtless be good reasons why property destined for benevolent uses should be retained till death, and he is justly honored who then gives it a wise direction; but giving thus cannot furnish either the same test or discipline of character, or the same enjoyment, nor can it always accomplish the same ends. By his course, Mr. Lawrence put his money to its true work long before it could have done anything on the principle of accumulation; and to a work, too, to which it never could have been put in any other way. He made it sure, also, that that work should be done; and had the pleasure of seeing its results, and of knowing that through it he became the object of gratitude and affection. So doing, he showed that he stood completely above that tendency to accumulate which seems to form the chief end of most successful business men; and which, unless strongly counteracted, narrows itself into avarice, as old age comes on, almost with the certainty of a natural law. He did stand completely above this. No one could know him, without perceiving, that, in his giving, there was no remnant of grudging or reluctance; that he gave, not only freely, but with gladness, as if it were the appropriate action of a vital energy. And in so doing, and in witnessing the results, and in the atmosphere of sympathy and love thus created, there was a test and a discipline and an enjoyment, as well as a benefit to others, that could have been reached in no other way.

"The second peculiarity in the bounty of Mr. Lawrence, and in which he was preëminent, was the personal attention and sympathy which he bestowed with it. He had in his house a room where he kept stores of useful articles for distribution. *He* made up the bundle; *he* directed the package. No detail was overlooked. He remembered the children, and designated for each the toy, the book, the elegant gift. He thought of every want, and was ingenious and happy in devising appropriate gifts. In this attention to the minutest token of regard, while, at the same time, he could give away thousands like a prince, I have known no one like him. And, if the gift was appropriate, the manner of giving was not less so. There was in this the nicest appreciation of the feelings of others, and an intuitive perception of delicacy and propriety. These were the characteristics that gave him a hold upon the hearts of many, and made his death really felt as that of few other men in Boston could have been. In this, we find not a little of the utility, and much of the beauty, of charity. Even in his human life, man does not live by bread alone, but by sympathy and the play of reciprocal affection, and is often more touched by the kindness than by the relief. Only this sympathy it is that can establish the right relation between the rich and the poor; and the necessity for this can be superseded by no legal provision. This only can neutralize the repellent and aggressive tendencies of individuals and of classes, and make society a brotherhood, where the various inequalities shall work out moral good, and where acts of mutual kindness and helpfulness may pass and repass, as upon a golden chain, during a brief pilgrimage and scene of probation. It is a great and a good thing for a rich man to set the stream of charity in motion, to employ an agent, to send a check, to found an asylum, to endow a professorship, to open a fountain that shall flow for ages; but it is as different from sympathy with present suffering, and the relief of immediate want, as the building of a dam to turn a factory by one great sluiceway is from the irrigation of the fields. By Mr. Lawrence both were done.

"The third characteristic referred to of the bounty of Mr. Lawrence was, that he gave as a Christian man, — from a sense of religious obligation. Not that all his gifts had a religious aspect: he gave gifts of friendship and of affection. There was a large enclosure, where the affections walked foremost, and where, though they asked leave of Duty, they yet received no prompting from her. Whether he always drew this line rightly; whether, in the measure and direction of his charities, he was always right; whether so much of diffusion and individuality was wise,— it is not for me to say. Certain it is, that this form of charity holds a place in the church now less prominent relatively than it did in the early ages; and it may be that the proportions of Christian character, in portions of the church, need to be remodelled and recast in this respect. These are questions for each individual. It is sufficient to know that Mr. Lawrence looked the great doctrine of stewardship full in the face, and prayed earnestly over it, and responded to it practically, as few have done. * * * *

"Undoubtedly, he was a man of great original powers. On this point, I have had but one opinion since knowing him. His mind was not speculative, discursive, metaphysical: but, in the high moral qualities; in decision and energy; in intuitive perception, and sound, practical judgment; in the sensibility and affections, and in the imagination,— he was great. Like all remarkable men who are not one-sided, he had large faculties, which found their harmony in their conflict, or rather in their balance. He was quick and tender in his feelings, yet firm; ardent in his affections, yet judicious; large in his gifts, yet discriminating; he was a keen observer, yet kind in his feelings; he had a fertile and shaping imagination: he built air-castles, and they vanished, and then he built others; but, when he decided to build anything on the ground, it was well-planned and promptly finished. His tastes were natural and simple, his habits plain, and his feelings always fresh, genuine, and youthful. Not even the smell of the fire of prosperity had passed on him. He shunned notoriety. He had a strong repugnance to all affectation and pretence and misplaced finery. A young man with rings on his fingers had small chance of favor or employment from him. He was impatient of talk when action was called for, and of all attempts to substitute talk for action. His command over the English language, especially in writing, indicated his power. Style is no mechanical product, that can be formed by rules, but is the outgrowth and image of the mind; and his had often great felicity and strength. When he wrote under the impulse of his feelings, he seemed to impregnate the very paper, and make it redolent of them. He loved nature; and, instead of becoming insensible to it as years came on, it seemed rather to open upon him like a new revelation. It was full of life and of teaching, and the charms of natural beauty were heightened by those associations which his quick imagination connected with its objects and scenes. After the death of two of his children, he says: 'Dear S. and R. speak in words without sound through every breeze, and in every flower, and in the fragrance of every perfume from the fields or the trees.' Years ago, after a long confinement, with little hope of recovery, he visited, when first able to get out, the Panorama of Jerusalem, then on exhibition in Boston, and remained there till the scene took full possession of his mind. Shortly after, on a fine day, he rode out to Brookline; and, as returning health threw over those hills a mantle of beauty that he had never seen before, they were immediately associated in his mind with the Panorama of Jerusalem, and then with the glories of the Jerusalem above. This association was indissoluble, and he would take his friends out to see his 'Mount Zion.' In 1850, he says, 'It really seems to me like the sides of Mount Zion, and that I can cling to them as I view them.' * * * * *

"He was a deeply religious man. His trust in God, and his hope of salvation through Christ, were the basis of his character. He believed in the providence of God as concerned in all events, and as discriminating and retributive in this world. He felt that he could trust God in his providence, where he could not see. 'The events of my life,' he writes, 'have been so far ordered in a way to make me feel that I know nothing at the time, except that a Father rules; and his discipline, however severe, is never more so than is required.' He believed in the Bible, and saw rightly its relation to all our blessings. 'What,' he writes again, 'should we do, if the Bible were not the foundation of our self-government? and what will become of us, when we wilfully and wickedly cast it behind us?' He read the Bible morning and evening in his family, and prayed with them; and it may aid those who are acquainted with the prayers of Thornton, in forming a conception of his religious character, to know that he used them. Family religion he esteemed as above all price; and, when he first learned that a beloved relative had established family worship, he wept for joy. He distributed religious books very extensively, chiefly those of the American Tract Society, and of the American Sunday School Union. * * * * Of creeds held in the understanding, but not influencing the life, he thought little; and the tendency of his mind was to practical rather than doctrinal views. He believed in our Lord Jesus Christ as a Saviour, and trusted in him for salvation. He was a man of habitual prayer. The last time I visited him, he said to me, that he had been restless during the night, and that the only way in which he could 'get quieted was by getting near to God,' and that he went to sleep repeating a prayer. During the same visit, he spoke strongly of his readiness, and even of his desire, to depart. He viewed death with tranquillity and hope and preparation, for it was habitual with him. What need I say more ' At midnight the summons came, and his work was done."

CHAPTER XL.

CONCLUSION.

Mr. Lawrence was of about the medium height, and, until reduced by sickness, was erect in person, and active and vigorous in his movements. The expression of his countenance was mild and cheerful, partaking of that benevolent cast which one would have been led to expect from the tenor of his daily life. His affections were warm, and his feelings quick and ardent. His temperament was of a nervous character, thereby inclining him to impatience. With this defect he had to struggle much in early life. It is related of him, that he once, by some hasty reply, wounded the sensitive feelings of a cherished sister, who afterwards died; and so much did he regret his impatience, that he made a resolution to persevere in his efforts until he had conquered the fault. A great change was soon remarked in him in this respect; so much so, that a relative, who passed several months under his roof during his early married life, was surprised at not seeing the least evidence of this tendency. During his latter years, when weakened by disease, and when his nervous system had been shattered by his violent and peculiar attacks of illness, he had more difficulty in controlling his feelings and expressions. On the second, sober thought, however, no one could have been more ready to confess the fault, and to make such reparation as the case demanded.

His daily actions were guided by the most exalted sense of right and wrong; and in his strict sense of justice, Aristides himself could not surpass him. He was a living example of a successful merchant, who had, from the earliest period of his business career, risen above all artifice, and had never been willing to turn to his own advantage the ignorance or misfortune of others. He demonstrated in his own case the possibility of success, while practising the highest standard of moral obligation. He had ever commanded the confidence of those around him. When an apprentice in his native town, many of his customers relied upon his judgment rather than their own. He never deceived them, and early adopted as his rule of life, to do to others as he would have them do to him. Thus he stood high in the confidence, as well as in the estimation, of his neighbors. What "Amos" said was right, and no one could gainsay.

If any one thing was, more than another, the means of promoting his success in life, we should say it was this faculty of commanding the confidence of others. To this can be traced the prosperity of his earliest business years; and, as his sphere enlarged, and his financial operations were extended, the same feeling of confidence gave him the unlimited command of the means of some of the wealthiest capitalists in New England, who, through the most critical seasons in the mercantile world, placed implicit confidence in the house of which he was the senior partner.

Mr. Lawrence had no fluency in conversation. His mind was ever active; but the volume of thought found no corresponding channel of utterance. The very number of ideas seemed to impede the power of expression.

Had his talents been devoted to literary or scientific pursuits, he would have earned distinction by his pen. His mind was not of that logical cast, which, from patient reasoning, can deduce effects from a succession of causes; but arrived at its conclusions by a kind of intuition, somewhat like those rare instances of mathematicians who solve a difficult problem, and yet can give no account of the mental process by which the solution has been reached.

As a husband and father, he was ever kind and affectionate. He was domestic in his tastes, and found his greatest enjoyment in his home. Here he was eminently favored, and ever found the warmest sympathy, and that considerate care and kindness so necessary in latter years to his feeble health. No one who has read the preceding correspondence can have failed to see the interest which he ever took in all that concerned the welfare of those whom Providence had committed to his keeping. His letters to his children would fill many volumes, and are in themselves an enduring testimony to his fidelity and watchful care during a long series of years. His motto was, "Line upon line, precept upon precept;" and thus his constant aim was to impress upon their minds the great principles of religion and morality. No parent could be more indulgent when such indulgence was consistent with the true welfare of his children, or more resolute in denying what was hurtful. Their present happiness was a great object; but his desire for their ultimate good was still greater.

As a friend, he was most faithful and sympathizing; and many now living can testify to the value of his friendship. Few, perhaps, have had more friends. Their affection for him was not founded so much upon gratitude for his constantly recurring favors, as upon the warm sympathy and affection with which his heart was filled toward them and theirs.

As a citizen, his views were comprehensive, and were bounded by no lines of sectional or party feeling. He was most deeply interested in all that concerned the honor and prosperity of his country, and keenly sensitive to the injury inflicted by such measures as tended to depreciate her standing in the estimation of other nations, or of good men among her own citizens. He was a true patriot, and had adopted the views and aims of the best men of the republic in former days, while he viewed with distrust many of the popular movements of more modern times. From his father he had inherited the most profound veneration for Gen. Washington, and faith in his public policy ; while the political principles of Alexander Hamilton and John Jay were those alone by which he thought the permanent happiness and prosperity of the country could be secured.

As a Christian, he endeavored to walk in the footsteps of his Master. He had no taste for the discussion of those minor points of doctrine upon which good men so often differ, but embraced with all his heart the revealed truths of the Gospel, which the great body of Christians can unite in upholding. He sought those fields of labor where all can meet, rather than those which are hedged in by the dividing lines of sect and party.

He reverenced the Bible, and, from the first chapter of the Old Testament to the last chapter of the New, received it as the inspired Word of God. This was his sheet-anchor ; and to doubt was, in his view, to leave a safe and peaceful haven, to embark upon an unknown ocean of danger and uncertainty.

Religion was for him a practical thing for every-day use, consisting not so much in frames and emotions as in the steady and persevering performance of the daily duties of life. His view of duty did not limit him to the common obligations of morality, but included the highest sense of duty towards God ; or, as he has expressed it in one of his early letters, " to be a moral man merely, is not to be a Christian." He was an active helper in all that tended to promote the cause of Christianity among nations, as well as to promote spiritual progress among individuals. The Christian banner, in his view, covered many denominations; and, with this belief, his charities were directed to the building up of institutions under the influence of the various sects differing from that under which he himself was classed.

What has been said of John Thornton might be applied to him ·

"He was a merchant renowned in his generation for a munificence more than princely. He was one of those rare men in whom the desire to relieve distress assumes the form of a masterpassion. Conscious of no aims but such as may invite the scrutiny of God and man, he pursued them after his own fearless fashion, yielding to every honest impulse, choosing his associates in scorn of mere worldly precepts, and worshipping with any fellow-Christian whose heart beat in unison with his own, however inharmonious might be some of the articles of their respective creeds. His benevolence was as unsectarian as his general habits; and he stood ready to assist a beneficent design in every party, but would be the creature of none. He not only gave largely, but he gave wisely. He kept a regular account (not for ostentation, or the gratification of vanity, but for method) of every pound he gave. With him, his givings were made a matter of business, as Cowper says, in an 'Elegy' he wrote upon him, —

'Thou hadst an industry in doing good,
Restless as his who toils and sweats for food'"

Those who were not acquainted with Mr. Lawrence might suppose that his long continued ill-health, extending through a period of twenty-one years, permitted the formation of a character which few could attain who should not be called upon to pass through a similar discipline.

That the isolation from the business-world, and freedom from the cares and struggles of active life, to which most men are subjected, tended to give him a more just and dispassionate view of his relations to God, as well as to his fellow-men, cannot be doubted.

The peculiar elevation and spirituality of mind which he acquired must not, however, be looked upon as the hot-bed growth of the invalid's chamber; but rather as the gradual development of a character whose germ was planted far back in the years of childhood. The principles of religion and truth which were inculcated by a faithful and sensible mother upon the heart of the child, shone forth in all the events which marked the life of the future man.

Of Mr. Lawrence's religious opinions respecting those doctrinal points upon which Christians are divided, the writer will not speak; though, from repeated conversations with his father on the subject, in the hours of health as well as of sickness, he might consistently do so. Rather than make assertions which might lead to discussion, it is more grateful to his feelings to leave the subject to the unbiassed judgment of those who shall read the preceding correspondence.

Let it rather be the aim of those who loved and honored him in life to imitate his example, now that he is dead. They may rejoice that they were permitted to claim as a relative, and to have daily intercourse with, one who has exhibited, in such an abundant degree, those fruits which are the truest and best evidence of a genuine faith.

In completing this volume, the editor feels that he has fulfilled a sacred trust; and his great regret is, that the work could not have been undertaken by some one more fitted, by his qualifications and past experience, to do justice to the subject. For reasons given in the Preface, this could not be; and it is, therefore, with great diffidence that these pages are submitted as a memorial of one whose life and character deserve more than a passing record.

If, however, what has been done shall be the means of directing the attention of those for whom the volume has been prepared to the consideration of the precepts here recorded; and, above all, if those precepts shall be the means of influencing them for good in their future course in life, — the effort will not have been in vain.

INDEX.

Abstinence, total, from tobacco and intoxicating drinks, by Mr. Lawrence, ... 25
Accounts, benefit of keeping, illustrated, 86
Adams, Amos, ... 44
Adams, Samuel, ... 140
Advice, letters of, to Abbott Lawrence, 48—53
Amherst College, effort of Mr. Lawrence in behalf of, ... 243
A'min Bey, letter to, from Mr. Lawrence, 285
Anatomy, views of Mr. Lawrence respecting the dissection of human bodies, ... 218
André, Major, ... 217
Appleton, Jesse, ... 190
Appleton, Mrs., death of, ... 190
Athenæum, in Boston, Mr. Lawrence's plans for benefit of, ... 200
Baldwin, Loammi, ... 338
Baltimore, derangement of business in, 73
Bangor Theological Seminary, donation by Mr. Lawrence to, . . . 310
donation for students in, ... 337
Banks, suspension of in 1837, ... 141
Bible, Mr. Lawrence's estimate of the, 257
Birth-place, attachment to expressed by Mr. Lawrence, ... 151
of Mr. Lawrence, engraving of, . 151
Blagden, George W., note from, respecting Rev. Dr. ——, of Scotland, ... 313
letter from Mr. Lawrence to, . . 316
Blake, George, ... 84

Bondsmen, advice respecting fathers becoming, ... 37
Book-keeping by double entry, adopted by Mr. Lawrence, ... 61
Boston, religious controversy in, . . . 55
Mr. Lawrence elected representative of, ... 77
wooden buildings in, ... 78
post-office, dead letters from, . . 154
Bowdoin College, donation by Mrs. Lawrence to, ... 244
Brattle-street Church, Mr. Lawrence's connection with, ... 184
Brazer, James, ... 22, 221
his store described, ... 23
Bridgman, Laura, ... 235
Briggs, George N., ... 214, 281
presentation of a cane to, by Mr. Lawrence, ... 227
Brooks, Peter C., death and character of, 263
Buckminster, J. S., remains of removed to Mount Auburn by Mr. Lawrence, ... 145
Bunker Hill, desire of Mr. Lawrence to retain for posterity the battle-field, ... 99
Bunker Hill Monument, Mr. Lawrence's interest in, ... 84
objection to a lottery for, ... 91
completion of, ... 169
Mr. Lawrence's agency in securing the completion of, ... 110
note from Mr. Lawrence respecting early history of, ... 332

362 INDEX.

Bunker Hill Monument, history of the plan of, ... 338
Burial-places, Mr. Lawrence's views respecting, ... 129
Business, secret of Mr. Lawrence's success in, ... 145
Buxton, Lady, letter from, to Mr. Lawrence, ... 298
   letter from, to Mr. Lawrence, . 324
Buxton, Sir Thomas Fowell, ... 298
Cabot, Samuel, ... 268
Cambridge Theological School, views respecting, ... 163
Canada, journey of Mr. Lawrence to, . 89
Canadian Boat-song, ... 261
Canfield, Mr., ... 38
Carroll, Charles, ... 276
Caswell, Oliver, ... 235
Chaplin, Daniel, ... 18
Chapman, Jonathan, ... 192
Charities, memorandum of, . . . 92—95
   proportion of, in 1835, ... 137
   money for, ... 178
   "odds and ends" for, . . . 186—187
   correction of a public statement respecting Mr. Lawrence's, . . 198
   amount expended during ten years in, ... 311
   total amount expended in, . . 312
Charity, systematic, inculcated by Mr. Lawrence, ... 118
Children, fondness of Mr. Lawrence for, ... 225—226
   hospital for, founded by Mr. Lawrence, ... 230—233
Christ, object of his death, ... 266
Christmas, Mr. Lawrence's view of, . . 91
Cobb, Gershom, introduces book-keeping by double entry, ... 61
Codman, Dr., ... 253
Colebrooke, Lady, ... 217
   death of, ... 304
Colebrooke, Sir William, letter to, from Mr. Lawrence, ... 240
   letter from Mr. Lawrence to, . . 304
Colonization of Africa, aided by Mr. Lawrence, ... 299, 318
Concord, Mr. Lawrence's account of the fight in 1775 at, . . . 215—217

Controversy, religious, in Boston, . . 55
Copartnership, offer of Amos Lawrence to dissolve, — declined by Abbott Lawrence, ... 47
Copartnership of A. & A. Lawrence dissolved by death, ... 340
Cornhill-street, store of Mr. Lawrence in, ... 29
Credit system, Mr. Lawrence's view of, 35
Cresson, Elliott, letter to, from Mr. Lawrence, ... 299
Darley, Mrs., ... 39
Darracott, George, ... 172
Davis, John, loan of $500 by Mr. Lawrence to, ... 330
   letter from, to Mr. Lawrence, . . 330
Dearborn, H. A. S., ... 84, 338
Debts, Mr. Lawrence's promptness in paying, ... 31
Dexter, Franklin, estimate of his argument on the fugitive slave law, 287
Dexter, Madam, ... 75
Diet of Mr. Lawrence, ... 123, 326
   table of, kept by Mr. Lawrence, . 124
Dorchester Heights, reflections on, . . 140
Drinking habits in Mr. Lawrence's early days, ... 23
Dwight, Edmund, ... 332
Dwight, Louis, ... 308
   testimony of Mr. Lawrence respecting, ... 219
Ellis, Judge, ... 77
Ellis, Mrs. Nancy, marriage of Mr. Lawrence to, ... 77
Epicureanism, Mr. Lawrence's notion of, ... 124
European fashions, introduction of discountenanced, ... 90
Everett, Edward, ... 172, 338
Expenditures, by Mr. Lawrence, in 1849, ... 278
   from 1842 to 1852, ... 311
Fac-simile of Mr. Lawrence's handwriting, ... 248
Family worship, Mr. Lawrence's remarks on, ... 150
Farwell, Captain, ... 17, 301
Fillmore, Millard, ... 256
Foreign gold, exchange of negotiated, 75

INDEX. 363

Fraternal affection, example of, . . . 147
French Revolution of 1830, Mr. Lawrence's sympathy with, ... 101
Fugitive slave law, Mr. Lawrence's opinion of the, ... 287
Funeral ceremonies at the death of Amos Lawrence, . . . 341, 342
Gannett, Ezra S., letter to, ... 45
Gannett, Caleb, ... 45
Gannett, Mrs., hymn for her little boy by, 46
Goddard, N., ... 76
Granger's Coffee House, ... 38
Gray, Mrs. Martha, present from Mr. Lawrence to, ... 214
Gray, Robert, ... 214
Green, Wm. L., death of, ... 251
Greenough, Horatio, ... 338
Greenwood, Rev. Dr., ... 123
Groton, scenery in, ... 152, 153
Groton Academy, donations of Mr. Lawrence to, preamble of the deed, ... 221
   amount of donations to, by Mr. Lawrence, ... 222
   donations of $45,000 by William Lawrence to, ... 222
   extract from address at jubilee of, 223
Gurney, Hannah (see Buxton, Lady), 299
Haddock, Charles B., letter from Mr. Lawrence to, ... 305
Hallock, Rev. Mr., ... 279
Hamilton, James, letters from Mr. Lawrence to, ... 269, 279, 322
   letter from, to Mr. Lawrence, . . 293
Hancock, John, ... 140
Harris, Colonel, ... 268
Harvard College, donation of $50,000 by Abbott Lawrence to, . . . 244
Heaven, reünion of friends in, . . . 157
Hillsborough Bank, Mr. Lawrence's draft on for specie, ... 36, 37
Hone, Isaac, ... 76
Hone, Philip, ... 76
Hopkins, Mark, President of Williams College, ... 341
   letters to, from Mr. Lawrence, 124, 183, 213, 214, 255, 257, 258, 259, 265, 272, 280, 285, 292
   lectures in Boston, ... 182

Hopkins, Mark, extract from his sermon on death of Mr. Lawrence, 287
   peculiarities of Mr. Lawrence's bounty sketched by, . . 346—360
Howe, Dr., ... 235
Hubbard, Judge, ... 253
Hubbart, Tuthill, ... 154
Hulsemann, Chevalier, interview of Mr. Lawrence with, ... 158
Immigration from Europe, Mr. Lawrence's view of, ... 258, 270
Income, net, of Mr. Lawrence in the first two years, ... 36
   practice of spending it, adopted by Mr. Lawrence, ... 263
Intoxicating liquors, total abstinence from, by Mr. Lawrence, . . . 25
Ireland, Mr. Lawrence's contributions to the famished in, . . . 236, 238
Johnson School, donation to, by Mr. Lawrence, ... 224
Kast, Dr., ... 302
Kent, Chancellor, ... 76
   ride with — character of, ... 158
Kenyon College, aid to by Mr. Lawrence, 177
Lafayette, General, Mr. Lawrence's opinion of, ... 84
   message to, ... 96
Lothrop, Samuel K., . 122, 138, 175, 342
   extract from his sermon on the death of Mr. Lawrence, . . . 185
   sketch of character of Mr. Lawrence by, ... 343—346
Lawrence, Abbott, ... 30, 131, 138
   letters to, 48, 49, 51, 52, 55, 56, 72, 73, 189, 244, 266, 267
   becomes partner with Amos, . . 38
   character as an apprentice, . . . 38
   declines offer to dissolve copartnership, ... 47
   sails for Europe, ... 48
   his dispatch of business, ... 52
   his military service in the last war with Great Britain, . 56, 295
   donation of $50,000 to Harvard College, ... 244
   candidate for the Vice-Presidency, 256
   tendered the office of Secretary of the Navy, ... 266

364 INDEX

Lawrence, Abbott, appointed Minister
    to the Court of St. James, . . 269
  his popularity in Great Britain, . 295
  likeness of, ... 295
Lawrence, Mrs. Abbott, ... 280
Lawrence, Amos, when and where born, 15
  ancestry of, ... 15
  early instruction of, ... 20
  his mechanical skill in boyhood, . 20
  anecdote of his school-days, . . . 22
  enters Groton Academy, ... 22
  becomes a merchant's clerk, . . . 22
  adopts the principle and practice
    of total abstinence, ... 24
  wounded by a gunshot, ... 26
  apprenticeship terminated, . . . 28
  accepts a clerkship in Boston, . . 29
  commences business in Boston, . 29
  his boarding-house rule, ... 30
  his promptness in paying bills, . 31
  motive for daily study, ... 32
  his remarks on letter-writing, . . 32
  his distinction between morality
    and religion, ... 34
  his mercantile principles, ... 35
  view of the credit system, . . . 35
  net income of first two years, . . 36
  advice against parents becoming
    bondsmen for their sons, . . . 37
  his opinion of the theatre, . . . 39
  assists to establish his brother
    William in business, ... 39
  flying visits to Groton, ... 40
  alarming illness, ... 40
  engagement of marriage, ... 43
  marriage, ... 46
  offer to dissolve copartnership de-
    clined, ... 47
  letter on the death of his sister, . 54
  letter on the birth of his daugh-
    ter, ... 57
  recommends marriage, ... 57
  domestic attachments, ... 60
  adoption of book-keeping by
    double entry, ... 61
  leniency to unfortunate debtors, . 61
  second alarming illness, ... 62
  resignation in prospect of his
    wife's death, ... 64

Lawrence, Amos, tour through the Mid-
    dle States, ... 68
  appreciation of the right of suffrage. 70
  delegate to assist in settlement of
    Jared Sparks, ... 71
  becomes an inmate of his broth-
    er's family, ... 74
  negotiates an exchange of foreign
    gold, ... 75
  narrow escape from shipwreck, . 75
  second marriage of, ... 77
  resumes housekeeping, ... 77
  representative in the Legislature, 77
  letter to Mr. Wolcott respecting
    his son, ... 78
  becomes a manufacturer, ... 79
  curtailment of his business, . . . 81
  extent of his correspondence, . . 83
  opinion of Lafayette, ... 84
  interest in Bunker Hill Monument, 84
  journey to Canada, ... 89
  objection to European fashions, . 90
  objection to a lottery for Bunker
    Hill Monument, ... 91
  presentation of plate to Daniel
    Webster, ... 102, 103
  dangerous illness of, ... 105
  feelings in sickness, . . 106, 107, 111
  visit to New Hampshire, ... 109
  his life in a sick chamber, . . . 112
  his submission under divine chas-
    tisements, ... 112—114
  inculcates systematic charity, . . 118
  secret of his success, ... 118
  exercise on horseback, ... 122
  his diet, ... 123
  improvement of health, ... 125
  avoids the appearance of evil, . . 126
  his views of burial-places, . . . 129
  advice about selecting a wife, . . 130
  advice to his daughter, . . . 131, 132
  gratitude towards his mother, . . 135
  visit to Washington, ... 138
  aversion to matrimonial specula-
    tions, ... 138
  estimate of Congressional debates, 139
  visit to Rainsford Island, ... 139
  reflections on completing thirty
    years of business, ... 141

INDEX.

Lawrence, Amos, pecuniary condition,
  January 1st, 1838, ... 142
habits of promptness, ... 144
prospects on December 31st, 1838, 146
reflections on the death of his
  brother, ... 149
advocates family worship, . . . 150
engraving of his birth-place, . . 151
character in the bestowal of gifts, 153
enjoyment of natural scenery,
  155, 156
belief in reünion of friends hereafter, ... 157
annoyances arising from his reputation for benevolence, . . . 159
his religious belief, ... 160
interest in a young colored lawyer, ... 165—6
reflections on his fifty-eighth
  birth-day, ... 167
his agency in securing completion of Bunker Hill Monument, ... 170—174
poetical toast to, ... 174
renders aid to Kenyon College, . 177
acquaintance with Pres. Hopkins, 182
presents sent to President Hopkins, ... 183—4
his aversion to public commenda-
  tion of himself, ... 189, 229
advice respecting his grandchildren, ... 191
opposes annexation of Texas, . . 192
joy at birth of twin grand-
  daughters, ... 193
letter on death of his daughter,
  194—196
sentiments in view of his prosperity, ... 197
his view of keeping the Sabbath, 202
offer of his remains for the dissect-
  ing-room, ... 218
his interest in the Johnson School, 224
fondness for children, ... 226
provides a hospital for sick children, ... 230
his gratitude for prosperity, . . . 234
contributes to the famished in
  Ireland, ... 236

Lawrence, Amos, his application in
  behalf of Amherst College, . . 242
congratulates Abbott Lawrence
  on his donation to Harvard
  College, ... 244
his attendance at church, . . . 246
his exactness in business, . . . 247
kindness to an old debtor, . . 248
fac-simile of his hand-writing, . 248
sentiments respecting a religious
  awakening in college, . . 255, 312
objects to his brother's taking
  political office, . 256—257, 258, 266
estimate of the Bible, ... 257
prefers Gen. Taylor for President, 258
treatment of an applicant for aid, 260
joy at a revival of religion among
  Unitarians, ... 267
interview with Father Mathew, . 270
adds a codicil to his will, ... 271
illness, ... 272
desire for death, ... 272
keeps Christmas with children, . 277
circulates Dr. Hamilton's works, 279,
  291, 292, 294
lameness, ... 281
attentions to children, ... 292
circulates Buxton's Life, ... 298
cancels a note for $500 against a
  clergyman, ... 300
interest in Wabash College, . . . 309
controversy with a Scotch clergyman, ... 313—315
his ground of religious hope, . . 316
circulates Uncle Toby's Stories on
  Tobacco, ... 319
his diet, ... 326
prefers Scott for President, . . . 327
solicits aid for Williams College,
  from Jonathan Phillips, . . . 328
relieves the straitened circumstances of Gov. Davis, ... 330
chosen presidential elector, . . . 333
votes for Scott and Graham, . . 334
intercourse with Franklin Pierce, 335
his last writing, ... 339
death of, ... 340
funeral ceremonies, ... 341, 342
sketches of his character, ... 343

INDEX.

Lawrence, Amos, personal appearance, 352
   character of John Thornton applied to, ... 357
   general character, ... 352—359
Lawrence, Amos A., ... 288
Lawrence, Arthur, ... 235
Lawrence, John, ... 15
Lawrence, Luther, value of his property, 30
   Speaker of House of Representatives, ... 148
   Mayor of Lowell, ... 148
   death of, ... 148, 149
Lawrence, Robert, illness of, ... 205
   letters of Mr. Lawrence respecting, ... 206—210
Lawrence, Samuel, Sen., ... 30
   account of, ... 16
   sketch of his military career, . 17, 18
Lawrence, Samuel, presentation of a gold box to, by Mr. Lawrence, 235
Lawrence, Mrs. Sarah, illness of, . . 62
   letter to her husband, ... 63
   her condition described by Mr. Lawrence, ... 64
   death of, ... 65
   her death-bed scene described, 65—6
Lawrence, Mrs. Susanna, character of, 19
   death of, ... 199
Lawrence, William, ... 30, 252
   commences business in Boston, . 39
   donations of $45,000 to Groton Academy by, ... 222
   death and character of, . 261, 262
Lawrence Association, in the Mather School, note to, ... 237
   contributions for Ireland by, . . 238
   presentation of a silver cup to Mr. Lawrence by, ... 277
   hymn sung at funeral of Mr. Lawrence by, ... 342
Letsom, Dr. C., ... 302
Letters from Amos Lawrence, ... 47
   to a friend, 17, 57, 70, 73, 126, 130, 157, 186, 187, 190, 201, 215, 245, 246, 252, 262, 267, 283
   to his son, 20, 30, 85, 99, 100, 101, 112, 114, 115, 124, 152, 190, 194, 200, 205, 206, 207, 332
   to a college student, ... 24, 25

Letters to Gen. Henry Whiting, . 30, 273, 276
   to a sister, 32, 33, 42, 68, 71, 73, 130, 166, 145
   to Dr. Gannett, ... 45
   to Abbott Lawrence, 48, 49, 51, 52, 55, 56, 72, 73, 189, 244, 266, 267
   to his wife, ... 52, 63, 126
   to a brother, ... 54, 68
   to his mother-in-law, ... 63
   to his sister-in-law, . 69, 112
   to Frederic Wolcott, ... 78
   to his eldest son, abroad, 83, 87, 90, 91, 96, 98, 103, 106
   to his second son, at Andover, 86, 117, 118, 125
   to Daniel Webster, ... 97, 102
   to his mother, 106, 107, 109, 110, 134, 141
   to his daughter, 119, 127, 129, 131, 133, 150, 152
   to his youngest son, ... 143
   to his sisters, ... 149, 151
   to a connection, ... 149
   to his second son, in Europe, . . 154
   to Rev. Charles Mason, ... 155
   to Rev. Robert Turnbull, D.D., . 160
   to Hon. Robert C. Winthrop, . . 165
   to General ———, ... 168
   to Mr. Parker (a partner), . 177, 204
   to the Mechanic Apprentices' Library Association, ... 181
   to President Hopkins, 183, 213, 214, 255, 257, 258, 259, 265, 272, 280, 285, 292
   to his partners, ... 196, 245
   to his children in France, ... 196
   to his grandson, ... 209
   to R. G. Parker, ... 224, 229
   to Gov. Briggs, ... 227
   to Alexander S. McKenzie, . . . 234
   to J. A. Stearns, for Lawrence Association, ... 237
   to Madam Prescott, ... 239
   to Sir Wm. Colebrooke, . . 240, 304
   to a wealthy bachelor, ... 242
   to Prof. Packard, ... 243, 338
   to Mr. G——, ... 251
   to Mr. and Mrs. Green, . . . 252

INDEX. 367

Letters, to a physician, ... 253
   to a newspaper editor, ... 257
   to Rev. James Hamilton, D.D., 269,
                 279, 294, 296, 322
   to his sons, ... 272
   to Robert Barnwell Rhett, . . . 274
   to a country clergyman, ... 280
   to an aged clergyman, ... 292
   to Elliott Cresson, ... 299
   to Lady Buxton, ... 300
   to a lady in Philadelphia, . . . 301
   to Charles B. Haddock, ... 305
   to Rev. Dr. Scoresby, ... 307
   to Rev. Geo. W. Blagden, D.D., . 316
   to a friend in South Carolina, . . 317
   to Benjamin Seaver, ... 320
   to a lady in Florida, ... 326
   to Jonathan Phillips, ... 327
Levelling, Judge Story's maxim of, . 266
Loan of money to Mr. Lawrence by
   his father, ... 36
Lowell, Charles, letter to Mr. Lawrence from, ... 321
Lowell, John, ... 78
Lunatic Asylum, plan for the new, . . 308
Manufactures, engagement of Mr.
   Lawrence in, ... 79
   largeness of his interest in, . . . 104
   fluctuations in, ... 236
   views of Mr. Lawrence respect-
      ing coarse and fine, ... 275
Marriage of Amos Lawrence, ... 46
Mason, Charles, ... 193
   letter from Mr. Lawrence to, . . 155
Mason, Jeremiah, ... 109, 117
   remarks of, on Rev. Dr. ———'s
      lectures, ... 219, 220
   death and character of, . . 261, 262
Mason, Mrs. Susan, Mr. Lawrence's
   letter on the death of, . . 194—196
Massachusetts General Hospital, place
   of Trustee resigned by Mr.
   Lawrence, ... 116
Mather School, character of, ... 276
Mathew, Father, ... 270
Matrimonial speculations, aversion of
   Mr. Lawrence to, ... 138
Maxims of business — speculation
   condemned, ... 72

McIlvaine, Charles P., letter from, to
   Mr. Lawrence, ... 177
McKenzie, Alexander S., letter to,
   from Mr. Lawrence, ... 234
   present of a cane to Mr. Law-
      rence from, ... 260
   death of, ... 261
Means, James, extract from address
   at jubilee of Groton Academy,
   by, ... 223
Means, Robert, ... 77
Mercantile principles adopted by Mr.
   Lawrence, ... 35
"Milo," arrival of ship, ... 52
Money, advice about spending, . . . 143
Morality and religion, Mr. Law-
   rence's distinction between, . . 34
Mortgage of his father's farm, . . . 36
Mount Auburn, interest taken in, by
   Mr. Lawrence, ... 175
National character, reflections upon,
                   133, 134
Native Americans, Mr. Lawrence's
   view of, ... 199
Natural History Society, donation to,
   by Mr. Lawrence, ... 231
Old Ladies' Home, donation to, by Mr.
   Lawrence, ... 321
"Old Oak," in Mount Auburn, . 207, 208
Paine, Robert Treat, ... 38
Parker, C. H., letter to, ... 177
Parker, Daniel P., ... 268
Parker, R. G., letter from to Mr. Law-
   rence, ... 225
Parker, Susanna, ... 16
Parkman, Messrs., ... 37
Percy, Lord, ... 217
Perkins, Thomas H., ... 338
Pestilence, Dr. Shattuck's account of
   the, ... 40—42
Phelps, Mrs., ... 325
Phillips, Jonathan, letter from Mr.
   Lawrence to, respecting aid to
   Williams College, ... 327
   donation from, to Williams Col-
      lege, ... 229
Pierce, Benjamin, son of President
   Pierce, note from, to Mr. Law-
   rence, ... 336

INDEX.

Pierce, Benjamin, sudden death of, . 336
Pierce, Franklin, character of, . 318, 326
   his intercourse with Mr. Lawrence, 335
Pitcairn, Major, account of his death, 302
   removal of his remains to England, ... 303
Pitcairn, William, ... 302
Pond, Rev. Dr., ... 310
Prayer adopted by Mr. Lawrence, . . 248
Prescott, General, ... 17
   Madam, note from Mr. Lawrence to, ... 239
   her views on the comforts of old age, ... 239
Presidential Elector, Mr. Lawrence chosen in 1852, ... 334
Prince, Martial, ... 268
Property, memorandum-book of Mr. Lawrence respecting his, . . . 80
Prudhoe, Lord, ... 217
Rainsford Island, visit to, and description of scenery, ... 139
Religion. (See Morality.)
   its cultivation urged upon his daughter, ... 119—121
Representative, Mr. Lawrence elected, 77
Richards, Giles, his card manufactory, 44
Richards, Sarah, Mr. Lawrence's engagement of marriage with, . 43
Richardson, Captain, ... 22
Sabbath, Mr. Lawrence's view of keeping the, ... 202
Savings Institution. (See Athenæum.)
Scenery, Mr. Lawrence's enjoyment of, ... 155, 156
Scoresby, Wm., letter from Mr. Lawrence to, ... 307
Sea-serpent seen at Hampton Beach in 1830, Mr. Lawrence's belief in the, ... 100
   Mr. Lawrence's belief in the existence of the, ... 268
Sectarianism, Mr. Lawrence's freedom from, ... 161
Sharp, Daniel, ... 253, 342
   letters from, to Mr. Lawrence, . 176, 203, 282
Shattuck, George C., his account of the New England pestilence, 40—42

Shaw, Robert G., ... 333, 334
Shipwreck, narrow escape of Mr. Lawrence from, ... 75
Slavery, views of Mr. Lawrence on questions of, ... 275
   view of its tendencies, ... 318
   contribution for freeing a negro from, ... 334
South Carolina, manufactures in, encouraged by Mr. Lawrence, . . 275
Sparks, Jared, Mr. Lawrence a delegate to assist in the settlement of, 71
Story, Joseph, ... 169
   letter from, to Mr. Lawrence, 179, 180
   his maxim of "levelling," . . . 266
Stone, John S., ... 123
   letter from to Mr. Lawrence, . 162
Stowe, Harriet Beecher, ... 325
Strachan, Lady, ... 237
Stuart, Moses, letter of thanks from, . 263
Sullivan, William, ... 84
Tarbell, Thomas, tribute to the memory of, ... 320
Taylor, Father, ... 123
   Zachary, preferred for President by Mr. Lawrence, ... 258
Tennett, Mr., ... 38
Texas, letter of Mr. Lawrence to Mayor Chapman, on the annexation of, ... 192
Ticknor, George, ... 338
Tobacco, total abstinence from, by Mr. Lawrence, ... 25
   book against, circulated by Mr. Lawrence, ... 319
   letter respecting use of, ... 319
Touro, Judah, his donation for Bunker Hill Monument, ... 173
Turnbull, Robert, letter from Mr. Lawrence to, ... 160
Uncle Tom's Cabin, Lady Buxton's testimony respecting, ... 325
Unitarianism, Mr. Lawrence's opinion of, ... 246, 247
Van Schaick, M., ... 76
Vinton, Alexander H., ... 341
Wabash College, donation from Mrs. Lawrence to, ... 309
Ward, General, ... 140

INDEX. 369

Ware, Henry, Jr., ... 163
Warren, John C., ... 84, 170, 218
Washington, General, ... 44
   celebration of his birth-day, . . 116
Webster, Daniel, letter from Mr.
   Lawrence respecting, . . . 68, 69
   Mr. Lawrence's view of his speech
   in reply to Hayne, ... 97
   letter to Mr. Lawrence from, . . 97
   letter to, from Mr. Lawrence, accompanying a presentation of plate, ... 102
   letter from to Mr. Lawrence, . . 103
   remarks on his address at Plymouth, ... 208
   view of his character by Mr. Lawrence, ... 327
   of his preparation for death, . . 337
White, Charles, account of his play, the "Clergyman's Daughter," 38, 39
White, Charles, President of Wabash College, ... 309

Whiting, Henry, clerk to Mr. Lawrence, ... 29
Will of Amos Lawrence, codicil to, . 271
Williams College, Mr. Lawrence's interest in, ... 182
   donation of $10,000 to, by Mr. Lawrence, ... 197
   donation of $5,000 by Mr. Lawrence, for a library building at, ... 213
   enlargement of library building proposed, ... 215
   scholarships established in, by Mr. Lawrence, ... 245
   account of Mr. Lawrence's benefactions to, ... 287—291
   donation to, by Jonathan Phillips, ... 329
Winship, Dr., ... 302
Wolcott, Frederic, letter to, from Mr. Lawrence, ... 78